Jim Wirley

The *Blackwell Great Minds* series gives readers a strong sense of the fundamental views of the great western thinkers and captures the relevance of these figures to the way we think and live today.

1 **Kant** by Allen W. Wood
2 **Augustine** by Gareth B. Matthews
3 **Descartes** by André Gombay
4 **Sartre** by Katherine J. Morris
5 **Charles Darwin** by Michael Ruse
6 **Schopenhauer** by Robert Wicks

Forthcoming
Aristotle by Jennifer Whiting
Nietzsche by Richard Schacht
Plato by Paul Woodruff
Spinoza by Don Garrett
Wittgenstein by Hans Sluga
Heidegger by Taylor Carman
Maimonides by Tamar Rudavsky
Berkeley by Margaret Atherton
Leibniz by Christa Mercer
Shakespeare by David Bevington
Hume by Stephen Buckle
Kierkegaard by M. Jamie Ferreira
Mill by Wendy Donner and Richard Fumerton
Camus by David Sherman
Socrates by George H. Rudebusch
Hobbes by Edwin Curley
Locke by Gideon Yaffe

blackwell great minds
edited by Steven Nadler

blackwell great minds

schopenhauer

Robert Wicks

BLACKWELL PUBLISHING
350 Main Street, Malden, MA 02148-5020, USA
9600 Garsington Road, Oxford OX4 2DQ, UK
550 Swanston Street, Carlton, Victoria 3053, Australia

First published 2008 by Blackwell Publishing Ltd

1   2008

Library of Congress Cataloging-in-Publication Data

Wicks, Robert, 1954–
   Schopenhauer / Robert Wicks.
      p.   cm. — (Blackwell great minds series ; 6)
   Includes bibliographical references and index.
      ISBN 978-1-4051-3479-8 (hardcover : alk. paper) – ISBN 978-1-4051-3480-4
(pbk. : alk. paper) 1. Schopenhauer, Arthur, 1788–1860. I. Title.

   B3148.W53 2008
   193–dc22

                                                                2007024792

A catalogue record for this title is available from the British Library.

Set in 9.5/12pt Trump Medieval
by Graphicraft Limited, Hong Kong
Printed and bound in Singapore
by C.O.S. Printers Pte Ltd

The publisher's policy is to use permanent paper from mills that operate a sustainable forestry policy, and which has been manufactured from pulp processed using acid-free and elementary chlorine-free practices. Furthermore, the publisher ensures that the text paper and cover board used have met acceptable environmental accreditation standards.

For further information on
Blackwell Publishing, visit our website at
www.blackwellpublishing.com

Materialism is the philosophy of the subject who forgets to take account of himself.

WWR (II), Chapter I, "On the Fundamental View of Idealism,"
P 13, HK 176, ZA 21

All thought is a physiological function of the brain, just as digestion is a function of the stomach.

PP (I), "Fragments for a History of Philosophy," §4, P 46, ZA 59

contents

preface

Arthur Schopenhauer (1788–1860) has endured a long reputation as a dyed-in-the-wool pessimist, combative curmudgeon, misanthrope, and vitriolic critic of German Idealist philosophers such as his University of Berlin teacher J. G. Fichte (1762–1814), his near-contemporary, F. W. J. Schelling (1775–1854), and his rival associate on the philosophy faculty at Berlin G. W. F. Hegel (1770–1831). Schopenhauer is also known for his sexism and, in anecdotes, for having been involved in a lawsuit that issued from a brief shoving-match with a seamstress who was living in his Berlin apartment house. Scholars of Friedrich Nietzsche (1844–1900) will also recall Nietzsche's teasing query in *Beyond Good and Evil* that asked how Schopenhauer could be a genuine pessimist if he enjoyably played the flute almost every day![1] Those aware of Schopenhauer's fashionable upbringing might also puzzle about how someone who was raised in such outstandingly privileged and socially comfortable surroundings could conclude that the world is fundamentally a frustrating and miserable penitentiary, the only rational reaction towards which should be a quest for detachment and inner peace.

The present philosophical portrait of Schopenhauer tempers the above characterization by acknowledging Schopenhauer's asceticism, while positively highlighting the tranquil virtues of Buddhist detachment as they stand opposed to a dim estimate of human potentialities. Anyone who is knowledgeable of the details of Buddha's life will not be alarmed at how an aristocrat, as was Buddha himself, could prescribe a supremely detached attitude in view of the futility involved in clutching constantly for material satisfactions. Nor will there be any surprise at how Schopenhauer's thought focuses so centrally on aesthetic experience and values, given how Buddha so sublimely and silently held up a flower to illustrate the enlightened mentality.

In reference to Schopenhauer's aesthetics and his philosophical outlook as a whole, we will see how his leading aesthetic concept is sublimity, rather than beauty. Schopenhauer devotes much of his thought to artistic matters, but this is informed by a culminating interest in religious asceticism – one characterized by states of enlightened awareness that involve a distinctively sublime mixture of pain and tranquility. This ascetic quality of Schopenhauer's outlook will be presented in mainly Buddhistic terms, giving a subordinate role to his philosophy's affinities to Christian quietism, mysticism, pantheism, and the yogic style of consciousness encountered in classical Indian thought. Schopenhauer read the Upanishads during the evenings in the way many read the Bible, and this invites confident, useful, and coincident reflections about the affinities between *The World as Will and Representation* (WWR) and the pre-Buddhistic, Vedic tradition. From the standpoint of philosophical consistency, however, the Buddhist outlook, rather than the Hindu, will provide us with a more coherent interpretation of Schopenhauer's metaphysics.[2]

We will acknowledge Schopenhauer's well-known view that the world is the manifestation of a blind, driving, and senseless force that can be characterized as "Will" and that our direct awareness of this Will closely reflects how reality is in itself. Schopenhauer admits that our contact with the world in itself is not absolute, but he typically assumes that it is close to being absolute, notwithstanding our human finitude.

From this philosophical angle, his pessimistic account of the daily world as a world of frustration and suffering emerges in connection with his account of human nature and its pursuit of scientific knowledge. Schopenhauer maintains that we can apprehend the nature of things only through our finite human situation, but it remains an open question whether our human finitude enables, impedes, or precludes our awareness of how things absolutely are. The most consistent way to answer this question in Schopenhauerian terms, it will be argued, is to presume that we apprehend the ultimate nature of things as if we were looking through a mildly translucent glass or through a sheet of colored cellophane. At one extreme, this differs from saying that we are facing an opaque wall, where the absolute truth remains inaccessibly on the other side. At the other, neither is it to say we can apprehend the absolute truth without any distortion, as if our own presence and activity of perceiving were like a perfectly polished mirror that makes no difference to the presentation of what we apprehend.

Schopenhauer agrees that the human factor always affects our apprehension of anything whatsoever, so whether we are perceiving an ordinary object, or whether we are trying to grasp the subtle underlying reality of that object, this factor must be taken into account in any accurate presentation of his outlook. The theory of sublimity will clarify this human factor's role and it will be at the forefront of the exposition. A consequence will be that Schopenhauer's ideal types of awareness – the aesthetic, the moral, and the religious – will emerge as sublime, rather than beautiful, modes of consciousness. This will imply that the highest levels of salvation and inner peace are not painless. Neither will they be detached absolutely and unrealistically from the human perspective.

Two further reflections underlie our emphasis upon sublimity and the idea that it is possible only to approach the knowledge of how things absolutely are, even if this approach is very close. The first focuses upon the theory of perception expressed by Immanuel Kant (1724–1804), whose influence on Schopenhauer cannot be underestimated. Kant's account of our perception of ordinary objects will stand for us as a model for understanding Schopenhauer's characterization of our apprehension of the absolute truth, of our own inner timeless nature, and of the time-less essences of other things. Schopenhauer highlights the importance of perception as opposed to pure conception, and he virtually invites us to explore how Kant's own theory of perception sheds light on his own philosophic perspective.

Secondly, at the foundation of Schopenhauer's outlook, we will iden-tify a prevailing logical relationship that yields a more consistent expres-sion of his various metaphysical claims, all of which aim to reveal the fundamental unity of the world. This contrasts with the more divisive logic of "cause and effect" where "cause" and "effect" remain differenti-ated from each other, just as one billiard ball moves another other upon contact. Schopenhauer's logic – a logic, as we shall see, is based on an alternative relationship of "manifestation" or "objectification" – is eminently suitable for expressing matters of degree, continuity, and identity between the elements in relation.

As a preview, we can succinctly appreciate this suitability by reflect-ing upon the relationship between ice cubes and water. Water does not "cause" ice cubes. Rather, ice cubes are a manifestation or objecti-fication of water. Ice cubes "are" water. Terms such as "manifestation" and "objectification" render it possible to say that the ice cubes and the water are identical in substance, but non-identical in form, since water can assume the form of liquid or steam as well. We will use this logic of manifestation as a key to understanding the main principles of Schopenhauer's philosophy, for he believes that "Will" is like the water described here.

This study divides into three parts: (1) Schopenhauer's theoretical philosophy, (2) Schopenhauer's practical philosophy, and (3) Schopen-hauer in perspective. The first part articulates the foundations of Schopenhauer's thought in issues concerning perception, explanation, and metaphysical speculation. The second sets forth the more familiar, wisdom-related aspects of his thought, such as his account of the world as involving endless frustration, and his prescriptions for salvation in aesthetic, moral, and ascetic experience.

The third part attends to some structural relationships and influ-ences between Schopenhauer's philosophy and three world-historical philosophers, namely, Friedrich Nietzsche (1844–1900), G. W. F. Hegel (1770–1831), and Ludwig Wittgenstein (1889–1951). Nietzsche, especially in his early years, was an enthusiastic advocate of Schopenhauer's philosophy. Hegel, in Schopenhauer's eyes, was an arch-enemy. Wittgenstein, who was highly influential in the twentieth century, was impressed by Schopenhauer's ascetic mysticism. The chapters on Nietzsche and Hegel present Schopenhauer's vision of the world through alternative Nietzschean and Hegelian lenses. The chapter on Wittgenstein reveals some of the debt that twentieth-century Anglo-American philosophy has to Schopenhauer. This chapter also shows the later Wittgenstein's positive relationship to Schopenhauer, advancing beyond the common opinion that Schopenhauer's influence on Wittgenstein's philosophical writings began and ended when the latter was still a young man.

Schopenhauer sympathized with the peaceful attitude of Christianity, Hinduism, and Buddhism, and the concluding proposal will be that cultivating a higher level of Schopenhauerian personal detachment and inner peace coheres with the moral aims of three of the world's major religions. This locates Schopenhauer's philosophy among those outlooks that carry a great reserve of untapped spiritual potential. The present adherents of Christianity, Hinduism, and Buddhism presently constitute over 50 percent of the present human population, and it stands to reason that a person's cultivated inner peace – however it is achieved – inevitably becomes redirected into the worldly social sphere within which that person is a living part. If this is so, then a Schopenhauerian attitude of detachment can lead to a more peaceful social end without the divisive burden of religious doctrinal details.

This, however, is not all. The great attractiveness of Schopenhauer's philosophy resides in its appeal to those who have strong moral sympathies, but who harbor doubts about God's existence, often as a result of perceiving painfully the world's violence and irrationality. Although it advocates universal compassion, his philosophy is decidedly atheistic. Such a mixture of propositions is itself sufficient to stimulate one's intellectual curiosity, since it is commonly believed that moral values cannot be reasonably defended or advanced unless one postulates for them an eternal, intelligent, good-natured, and realistic ground. If we add the large segment of the world's unaffiliated atheistic and agnostic population to the theistic population described above, then the potential benefit that Schopenhauer's philosophy can produce is immense, since he prescribes a moral attitude that coheres with the sentiments of anyone, atheist or not, who acknowledges the value of traditional morality.

Schopenhauer nonetheless believes that the core of the universe is meaningless and that bodily death annihilates our individual consciousnesses. The following pages articulate why he believes this. Part of the paradoxical and macabre attractiveness of Schopenhauer's outlook is his sympathy with the ethical, compassionate, core of the world's main religions, while admitting that from a metaphysical standpoint, individual personalities are insubstantial in a world that simply drives on meaninglessly. Among the world's main religions, the closest to this view is Buddhism, and we will emphasize this spiritual association in what now follows.

notes

1   Friedrich Nietzsche, *Beyond Good and Evil* (1886), §186.
2   In the Schopenhauer-Archiv in Berlin (c. 2006), it is revealing that the room containing the library of the Schopenhauer scholar, Arthur Hübscher (1897–1985) is arranged dramatically with Hübscher's large, museum-quality Buddha at the center of the wall of books. Schopenhauer's own study in Frankfurt also contained a 100-year-old statue of Buddha, either of iron or brass, originally painted black. Schopenhauer had ordered it from Paris and believed that it was probably from Tibet. He had it gilded in 1857, three years before his death.

acknowledgments

This presentation of Schopenhauer's philosophy would never have materialized, had not Ivan Soll helped me realize years ago how Arthur Schopenhauer deserved a far more widespread philosophical reception. I would like to dedicate this book to Ivan as a small measure of gratitude for many years of friendship and personal inspiration in both my professional and private life from Wisconsin to Germany, and through Arizona to Auckland. A. David Roth and Herbert Garelick also deserve respectful, if belated, thanks for having first introduced me to the cadaverous perfume of Schopenhauer's philosophy amidst memorably white and snowy Michigan surroundings. Similarly, Ronald Suter has been the source of some of my healthiest and formative philosophical memories; at exactly the right time in my education, his deep admiration of Wittgenstein's philosophy impressed itself upon me inspirationally.

In New Zealand, the University of Auckland Philosophy Department and Faculty of Arts kindly granted travel funds and a period of academic leave in Germany and New York, during which time most of this book was peacefully completed. Warm acknowledgment is also due to my students of Schopenhauer and of Asian philosophy in Auckland whose presence over the years stimulated many of the reflections contained herein. Among my good colleagues in Auckland, Julian Young has been an especially positive and supportive presence in connection with our mutual interest in Schopenhauer's thought. Many thanks go out to Julian, to Sean Kinsler, and to Markus Weidler for our conversations. The Schopenhauer Archives in Frankfurt also kindly assisted me with my research while I was in Germany during the summer of 2005. It is also a pleasure to acknowledge Steve Nadler's open-mindedness and encouragement during the beginnings of this project, along with Jeff Dean's keen literary eye, patience, and editorial wisdom, all of which contributed substantially to this book's development.

The translations from the German and French texts are my own. James Stewart's bodhisattva-like generosity and knowledge of the Pali language substantially informed the translation of Buddha's first noble truth. Thanks are due additionally to my colleague Chris Martin, who shared with me his professional expertise in Latin at crucial points. This is also the place to acknowledge the many productive conversations about Karl Marx that Paul Warren and I have had over the years, for they led me to appreciate the kinship between Schopenhauer and the intellectual tradition that so humanistically concerns itself with the plight of alienated labor.

Finally, my intellectual horizons have been broadened immeasurably by the presence of Kathleen M. Higgins and Robert C. Solomon during their yearly academic visits to Auckland during the last decade, their frequent guest-lecturing in my German philosophy classes, and the stimulating discussions we have had on Schopenhauer-related topics in nineteenth-century German Idealism and aesthetics in general. Bob's untimely death in January 2007 has been a great loss, and I hope that this study can somehow commemorate the inspiring presence and example that he was for me.

Auckland, New Zealand
March 2007

abbreviations

PSR Principle of Sufficient Reason

works by schopenhauer

BM "On the Foundations of Morality" [1840]
FFR The Fourfold Root of the Principle of Sufficient Reason [1813]
FW "On the Freedom of Human Will" [1839]
MSR (I–IV) *Arthur Schopenhauer, Manuscript Remains in Four Volumes*
PP (I) *Parerga and Paralipomena, Vol. I* [1851]
PP (II) *Parerga and Paralipomena, Vol. II* [1851]
WWR (I) *The World as Will and Representation, Vol. I* [1818]
WWR (II) *The World as Will and Representation, Vol. II* [1844]
ZA Arthur Schopenhauer, Zürcher Ausgabe, Werke in zehn Bänden.

other works cited

CPR Critique of Pure Reason [1781/87]
See the Bibliography for further details. In the references, supplementary page numbers will be provided for *Arthur Schopenhauer, Zürcher Ausgabe, Werke in zehn Bänden*, Diogenes, 1977 [*ZA*], along with the paginations for the translations by E. J. F. Payne [P] and R. B. Haldane and J. Kemp [HK], as appropriate. In all of the quotations, the italics are in Schopenhauer's original manuscript.

the philosophy of a nonconformist (1788–1860)

i the unsettled years: 1788–1831

As one of the most erudite and cosmopolitan thinkers in the history of western philosophy, Arthur Schopenhauer offers us an image of the world that is both astounding and sobering. He never left Europe in his 72-year lifetime, but he traveled extensively and observantly throughout the continent during his early years, with fluent linguistic abilities in German, French, English, Greek, Latin, and, in later years, Spanish. He had the good fortune to live when traditional religious texts from India were first reaching Europe in accessible translation, and he became notable as being among the first western philosophers to incorporate Vedic and Buddhistic themes into his philosophical outlook. His philosophical approach also displayed a distinctively universalist character in its effort to establish conclusions that apply to all times and places. Known popularly as one of philosophy's great pessimists, Schopenhauer – as the chapters ahead will reveal – can also be appreciated as representing a combination of hard-headed realism, artistic appreciation, and religious mysticism.

Schopenhauer entered the world surrounded by social prestige and privilege, having been born into a successful mercantile trading family in the free city of Danzig (now Gdansk, Poland) whose roots traced back to the Netherlands. His Anglophile father, Heinrich Floris Schopenhauer (1747–1805), planned that Arthur would follow in his footsteps to manage the family business and establish himself as the head of a patrician, ship-owning family. Young Arthur was educated accordingly with a strong dose of European travel at an early age, which combined later with an enrolment at an exclusive school in Hamburg whose curriculum helped train young teenagers for success in international business.

Danzig was a free trading city when Schopenhauer was born, but it was in Prussia's hands by the time Arthur had reached the age of 5. This forced the family to move to Hamburg – another free trading port where his anti-Prussian father could conduct business more comfortably.

Arthur's mother, Johanna Henriette Trosiener Schopenhauer (1766–1838), was nineteen years younger than her husband, and her relationship with Heinrich Floris expressed this distance in age. Immediately after Arthur was born, the 22-year-old Johanna lived on the family's suburban estate outside of Danzig while Heinrich Floris spent most of the weekdays in the city on business, returning on the weekends to visit his young wife and son. Johanna's own family, although it was less affluent than her husband's, was also well-placed in Danzig society. Her father was one of the city's senators, and the marriage to Heinrich Floris solidified upper-class social relationships. Johanna herself loved to entertain people in the high society of her time, abhorred boredom and being alone, and later displayed an impressive talent for writing fiction and travelogues. Her collected works were published in 24 volumes in 1831. Arthur would later use the same Leipzig publisher, Friedrich August Brockhaus, for his own writings.

Schopenhauer appears to have had a relatively lonely childhood, sometimes distraught by fears of abandonment. According to his own reports, the occasion upon which he felt consistently the happiest and most at home was neither in the company of his parents nor in Germany, but in France, from the ages of 9 to 11, when he stayed at the house of one of his father's business associates whose surname was Grégoires de Blésimaire. In Le Havre, he developed a friendship with the family's young son, Anthime Grégoires, and learned to speak French so fluently and naturally, that upon his return to Hamburg, he could hardly remember how to communicate in German.

Arthur witnessed for the next few years the large parties thrown by his parents for the Hamburg elite. He does not appear to have been inspired by these get-togethers and he showed increasingly less interest in becoming a member of this prestigious social group as time went on. This was unlike some of his schoolmates who grew up to assume respectable and powerful places in the Hamburg mercantile community. Arthur was more reflective and academically-inclined, much to his father's disappointment.

As Schopenhauer matured into his teenage years and the decision for embarking on a specific course in life became more pressing, his father agreed that Arthur could develop his interest in academics only if he would agree to miss out on yet another, more grand opportunity to travel extensively throughout Europe. The price of travel, however, was to include not only the abandonment of his academic pursuits but also the commitment to commencing an apprenticeship in the mercantile

trading business immediately upon return. Setting his academic dispositions aside, Arthur chose the attractive European travel and in 1803 at
age 15, he journeyed with his parents through the Netherlands, Belgium,
England, France, Switzerland, and Austria, returning for a brief time
to Le Havre, of which he had fond memories. While in England, he
was briefly enrolled in a boarding school in Wimbledon (June 30 to
September 20, 1803) while his parents traveled in Great Britain. Some of
Johanna Schopenhauer's published travelogues vividly describe the
cities and towns she and her husband visited in England and Scotland
during this trip.

These European adventures conveyed a more mature meaning for
Schopenhauer, for he became impressed painfully with the wretched
circumstances in which he saw many people living. The memories
never left him and he later wrote about how, at age 17, he had gravitated
into perceiving human life, as had Buddha, with its unceasing suffering
and pain. The belief in God became impossible for him, as he found it
inconceivable that this physical world could be the product of an all-
good, all-powerful, and all-knowing deity. Despite this, and although his
cosmopolitan experiences helped transform him into an atheist, it did
not undermine his sense of duty and respect, for Schopenhauer kept
his promise to his father upon returning from his travels and began his
business apprenticeship in earnest.

From his father, Schopenhauer believed, he had inherited a tendency
towards anxiety, and he probably had sufficient reason to interpret his
own personality in this way. Whether his father suffered from anxiety is
uncertain, but Schopenhauer's duty to his father was put to the test by
Heinrich Floris's death on April 20, 1805 at age 58; Arthur himself had
turned 17 two months before, almost to the day.

Heinrich Floris's body was discovered in a canal behind the Schopenhauer's house in Hamburg, whose rear constituted the warehouse for the
family business. He had apparently fallen from one of the upper floors.
The situation was ambiguous; the death was considered officially to
have been an accident, although it could well have been a suicide.
Heinrich Floris had been ill in the months preceding, he had displayed
memory losses, and his business had not been faring well. Arthur later
blamed his mother for his father's suicide, believing that she had seriously neglected her husband when he was ill and depressed. In light
of this tragic event, Arthur's negative view of the world only deepened,
and although he and his father did not seem to be close, Arthur suffered
emotionally from his father's absence.

Johanna sold the family business within a few months and moved to
Weimar with Adele, Arthur's younger sister (Luise Adelaide Lavinia
Schopenhauer, 1797–1849), a year later. In the meantime, Arthur con-
tinued in his business apprenticeship for two further years, then, with

his mother's support, he made the decision at age 19 to abandon the businessman's life that his father had virtually obligated him to. Schopenhauer then moved to Gotha, near his mother in Weimar, to attend preparatory school for entrance into university studies. The year was 1807.

Schopenhauer managed well in his initial studies, but his precociousness led to an unfortunate episode where he condescendingly mocked one of his teachers with a cutting poem, with the effect of alienating himself from the school environment. Thinking of escaping back to Weimar, he encountered resistance from his mother who did not want him to live with her lest he cause disruption at the intellectual salon she had been cultivating. Johanna was socially well-connected in Weimar and she took pride in having people such as Goethe, Wieland, the Brothers Grimm, and Schlegel visit her home for intellectual discussion.[1]

As a condition for supporting Arthur's presence in Weimar, Johanna insisted that he live in a separate house from which he could visit her during the day. Accepting these stipulations, Schopenhauer moved from Gotha to Weimar and prepared himself for university studies with a private tutor who specialized in Greek literature, Franz Passow (1786–1833). At the end of 1809, at age 21, he enrolled as a medical student at the scientifically-renowned University of Göttingen, and remained there for two years before transferring to the University of Berlin in 1811 at age 23.

Schopenhauer studied philosophy in Göttingen with the skeptical philosopher Gottlob Ernst Schulze (1761–1833), who wisely advised him to study two of the most influential philosophers in the western tradition, namely, Plato and Kant. These fountainheads of western thought shaped Schopenhauer's philosophy, and although Plato and Kant offered opposing answers to the question of whether metaphysical knowledge is possible, they shared a universalistic and reason-respecting approach to life that grounds moral and scientific awareness upon general and necessary laws. Striving for a universalistic mode of awareness became one of the key ideas in Schopenhauer's philosophy as well.

From his earliest days, Schopenhauer was accustomed to social contact with powerful and influential people, so it is unsurprising that he became attracted to the University of Berlin, where one of the most popular philosophers of the day was lecturing, namely, J. G. Fichte. In late 1811 and early 1812, he attended Fichte's lectures "On the Facts of Consciousness and the Theory of Science" with painstaking dedication, writing the lecture contents in exact detail after almost every lecture.

Fichte's lectures slowly disillusioned Schopenhauer, however, and after months of intensive study and note-taking he concluded that Fichte's philosophy was obscurantist, incomprehensible, and ultimately implausible. It is rarely appreciated that Schopenhauer's knowledge of

Fichte's philosophy was impressively informed: his detailed reconstructions of Fichte's lectures almost verbatim, run to approximately 200 printed pages and constitute a small book in itself. Fichte's own words predominate in the manuscripts, but Schopenhauer's numerous quips and frustrated side-remarks reveal a young student with a penetrating, commanding, and challenging mind of his own.

In 1812, by the end of Schopenhauer's second year in Berlin, Napoleon's invasion of Russia and subsequent defeat led to a large influx into Berlin of badly wounded French troops. Schopenhauer witnessed their massive suffering. With the arrival of 1813, Napoleon's weakened military position was exploited by those seeking German independence and a campaign against the French resulted. With Berlin soon under direct threat from a French attack, Schopenhauer, now 25 years of age, left the university in May, and, after a brief stay in Weimar, retired to the small town of Rudolstadt, near Jena, where he spent several months writing a short doctoral dissertation with the esoteric title, *The Fourfold Root of the Principle of Sufficient Reason*.

In October, Schopenhauer submitted his manuscript for a doctoral degree at the University of Jena and was awarded his doctorate *in absentia*. This manuscript, he would later claim, contained the core of his mature philosophy. Printing it privately at his own expense, he returned to Weimar to live with his mother, and proudly sent a copy to Goethe, his mother's friend, hoping – correctly, as it turned out – that it would impress the literary giant and father figure. Goethe received Schopenhauer's dissertation well, and this led to numerous visits between the two men immediately thereafter.

Schopenhauer's departure from Weimar in May 1814 – only six months after his arrival – issued from a dispute with his mother over one of his mother's close traveling companions and border, a civil servant named Gerstenbergk, who, at age 33, was more like Schopenhauer's older brother than (as rumor had it he was) a prospective stepfather. The 26-year-old Schopenhauer and Gerstenbergk did not get along smoothly in his mother's house, and when Johanna eventually asked her son to seek alternative lodgings her preference for Gerstenbergk led to Arthur's angry and emotionally bruised departure from Weimar. Johanna, also upset, severed communications with Arthur in a parting letter that asked that he permanently go his own way. Arthur then left Weimar for Dresden, never to see his mother again for the rest of her life. She lived for another 24 years and did not remarry.

Schopenhauer's four years in Dresden (1814–1818) marked the gestation period and birth of his most famous and influential work, *The World as Will and Representation*, completed in early 1818 and published at the very beginning of 1819. The prelude to this major work was his *On Vision and Colors* (1816), in which he defended Goethe's theory of color. Schopenhauer's genuine friends seem to have been few during these four years, but he regularly attended the theater, frequented locales at which intellectuals gathered, and developed a social reputation as a candid and disputatious character.

Much of Schopenhauer's time in Dresden was spent reading, writing, and studying, with a particular interest in the materialist theories of Claude Adrien Helvétius (1715–71) and Pierre Jean Georges Cabanis (1757–1808) in addition to the Upanishads. The latter, South Asian texts were emerging in the avant-garde intellectual scene, having been first made available to the European audience in 1801–2 with the translation into Latin (from a Persian version) of the original Sanskrit writings. The translated work – done by the French orientalist Abraham Hyacinthe Anquetil-Duperron (1731–1805) – was presented in two thick volumes and bore the title *Oupnek'hat*; Schopenhauer would repeatedly refer to it in the years to come. Only shortly before, in 1813, he had begun enthusiastically reading the Duperron's translation of the Upanishads in Weimar, due to his conversations with the orientalist, Friedrich Majer (1771–1818), whom he knew from his mother's salon.

One of Schopenhauer's neighbors in Dresden was the philosopher, Karl Christian Friedrich Krause (1781–1832), whose personal and academic history was unusually similar to Schopenhauer's. Seven years older, Krause attended the University of Jena from 1797–1801, where he attended lectures by Fichte and Schelling. After receiving his doctorate in 1801, he offered his own philosophy lectures in Jena from 1802–4 where he was colleagues with Schelling and Hegel (who was still relatively unknown). From Jena, Krause moved to Rudolstadt in 1804 – the town where in 1813 Schopenhauer would write his dissertation – and then relocated to Dresden in 1805.

While in Dresden, Krause taught for a number of years at the engineering academy and fatefully joined the Freemasons. In 1812–13, almost a decade later, he spent a brief time in Berlin as a lecturer, with his move to Berlin having been stimulated and encouraged by Fichte, his former teacher, who was then rector of the university. After the disappointment of not receiving a permanent position teaching Fichtean philosophy in Berlin after Fichte's death in 1814, Krause returned to Dresden in 1815, where he moved into Schopenhauer's neighborhood. How Krause arrived in the same place as Schopenhauer and why Schopenhauer chose Rudolstadt to write his dissertation is unclear, but Krause and Schopenhauer were both at the University of Berlin in 1812–13, were involved in philosophical studies at that university and were connected to Fichte as either present or former students. The accumulated coincidences suggest that Schopenhauer and Krause might have already crossed paths in Berlin.

By the time Krause moved to Dresden in 1815, he had himself developed a unique interest in classical Indian philosophy, had learned Sanskrit, had acquainted himself with journal publications in Asian thought, and was a practitioner of yogic meditation. Having already been captivated by the Upanishads upon reading them in Weimar, Schopenhauer now had a neighbor in Dresden who shared his interests in Vedic thought and who had a similar philosophical history.

Despite their close domestic proximity for two years, the relationship between Krause and Schopenhauer must have been tempered by their noticeable difference in philosophical attitude. Krause, more like Hegel and Fichte, expressed an optimistic and developmental view that promised a harmonious and moral society; Schopenhauer, in contrast, could never seriously imagine the world to have a benevolent, moral, and rational source. This difference notwithstanding, Krause's "pan-entheism" ("all-in-god," in contrast to pantheism's "all-is-god") closely echoes the Upanishadic-mystical interpretation of Schopenhauer's philosophy that we will see in later chapters, as does his Masonic and universalist view of ethics. It is difficult to avoid speculating that Krause significantly influenced Schopenhauer and that his presence in Dresden affected the philosophical outlook Schopenhauer expressed in *The World as Will and Representation*.

Karl Friedrich Christian Krause has remained virtually unknown among academic philosophers in the English-speaking world, despite his historical association in Jena and Berlin with Fichte, Schelling, and Hegel. This is partly owing to the professional damage Krause incurred from a controversial book he published on freemasonry: it publicly discussed Masonic symbolism that the secret brotherhood preferred to keep private. Krause also published works on legal and political philosophy, and through these he later became influential in Spain and Latin America. This influence extended well into the twentieth century and, according to some authors, Krause's views served as an ideological basis for the Cuban revolution during the late 1950s.[2] His main doctrine – one expressive of German Idealistic optimism – became known in Spain and Latin America as "Krausism" (*krausismo*) and it maintained that society is rationally perfectible, much in the spirit of Marxist and Hegelian social theory.

In early 1818, Schopenhauer sent the completed manuscript of *The World as Will and Representation* to Brockhaus, the publisher of his mother's numerous manuscripts, and departed in October on the first of his two trips to Italy. Krause himself had left Dresden and had traveled to Italy the year before. Schopenhauer's nine months there were refreshing, but they were punctuated with unproductive experiences and troubling news. While in Venice, for instance, he carried a letter of introduction to Lord Byron, written by Goethe, but during one occasion when he was accompanied by a female companion, he bypassed an opportunity to meet Byron on the Lido beach.[3]

Traveling then to Bologna, Rome, Naples, Florence, and then back to Venice, and fraternizing with the German community in Rome at some length, Schopenhauer established a reputation as a tough conversationalist. Throughout this time, while keeping an eye out for a potential wife, he more soberingly learned about the birth of a daughter in Dresden – the consequence of an affair he had had with a young woman whom he had no intention to marry. The child unfortunately died a few months later, in September.

While in Milan, near the end of his trip, Schopenhauer also learned of the near-bankruptcy of the Danzig investment house where his mother and sister had their fortunes invested, and to which he had entrusted a portion of his own. Schopenhauer endured the financial threat reasonably well, but his mother and sister were less fortunate. He returned to Germany in July 1819 shortly before the death of his daughter and decided in Heidelberg to enter into university life.

After some deliberation, Schopenhauer chose Berlin as the forum to present his views – a city where the philosophical culture was coming under the powerful influence of Hegel, who had assumed Fichte's chair in philosophy. He subsequently submitted his application to Berlin along with a sample of his writing, delivered an exemplary lecture and oral defense (which Hegel attended), and was consequently given a position as a *Privatdozent* to teach six hours per week. His course, whose first meeting was during the spring of 1820, was entitled "*doctrina de essentia mundi et mente humana*" ["theory of the nature of the world and the human mind"].

Schopenhauer ambitiously scheduled his course at the same time that Hegel delivered his main lecture, and few students attended Schopenhauer's class. The course never reached its conclusion during the semester and Schopenhauer's debut as a university lecturer began, and virtually ended, with disappointment. He never seemed to have had much respect for Hegel, but from 1820 onwards, kind words towards him cannot be found within Schopenhauer's writings.

Schopenhauer had a combative personality, but he was emotionally sensitive and sometimes suffered from nightmares and fears, one of which was the fear of a financially devastating lawsuit. These liticaphobic worries were partly motivated by a disagreeable episode between him and a 47-year-old woman, Caroline Luise Marguet, who lived in his rooming house. The incident occurred approximately a year and a half after Schopenhauer offered his short-lived course at the university in competition with Hegel. Within popular Schopenhauer lore, there is some misunderstanding about what happened.

Schopenhauer had at an earlier time asked his landlord to manage the noise outside of his rooms, often caused by Ms Marguet and her friends. When this request had little effect, and when the women were again making noise outside of his room in a lobby area that Schopenhauer also rented, Schopenhauer asked them to leave. Ms Marguet would not consent, and this led to Schopenhauer's seizing her physically and dragging her out of the lobby area. She re-entered the room – in Schopenhauer's perception, outrageously – to retrieve some belongings left behind and this caused him to remove her from his lobby for a second time, at which point she was screaming and causing others to take notice. On this occasion she fell down. Ms Marguet subsequently brought Schopenhauer before the courts, and a decision six months later ended with a small fine and Schopenhauer's acquittal for any major wrongdoing.

The legal affair did not end at this point, since Ms Marguet appealed the court's decision, with Schopenhauer asking the authorities for a quick settlement in turn. The settlement did not materialize rapidly and he left Berlin in May of 1822 on a year-long trip to Italy without waiting to hear from the court. Three years later, in May 1825, the courts finally called him back to Berlin. In the meantime, Ms Marguet claimed to have suffered serious injuries from her fall that affected her ability to work, and Schopenhauer had lost the appeal in his absence. His assets were frozen and after appealing for a reconsideration upon his return to Berlin, the final decision went against him after a series of hearings. In May 1827 – at this point almost six years after the original incident and two years since his more recent return to Berlin – Schopenhauer was ordered to pay a continual compensation to Ms Marguet which lasted until the end of her life, twenty years later.

Schopenhauer retained his interest in becoming a university professor and in settling down to lead a bourgeois, married life. He never seemed to find the appropriate university or the appropriate woman, however. While in Berlin, he applied in 1827 for professorial positions in Würzburg and Heidelberg, without success. He also maintained his contact with an actress to whom he was romantically attracted, Caroline Richter (1802–82), whom he had met in 1821. In addition to concerns about Caroline's health, and despite her unmarried and available status, he was put off by her already having had two children (in 1820 and 1823).

Amidst these frustrating episodes, Schopenhauer tried to secure contracts for translation work. In 1829 he made some efforts to secure an agreement to translate into English Kant's *Critique of Pure Reason*, his *Prolegomena*, and his *Critique of Judgment*, but the negotiations fell through. He also planned to translate Balthazar Gracian's (1601–58) *Oraculo Manual y Arte de Prudencia* (1647) [*The Art of Worldly Wisdom*]. This translation was eventually published decades later in 1862.

Schopenhauer was always wary of threats to his health, and when a cholera epidemic entered Berlin from Russia in 1831, he decided to leave the city. Putting his reservations and uncertainties aside, he asked Caroline to accompany him, but the plans fell apart: Schopenhauer would not agree to her request to bring along the younger of her two sons, 8-year-old Carl Medon. He consequently left Berlin alone and remained unmarried for the rest of his life. As an alternative to Berlin, Schopenhauer initially chose Frankfurt, which was cholera-free, where he lived for nine months. He then moved to Mannheim for a year, returning to Frankfurt to settle permanently in July of 1833. He was then 45 years of age and was never to leave the city for the next 27 years, except for small day trips.

ii the stable years: 1833–1860

Schopenhauer's apartment in central Frankfurt was in a building located attractively on a short segment of the long road that runs along the bank of the river Main. The apartment overlooking the river – on Schöne Aussicht near the Old Bridge (Alte Brucke) – was about three minutes walking distance from the Jewish quarter and about the same distance from the main cathedral in the old city. The restaurant at which Schopenhauer regularly took his lunch – the Englisher Hof – was about a fifteen-minute walk from his apartment, close to the Hauptwache near the city center. He always took his own silverware along with him.

During these final three decades, Schopenhauer tended to keep a regular routine. He would wake up early as a rule, write for several hours and then play the flute before lunch. Then he would lunch at the Englisher Hof, walk his poodle in the afternoon, visit a reading room to obtain the latest news, perhaps go to the theater or a musical performance upon occasion, have a light supper, and then return to his apartment for a quiet evening. He would often read the Upanishads before going to sleep. Schopenhauer also kept a pistol and sword nearby to protect against intruders. A bust of Kant, a statue of the Buddha, along with portraits of Goethe and Shakespeare provided some aesthetic and spiritual balance. His lifestyle expressed a desire to be free, to be left alone, and to make his own rules, combined with a noticeable predictability, consistency, and rhythm that could be interpreted as an effort to produce a feeling of inner balance and health, if not security.

Schopenhauer traveled much and saw much when he was young. He fraternized with an assortment of people, although his social choices did not bring him repeatedly before large institutional audiences as would accompany the roles of a teacher, politician, or soldier. He also experienced a measure of frustration in his social relationships, such as those with his mother, with his romantic partners, in his attempts to secure university work, and in his attempt to achieve widespread philosophical recognition. By the time he was 45, he had settled down by himself, keeping a Kantian regimen and devoting himself to his writing and leisure. An atmosphere of resignation defines a significant part of Schopenhauer's lifestyle at this point in his life.

Schopenhauer continued his philosophical work, and within three years he published *On the Will in Nature* (1836) – book that aimed to show how his metaphysical views defended almost two decades earlier in *The World as Will and Representation* had been confirmed by recent scientific advances. He was most enthusiastic about the chapter entitled "Physical Astronomy" and later referred to it as a useful encapsulation of his philosophy's key ideas. In 1838–9, he focused on the problem of the freedom of the will and submitted essays for two competitions sponsored respectively by the Royal Norwegian Society of Sciences and Letters and by the Royal Danish Society of Sciences.

Schopenhauer's first essay, "On the Freedom of Human Will" ("*Über die Freiheit des menschlichen Willens*") was awarded first prize by the Norwegian Society; the second, "On the Foundations of Morality" ("*Über die Grundlage der Moral*") was denied a prize by the Royal Danish Society, although his was the sole submission. Schopenhauer's supposed failure to answer the question combined with his verbal abuse of Hegel turned the judges against him. In an exemplary display of self-confidence, Schopenhauer published both essays together in 1841 under the title, *The Two Fundamental Problems of Ethics*.

By 1844 – the year of Friedrich Nietzsche's birth – Schopenhauer had written a second volume of *WWR* and successfully published it with the first volume in a combined second edition. The first volume of 1818 remained unchanged for the most part, except for additions to the appendix that critically outlined Kant's philosophy. The first edition appendix had been composed in light of Schopenhauer's reading of only the second edition of Kant's *Critique of Pure Reason* (1787), but later, after having read the first edition of Kant (1781), and having felt that this was a superior and more inspired rendition, Schopenhauer altered his critical appendix.

The supplementary second volume of *WWR* contains a series of essays that fall into line with the topics of the first volume and are intended to be read in conjunction with the first volume in sequence. As we shall note in Chapter 6, there is some scholarly disagreement about whether the views of the 56-year-old Schopenhauer in 1844 completely accord with the 1818 first edition that was published when he was 30. It will be argued here that the views of 1818 and 1844 are substantially the same.

In 1851, the fruits of Schopenhauer's subsequent six years of work were published with the unique title, *Parerga and Paralipomena* ("incidental and supplementary matters"). He directed these writings towards a more popular audience, and they contain highly readable aphorisms and entertaining reflections on the wisdom of life, women, ethics, metaphysics, religion, and sexuality. *Parerga and Paralipomena* successfully stimulated a wider popular interest in Schopenhauer's work, and, within scholarly circles, his recognition was initiated positively by an 1853 article in the *Westminster and Foreign Quarterly Review*, "Iconoclasm in German Philosophy" (by John Oxenford, published without signature) that drew an accurate association between Schopenhauer's and Fichte's philosophies.[4]

Schopenhauer finally received the intellectual recognition he had been seeking, and he published a third edition of *The World as Will and Representation* in 1859. At the University of Leipzig, the exposition and critique of his philosophy became the subject of an intellectual competition. Also in 1859, Schopenhauer's bust was done by the sculptor Elisabet Ney (1833–1907), along with a series of paintings and photographs by other artists that now often appear on the covers of Schopenhauer's publications. The philosophical ideas for which Schopenhauer is famous, it should be remembered nonetheless, were published when he was a relatively young man of 30.

Schopenhauer's life ended in the year when, far across the Atlantic Ocean, Abraham Lincoln was elected President of the United States – a nation whose advocacy of slavery Schopenhauer found morally repugnant.[5] He died peacefully at age 72 on September 21, 1860 in his apartment overlooking the river Main. He had been experiencing heart palpitations in April and had developed a lung inflammation in September. At the time of his death, both his mother and sister had been long gone, and he had neither a wife nor children to whom he could leave an inheritance. What remained of his estate he left in a fund for disabled Prussian soldiers and the families of those soldiers killed in the suppression of the 1848 revolution. Schopenhauer's supportive follower Julius Frauenstädt (1813–79) – who had earlier helped him find a publisher for *Parerga and Prolegomena* – brought new editions of Schopenhauer's works into print, and in 1873 he compiled the first complete edition (six volumes) of Schopenhauer's works. Schopenhauer scholarship later also became indebted to Arthur Hübscher (1897–1985), who compiled and edited Schopenhauer's works during the twentieth century.

notes

1 After he had been spurned by the Weimar community for having decided to marry his mistress, Christiana, Johanna Schopenhauer was among the few who would receive Goethe and Christiana invitingly and graciously into her house.

2　See Richard Gott, "Karl Krause and the Ideological Origins of the Cuban Revolution." University of London, Institute of Latin American Studies, Occasional Paper, No. 28, 1992.

3　This episode is nicely described by Rüdiger Safranski in his outstanding biography, *Schopenhauer and the Wild Years of Philosophy*, trans. Ewald Osers, to which this chapter is significantly indebted (Cambridge, MA: Harvard University Press, 1990, pp. 240–1).

4　Oxenford had written a review on Schopenhauer the year before as well, but it was the German translation of Oxenford's 1853 *Westminster Review* article in the *Vossische Zeitung* that began Schopenhauer's fame in Germany.

5　See, for example, *PP* (II), Chapter IX, "On Jurisprudence and Politics," §127, P 253, ZA 275.

further reading

Bridgwater, Patrick, *Arthur Schopenhauer's English Schooling* (London and New York: Routledge, 1988).

Copleston, Frederick, *Arthur Schopenhauer: Philosopher of Pessimism* (London: Burns Oates & Washbourne, 1946).

Gardiner, Patrick, *Schopenhauer* (Harmondsworth, UK: Penguin Books, 1967).

McGill, V. J., *Schopenhauer: Pessimist and Pagan* (New York: Haskell House Publishers, 1971).

Safranski, Rüdiger, *Schopenhauer and the Wild Years of Philosophy*, trans. Ewald Osers (Cambridge, MA: Harvard University Press, 1990).

Wallace, W., *Life of Schopenhauer* (London: Walter Scott, 24, Warwick Lane, 1890).

Zimmern, Helen, *Schopenhauer: His Life and Philosophy* [1876] (London: George Allen & Unwin Ltd., 1932).

schopenhauer's theoretical philosophy

historical background

i mind-dependent qualities versus mind-independent qualities

Schopenhauer's metaphysical outlook cannot be fully appreciated if we remain unaware of the philosophical problems it was intended to resolve. In the form in which Schopenhauer inherited them, these emerged during the seventeenth and eighteenth centuries from scientific reflections about the nature of perceptual experience. For example, Galileo Galilei (1564–1642) asserted that the external world – the daily, public world of tables, chairs, the sun, the moon, and so on – as it is *in itself*, is constituted *only* by shapes, motions, and their numerical relationships. Colors, tastes, sounds, odors, and textures he held to be nothing more than the aesthetic side-effects of the external world's contact with our sense-organs.[1]

By drawing such a penetrating distinction, Galileo not only advanced scientific thought dramatically, but he also generated some knotty philosophical perplexities about how we can become aware of the external world at all. Thinkers such as John Locke (1632–1704) subsequently developed philosophical theories that tried to explain how we can become aware of an objective, public world that has in itself neither color, taste, sound, odor nor texture, and that contains only qualities associated with space and solidity, such as extension, figure, number, and motion. As a summary quote from Schopenhauer at the end of this chapter will show, Schopenhauer highly respected Locke's philosophical efforts and took some inspiration from them.

We can begin by considering the philosophical implications of Galileo's and Locke's analysis of human perception. This involves tracing the problems that arise when we sharply distinguish qualities such as a stone's felt smoothness and perceived color from qualities such as its three-dimensional shape and mathematically-describable weight. Here, the fundamental contrast is between *mind-dependent* qualities and *mind-independent* qualities, and in the present instance, it requires that we relocate some qualities of daily experience that are often considered to be mind-independent, such as colors, into the mental realm of what is mind-dependent.

Mind-dependent qualities are such that if we were not present, then neither would those qualities be present, even though the external objects that cause them would remain just as they are. We can focus and unfocus our eyes, move our heads back and forth, put on and take off sunglasses, turn the lights on and off, and create all sorts of variations in our perceptions of a set of objects on a table. Throughout these variations, the objects remain in themselves unaffected by our changing perception of them, and this allows us to distinguish between the qualities that depend on our perception and the mind-independent qualities of the objects as they are in themselves.

Locke appreciates how we perceive external things as *seeming* to have in themselves colors, textures, odors, tastes, or sound qualities, but he is convinced that these qualities, as experienced, cannot really be located in the objects. An instructive example is how room-temperature water feels warm to a cool hand and cool to a warm hand, but cannot in itself be both warm and cool. The warmth and coolness are in us, invoked through our relationship to the water, and are not in the water as it is in itself.

To clarify such situations, Locke advances a radical philosophical postulate: the *immediate* objects of our awareness are not mind-independent external objects at all. What we perceive immediately, he claims, are *our own mental images* that stand between our originary point of consciousness and the mind-independent objects that populate the external world. That is, we perceive directly our mental images and do not directly perceive external objects. To establish a perceptual connection between our mental images and those objects, he adds that they resemble them to various degrees.

On this model, perception is like looking at a photograph album, where the "photographs" are mental images that resemble external objects in their mathematical and geometrical contours, but have other, non-resembling properties besides. Following this analogy, Locke concludes that by examining the qualities of our mental images alone, we can *indirectly* apprehend the qualities of their external cause, and thereby explain how we can perceive external material objects.

In accord with this theory, when perceiving a yellow pencil, for instance, we would not regard the yellowness in our image of the pencil as actually being on the surface of the material pencil. We would infer, instead, that the material pencil corresponding to it is thin and cylindrical, but that it has other, imperceptible qualities (for example, the movements of non-perceivable, tiny atoms) that are causing our experience of yellowness. Like the warmth and coolness in the example mentioned above, the yellowness is only in us, and for a being with a different kind of eye (a fly, for instance), the perception of the very same pencil could yield a different type of visual experience. By appealing to this distinction between mind-dependent qualities and mind-independent qualities, Locke develops a theory of perception that is consistent with Galileo's scientifically-motivated distinctions.

A philosophical obstacle unfortunately arises when we regard our mental images as opaque, and locate them in an intermediary position (presumably somewhere in our head) between our perceiving consciousness and the external world. It is as if we were locked in a prison-cell watching a video monitor assumed to be showing images from outside of the cell. The problem is that since we are unable to leave the cell, we cannot make reliable inferences from the contents of our mental images, or from our private monitor, to the objective material things that they supposedly represent.

The representative theory of perception assumes that our mental images are more like pictures, photographs, or television screens, and less like transparently colored eyeglasses or tinted windows through which we can directly view mind-independent things. The theory consequently provides no way for us to check an image's accuracy by comparing it independently and directly to the external object of which it is supposedly the representation. For all we know, continuing with the above analogy, as we sit isolated in the prison-cell, the video monitor could be playing some previously recorded footage instead of actively monitoring the happenings outside the cell. We would not be perceiving what is happening outside, although it would look that way on the monitor.

If our mental images are the immediate objects of perception, it becomes easy to doubt, and impossible to prove by inspecting those images, that there is a material, mind-independent world, let alone one that is constituted primarily of extension, figure, and motion. This reveals an undesirable consequence of Locke's representative theory of perception, namely, that it leads to skepticism about the existence of the external world. He formulates the theory in view of such a scientifically measurable world, but the theory imprisons us in the private theater or photograph album of our mental images without sufficient connections to the outside world.

Among the British empiricist philosophers who react to this skeptical conclusion is Bishop George Berkeley (1685–1753). Rather than explaining how we can perceive the external material world with greater confidence than Locke's theory allows, Berkeley rejects the hypothesis of an external material world altogether, initially remaining content to leave each of us alone in the world of our private mental images, or "ideas" as he calls them. Agreeing with Locke that we are each immediately aware of only our ideas, he adds crucially that an idea can resemble only another idea, and that ideas are themselves entities that can only occur in, and can only be caused by, a consciousness or spirit.

Berkeley finds it inconceivable that a non-physical, mental entity such as an idea could resemble *any* form of inanimate matter. He also denies that non-living, unintelligent matter could cause a non-material entity such as an idea to appear, let alone cause a series of ideas in us that are predictable and well-organized. To him, the thought of a mind-independent material world composed exclusively of extension, figure, and motion that causes our ideas is a repugnant contradiction, philosophically useless for explaining the nature of our experience.

Berkeley concludes that if the immediate objects of perception are ideas, and if we can draw inferences to an external world only by inspecting these ideas, then we cannot infer that an inanimate, external, and material world is the cause of the ideas that we do not imaginatively cause ourselves. To explain the origin of the latter, it makes better sense to assume that their cause is independent of our own minds, but that it is intelligent, supremely powerful, and spiritual. The mind-independent cause of these ideas must be of the same mental substance as are the ideas themselves, and since we do not cause these ideas, Berkeley infers that another mind must cause them.

In Berkeley's mind, the best candidate for this spiritual cause is God, and he reformulates Locke's position by locating God in the philosophical place where the mind-independent material world formerly stood. With this substitution, all of creation becomes the expression of a divine, spiritual substance, and through this, Berkeley claims, the sensory objects of the "external world" that you or I experience – since they have now become nothing more than collections of our own ideas – have in themselves exactly the qualities that they appear to have. The sensible objects of experience are in fact green, blue, loud, soft, sweet, sour, hard, or sharp, just as common sense describes them. They are not indirectly-apprehended, ghostly entities that have only the scientifically measurable qualities of extension, figure, and motion.

Berkeley's account allows us to approach saying in an idealist manner – one that Schopenhauer echoes a century later – that "the world is my idea," for according to Berkeley, there are only minds and their mental images, or as he describes it, spirits and their ideas. The situation invites a comparison to the realm of God and the angels, none of whom have physical bodies, but who together constitute a community of spirits governed by God.

In a broader sense, then, the Berkeleyian world is not exclusively the set of one's own ideas, since the idea-filled consciousnesses of other people exist and God – as the supreme, independent spirit – causes all of the ideas that, for each of us, constitute what we call the world of sensible, or ordinary, things. These things are merely collections of ideas, but they have an objectivity insofar as God causes them. The sun, moon, and stars are present only in our minds, but they are not our own mental productions.

Berkeley's theory of perception is more logically consistent than Locke's, but his theory becomes doubtful when we note weaknesses in the proof of God's existence – a proof upon which the bulk of Berkeley's theory rests. If we grant that the cause of the ideas that we do not cause ourselves must be extremely intelligent, powerful, and more like ourselves than lifeless matter appears to be, it remains that this governing intelligence need not be "God" as typically conceived. It could be finite, or not perfectly rational, or not perfectly good, or a group of spirits rather than a single one. When considering the question of God's existence, Schopenhauer asserts, moreover – and we can see a hint of Schopenhauer's own view in this – that if there is a spiritual ground to the world, then the presence of widespread suffering suggests that it is more devilish then angelic.

Once we recognize alternatives to the single, all-knowing, all-powerful, and all-good God that Berkeley postulates as the cause of those ideas that we do not cause ourselves, the resulting uncertainty about the existence of a mind-independent supreme spirit counterbalances Berkeley's own doubts about the presence of Locke's mind-independent material world. Given this stalemate, we need a more persuasive description of the cause of those ideas that we do not cause ourselves, not to mention a more persuasive way to account for their regular patterns.

One of the most acute observers and analyzers of experience within the British empiricist tradition, David Hume (1711–76), amplified these philosophical difficulties. With powerful arguments that challenge the legitimacy of postulating natural patterns (such as the laws of nature) that hold for our future experience, he does much to undermine the foundations of the very scientific thinking that originally motivates the British empiricist tradition. Hume's skeptical arguments also awaken Kant from his "dogmatic slumbers," inspiring him to formulate an influential alternative to British empiricism – one that leads us directly to Schopenhauer.

Hume assumes that for human knowledge and language to be meaningful, the meanings of our words must trace back to basic sensory experiences. Upon this empiricist assumption he asks incisively what the exact meaning of the relationship that underlies scientific inquiry – namely, the relationship between cause and effect – would then be. He notes that if we say that *A causes B*, then when *A* occurs, we assume that *B* will *necessarily* occur. Furthermore, if the above assumption about linguistic meaning is correct, then we require an observation corresponding to each element of this causal expression. Specifically, if "*A causes B*" is meaningful, then there should be an observation for *A*, an observation for *B*, and, most importantly, an observation for the relationship between *A* and *B* which, in this case, is assumed to be one of necessary connection.

Hume notices that it is easy to observe *A* and *B*, but that we never have any observation of a *necessary* linkage between *A* and *B*. We experience *A* (for instance, a drummer's moving a drumstick and striking a bass drum) and *B* (the boom of the drum), but with respect to the linkage between them, at best and at most, we experience a feeling of psychological transition between *A* and *B* that links them in our imagination. This feeling of transition becomes conspicuous especially after we habitually or customarily experience *B* always following *A*.

Such a feeling of transition establishes only a psychological connection, however, and there may be no objective, mind-independent link between the events themselves. So just as Locke denies that colors, sounds, textures, etc., reside objectively in the external world as such, Hume denies that there are necessary connections that hold objectively between events. In both cases, what are first thought to be objective features of the external world are shown to be subjective qualities that can vary from person to person.

If we accept the above argument, the "necessary connections" between events that we project in the formulation of scientific laws are in fact neither necessary nor mind-independent. So, either the world holds together for us because it just happens to hold together for no discernable reason, or because we psychologically hold it together by projecting associations between events – events that Hume maintains are in themselves entirely loose and separate, and that could proceed along entirely different lines at any given moment. Unfortunately for scientific predictability, psychological associations can be arbitrary and variable, and they lack the rigid quality needed to justify postulating natural laws.

As an advocate of scientific inquiry, Kant addresses the above philosophical situation, considering how to understand the mind-independent cause of our mental images and how to explain the nature of their intelligent and predictable sequences, for he realizes that science is now boxed into a philosophical corner. Berkeley's arguments undercut the idea that a mindless material world of extension, figure, and motion is the cause of the ideas that we do not cause ourselves, and Hume's criticism of the causal relationship itself undercuts the idea that the patterns of our past experience can reliably indicate how the future will unfold.

Such threats to the integrity of scientific thinking lead Kant to develop an innovative theory of the mind's operations that we will characterize in a moment. It is one that Schopenhauer largely advocates. In this effort, Kant succeeds in explaining more convincingly why our experience displays predictable patterns, and, through this, he legitimates scientific reasoning in a reply to Hume's skepticism. The price of saving science, though, is to render it mostly worthless for characterizing the mind-independent reality that underlies the world of daily experience. Kant leaves its nature completely open to speculation and as we shall also see, he makes himself vulnerable to criticisms from Schopenhauer.

The difference between Hume and Kant in the present context is as follows. Hume believes that we experience events that are in themselves loose and separate, and that we superimpose necessary connections upon them that we believe tie them together tightly. These connections, however, turn out to be merely psychological, customary, and mostly arbitrary. In contrast, Kant believes (in a sense that we will describe) that we *actively constitute* events as being related to each other in terms of necessary connections. He appreciates how Hume locates the source of the concept of causality in the operations of the mind itself, but he disagrees with his analysis of this concept in terms of merely psychological associations. Kant alternatively grounds the concept of causality upon much stronger, *logically* connective formats, rather than upon psychological associations, while preserving Hume's insight that we must look into ourselves and into our own mental operations to reveal the nature of causality.

Kant consequently accepts Hume's startling claim that relationships of necessary connection between events are not grounded in sensory experience. This implies either that they are objectively non-existent, as Hume claims, or that they derive from a different source. If one is committed to Locke's view that the mind is initially like a blank piece of paper and if one holds accordingly that knowledge both begins and arises from sensory experience, then Hume's skeptical conclusions are difficult to avoid.

Largely in accord with Locke and the British empiricist tradition, Kant admits that without experiential content, any so-called knowledge that remains would be, in an important sense, empty. He nonetheless indicates a crucial role for knowledge of a purely formal sort that lacks experiential content, stating that although all knowledge *begins with* experience, it does not all *arise from* experience.

To say that all knowledge begins with, but does not all arise from experience, compares to noticing that the experience of sugar's sweetness begins with the touch of the sugar crystals upon one's tongue, but that the crystals alone cannot account for the sweetness. One's tongue is not merely a passive receptor or mirror of the crystals' qualities. We must also refer to the tongue's intrinsic structure to account for our experience of sweetness, for with a differently structured tongue, the sugar crystals might not taste sweet. Kant maintains analogously (to the tongue's structure) that the human mind operates according to a set of constant, abstract forms through which we actively constitute our sensory experience. He adds that if we are to understand how human experience is put together, then we must refer not only to the sensations that are given to us, but also to the activity of these contentless, logical, spatio-temporal, comprehension-giving forms that we introduce into experience. He writes:

> There is no doubt that all of our knowledge begins with experience. For how could the faculty of knowledge otherwise be awakened into activity, if it were not through objects that affect our senses, partly of themselves producing representations, and partly bringing our understanding into activity to compare them – either to combine them or separate them – and thereby prepare the raw material of sensible impressions into the knowledge of objects which is called experience? Therefore in the order of time, there is in us no knowledge prior to experience, and with this everything begins.
>
> Although all of our knowledge is brought into being with experience, not everything contained in it arises from experience. For it could indeed be true [and Kant believes that this is the case] that our experiential knowledge is itself constituted by what we receive through impressions, and what our own faculty of knowledge . . . supplies from itself . . .
>
> It is therefore at least a question that requires a closer investigation, and that cannot be settled with a quick glance: whether there is knowledge that is accordingly independent of experience and even from all sensory impressions. One calls such knowledge *a priori*, and distinguishes it from empirical knowledge, which has its sources *a posteriori*, namely, in experience.[2]

Kant's reference to "what our own faculty of knowledge supplies from itself" implies that the British empiricists are only half-correct when they assume that prior to experience, the mind is empty. The term "empty" is ambiguous, for there are at least two ways that the mind can be empty. It can be empty in the way a mirror in a dark room reflects no light, and in connection with this, how, when the room is illuminated, the mirror reflects perfectly and without distortion whatever it happens to be directed towards. This sort of empty mirror closely approximates the British empiricist view of the mind upon which Locke's, Berkeley's, and Hume's views are based.

In another sense, the mind can be empty in the way a waffle-iron or cookie-cutter is empty in the absence of dough or batter to fill it. In the latter case, there is a prior, determinate form of the cookie-cutter, even though it stands initially as empty of dough (content). This sense of emptiness more closely approximates Kant's view of the mind as having in itself contentless, rational formats that give a basic shape to our experience. Schopenhauer accepts Kant's account of the mind's operations in its core outlines, especially with respect to the constitutive roles of space and time.

In his effort to ascertain the essential form of the human mind, that is, as it is structurally and independently of sensory content, Kant relies upon what, for him, are unquestionable and well-established conceptions from classical Greek philosophy. These define human beings generally as rational and reflective beings. Noting confidently that the principles of Aristotelian logic have been constant for 2,000 years and assuming that they will remain rock-solid, Kant asserts that abstract and elementary logical forms embody human rationality in its essential form. He believes that these forms identically regulate the mental processing of all human beings, whenever and wherever people might be. Examples are the conditional form, *"If A, then B"* where *A* and *B* typically describe actions or events (for example, "If one throws the ball into the air, then it will come down") and the categorical form, *"S is P"* where *S* is some individual and *P* is some universal quality (for instance, "The ball is white").

Kant describes in some depth how we rationally comprehend our sensations in accordance with our logical nature, and consequently apprehend the world as a set of causally-connected things with qualities. In response to Hume's difficulty in explaining how we can legitimately ascribe rigid connections between our experiences, Kant replies that these connections arise from logical projections through which we necessarily construct our experience according to the causally expressive, *"If A then B"* format.

In sum, both Hume and Kant agree that causal connections are not in the world as it is in itself, but are mind-*dependent* relationships. The difference between them is that in place of Hume's claim that causal connections are unreliable, non-necessary psychological associations, Kant claims that they express logical projections that reflect our rational nature. If we are rational beings and if our rationality is embodied in logical formats that we project comprehensively onto every given sensation, then science is not only a legitimate enterprise, it is an unavoidably human one. Its causal connections might not exist mind-independently, but every human being projects them in the same way, and this, for Kant, is sufficient to establish a stable, predictable scientific quality to our experience.

ii space and time

To complete his account of "what our faculty of human knowledge supplies from itself," Kant attaches to the various logical formats a complementary pair of abstract, sensation-related ones whose modes of organization further account for the kind of shared world we experience. These formats are none other than space and time, considered abstractly as prerequisite experiential forms that are devoid of any sensory content.

According to Kant, we cannot imagine any possible experience that is not in some space and/or time. We *can*, however, imagine space and time apart from any particular objects that an experience might contain. The experience of a cup, for example, depends upon the presence of space and time, but the space and the time that the cup happens to be in, do not depend on the existence of that particular cup. The spatio-temporal "container" in which the cup appears is a prerequisite for the cup's appearance and is a more fundamental constituent of experience than the cup. Unlike the cup, which may or may not be present, space and time are universal and necessary (that is, a priori) constituents of experience.

Kant's argument is that if B (for example, the cup) depends on A (for example, space and time), and if A does not depend on B, then A is necessary condition for B. Since in this case, space and time turn out to have no sensory content and are regarded as only formal structures, Kant concludes that space and time are features of the human mind and as far as we can know, are nothing more than styles of formatting our sensations:

> We can therefore speak about space, of extended things, etc., only from the human standpoint. If we depart from the subjective conditions under which we can alone have outer intuition, which is namely our capacity to be affected by objects, the representation of space has no meaning at all.[3]

> . . . the things which we intuit, are not in themselves what we intuit them as being. Nor are their relationships so constituted in themselves in the way they appear to us. And if the subject, or even only the subjective condition of the senses in general be taken away, the entire constitution and all of the relationships of objects in space and time, indeed space and time themselves, would disappear.[4]

The second excerpt above matches Galileo's remark that if tongues, noses, eyes, etc., were removed from existence, then there would be no tastes, odors, and colors. This is very close to what Kant asserts more radically about space and time, namely, that if there were no people, then space and time would have no meaning. Consider Galileo's remark in comparison to Kant's: "I think that tastes, odors, colors, and so on are no more than mere names so far as the object in which we place them is concerned, and that they reside only in the consciousness. Hence if the living creature were removed, all these qualities would be wiped away and annihilated."[5]

In *The World as Will and Representation*, Schopenhauer states frequently that life is like a dream. If we consider the mind-dependent quality of sugar's sweetness and interpret the experience of objects in space and time as akin to the experience of sweetness in its comparable mind-dependence, then the first line of Schopenhauer's main work, "The world is my representation," can be more readily understood and appreciated. For Schopenhauer and Kant, the spatio-temporal world of things in causal relationships does *not* represent how those things are in themselves, just as the sweetness of the sugar provides knowledge of neither the chemical nature of the sugar nor its crystalline structure.

If we were asked to infer from only the quality of its taste what sugar itself is mind-independently like, we would have nothing to say. For Kant, there is an analogous difficulty in drawing inferences from our immediate experience to the way things are in themselves. For, if we have only the world of sensory experience from which to make inferences, we can have no specific idea of what things are like in themselves. As we shall see, Schopenhauer maintains less skeptically that there is an alternative way to apprehend the true being of the objects that appear to us, even though he admits that Kant's account of space and time tempers such knowledge.

To summarize the road we have taken towards establishing the Kantian foundations of Schopenhauer's philosophy via the British Empiricists, we can now present Schopenhauer's own characterization of Kant as he stands in relation to Locke:

> Locke had proven that the secondary qualities of things such as sound, odor, color, hardness, softness, smoothness, and the like, insofar as they are grounded upon the affectations of the senses, do not belong to the objective body, to the thing in itself. To the latter, rather, he attached only the primary qualities, i.e., those presupposed by merely space and impenetrability, such as extension, figure, solidity, number, and movement.
>
> This easy-to-find Lockean distinction, which remains on the superficial surface of things, however, was only a youthful prelude to the Kantian distinction. Extending from an incomparably higher standpoint, the latter explains everything that Locke had regarded as *qualitates primarias* [primary qualities], that is, qualities of the thing in itself, as belonging only to the appearance of the thing-in-itself in our faculty of apprehension, and indeed so, because the conditions of this faculty, namely, space, time, and causality, are known by us *a priori*. Locke had therefore removed from the thing-in-itself the share that the sense-organs have in its appearance, whereas Kant further removed the share that the brain-functions have (although not under this name).[6]

We arrive at the following synopsis of Kant's view: there is a mind-independent reality whose features cannot be known to be either spatio-temporal or constituted by objects that are causally-interconnected. This is because space, time, and causality are knowable only as features of our own minds. Whatever mind-independent reality is in itself cannot be known, although we are aware that it is somehow partially responsible for our experience of causally-related things in space and time. We supply the generalized spatio-temporal and causal formats to our experience, and a mind-independent reality supplies its particular experiential contents. Our experience of an objective world of ordinary things such as tables and chairs is thus best described as the appearance of a mind-independent reality whose intrinsic quality is unknowable. Its *appearance* can be known, due to our specifically human way of perceiving things logically and in space and time. The mind-independent reality in itself, however, remains opaque to us. For any object that we perceive, we can know nothing positive about that object as it is in-itself or about things-in-themselves in general.

As mentioned above, Schopenhauer transforms this Kantian outlook to allow for knowledge of the thing-in-itself. For the present, it is important to note only that Kant conceives of our minds – in their given, generalized human quality – as being akin to cookie-cutters, where the intrinsic shape of the cookie-cutter is defined by the forms of space, time, and twelve conceptual categories that he derives from the basic forms of Aristotelian logical judgment, among which is the category of causality. These *a priori* contours of our minds shape everything that we experience, and we never experience anything without simultaneously experiencing our own spatio-temporal–causal reflection in the object we have constructed. The situation is roughly comparable to a red-hot cookie-cutter that not only cuts the dough, but sears it upon touching it, and can know the dough only by touching it. If it wishes to know what the unseared dough is like in itself, independently of the cookie-cutter's touch, it is wishing for the impossible. From the standpoint of the cookie-cutter, the dough in itself is unknowable.

Accepting this Kantian theory of knowledge, Schopenhauer usually refers to space, time, and the logical categories in a streamlined manner, using arguments that reduce Kant's twelve logical categories to the single category of causality, and introducing a single term that includes space, time, and causality under its heading. This all-inclusive term is "the principle of sufficient reason" – the subject of the next chapter – about which Schopenhauer wrote his doctoral dissertation. He would later write that,

> starting from the subject, and indeed without [appealing to] the knowledge of the object itself, the essential and therefore universal forms of all objects – time, space and causality – can be found and fully known. In Kant's language, they lie *a priori* in our consciousness. Having discovered this is one of Kant's main merits and it is an enormously significant one. I now claim beyond this that the principle of sufficient reason is the common expression of all these *a priori* forms of the object of which we are conscious, and consequently that everything we know purely *a priori* is nothing more than the content of that principle and what follows from it. Therefore, it in fact expresses all of our *a priori* and certain knowledge.[7]

Schopenhauer sometimes refers to space and time by themselves as "the principle of individuation" since he explains our awareness of individual things in reference to space and time. Sometimes he interchanges the narrower term, "principle of individuation" with the broader term, "principle of sufficient reason," producing some confusion. In what follows, we will need to remember that Schopenhauer's use of his key technical terms is sometimes inconsistent across his writings, but, with the above characterizations in mind, we can now turn to the specific contents of his doctoral dissertation, *The Fourfold Root of the Principle of Sufficient Reason*, to solidify the conceptual underpinnings of his philosophical outlook.

notes

1   See Galileo's 1623 essay, "Il Saggiatore" ("The Assayer").
2   *CPR*, B1.
3   *CPR*, A26/B42.
4   *CPR*, A42/B59.
5   "Il Saggiatore" [1623] ("The Assayer") in *Discoveries and Opinions of Galileo*, trans. Simon Drake (Anchor/Doubleday Press, 1957), p. 274.
6   *WWR* (I), "Appendix – Criticism of the Kantian Philosophy," P 418, HK 6–7, ZA 514–15. Schopenhauer repeats this characterization, close to verbatim, in *PP* (I), "Sketch of a History of the Doctrine of the Ideal and the Real," P 17, ZA 26. In both instances, Schopenhauer is reciting a passage from Kant's *Prolegomena* (§13), where Kant describes his own views as a development of Locke's.
7   *WWR* (I), Book I, §2, P 5–6, HK 6, ZA 32.

further reading

Berkeley, George, *A Treatise Concerning the Principles of Human Knowledge* [1710] (Oxford: Oxford University Press, 1998).
Hume, David, *A Treatise of Human Nature* [1739–40] (Oxford: Oxford University Press, 1978).
Kant, Immanuel, *Critique of Pure Reason*, trans. Paul Guyer and Allen W. Wood (Cambridge: Cambridge University Press, 1999).
Locke, John, *An Essay Concerning Human Understanding* [1689] (Oxford: Oxford University Press, 1979).
Schopenhauer, Arthur, "Sketch of a History of the Doctrine of the Ideal and the Real," in *Parerga and Paralipomena*, Vol. I. [1851] (Oxford: Oxford University Press, 1974).

the principle of sufficient reason

i the root of all explanation

In Schopenhauer's preface to *The World as Will and Representation* (*WWR*), we learn that to appreciate the philosophy contained therein, we must read the book twice, and familiarize ourselves not only with Kant, but with the contents of his PhD dissertation, *The Fourfold Root of the Principle of Sufficient Reason*, written five years earlier. Schopenhauer's advice is useful, for his dissertation significantly illuminates the main argument of his 1818 work. We considered Kant's views in the previous chapter; we will now look at Schopenhauer's dissertation in accord with his wishes.

A second edition of the *Fourfold Root* appeared in 1847 that expands the initial 1813 version.[1] Our emphasis here will be on the more succinct first edition that stands literally as a preliminary study to the *WWR*, attending specifically to the sections of the *Fourfold Root* whose themes are not more highly developed in *WWR*, but that nonetheless crucially inform the exposition in *WWR*. The themes shared between the *Fourfold Root* and the *WWR* that are more developed in the latter, we will discuss in later chapters.

The technically worded title of Schopenhauer's dissertation tells us exactly what his book is about: it concerns the principle of sufficient reason (hereafter, PSR), which he analyzes into a "root" with four different aspects. In the *Fourfold Root*, he reflects upon the relationships between the PSR's four defined aspects and draws conclusions for the fields of metaphysics and the theory of knowledge.

The PSR is in historical company with the Laws of Thought that come to us from Aristotle and the long history of Aristotelian logic. Both the PSR and the Laws of Thought aim to be philosophically basic, and they are the result of abstractive efforts to identify the most elementary rules or principles of human thought. They apply to *all* thought, so they are presupposed in their very own formulation. This makes it impossible to "prove" that the PSR or the Laws of Thought are true, since any proof would presuppose their truth to begin with. This would be like using logic to prove that logical proofs are intellectually valuable. Schopenhauer realizes this, and appreciates that every rational, articulated standpoint presupposes the PSR's truth. Even those radical viewpoints that aim to reject the PSR, never do so absolutely, insofar they remain in the realm of articulated concepts and coherent speech.

In ordinary terms, the Aristotelian Laws of Thought assert that we must assume that:

1 Whatever we think about retains its identity as we think about it. If this were not so, there would be nothing to pick out and refer to in our reflections. For example, even when we say that time flows endlessly, or, with Heraclitus, that one cannot step into the same river twice, we coherently identify and fix objects of attention called "time" and "the river."
2 Among the various qualities that there are, each quality has only one exact opposite, and if an object has either one of these, then it cannot have the other.
3 An object cannot have two exactly-opposing qualities at once, in the same respect.[2]

In formal terms, the first of these is the Law of Identity ("*A is A*"); the second is the Law of Excluded Middle ("*Either A or not-A*"); the third is the Law of Non-Contradiction ("*It cannot be that both A and not-A*"). When applied to thought and experience, these laws yield a thoroughly articulated world that contains a multitude of distinct objects, qualities, events, people, etc. Since the Laws of Thought have the effect of transforming our experience into a mosaic-like presentation in our efforts to comprehend our surroundings, it is *prima facie* difficult to express smooth fluctuations, fluidity or pure continuity, without transforming them to a more intellectually manageable series of step-by-step changes. When we comprehend the natural and continuous flow of time, for instance, we start with the fixed concept "time" to have something determinate to think about, and then divide the latter into centuries, decades, years, months, weeks, days, hours, minutes, seconds, split-seconds, and so on, to establish our bearings and increase our comprehension.

The PSR – a principle traceable to ancient Greek philosophy in pre-Socratic figures such as Anaximander (c. 540 BCE) – is a companion to the Aristotelian Laws of Thought that arises at a comparably elementary philosophical level. When the PSR extends to cover all subject matters, it asserts that for everything that is, there is a reason *why* it is, and that there are no genuine absurdities. It asserts that nothing happens by chance, or without a cause, or for no reason of all, or simply out of nowhere.

In its specific application, the PSR has some surprising and counter-intuitive implications. If all points in space are qualitatively the same, then one can argue that their uniform quality provides no reason why the Earth originally would have been moving in one direction as opposed to another. Hence, the Earth originally stood still. If all points in time are qualitatively the same, then one can argue that their uniform quality provides no reason why the universe would have been created at one point in time as opposed to another. Hence, the universe was not created at any particular point in time. Similarly, one can argue that no two individuals are exactly alike, since there would then be no reason why one individual would be in one place, and why the other would be in the other place.

The PSR, in effect, renders our experience rational and governs our practices of giving explanations. When we extend it to cover all subject matters, it asserts that everything is explainable. When we restrict its application, it asserts that everything is explainable within the circumscribed realm. The more we extend the principle, the more we assert that the world is a rational place. If we completely extend it, we assert that the real is the rational and that the rational is the real, as Hegel believed.

Whatever is beyond the scope of the PSR, if we acknowledge anything beyond it, is consequently rationally inaccessible and incapable of being explained philosophically, scientifically, psychologically, or in any other way. The PSR itself implies, quite consistently and yet intriguingly, that there can be no such realm of the inexplicable – the PSR cannot see beyond itself – but Schopenhauer acknowledges more reflectively that we can indicate a non-rational realm beyond the PSR's scope, and indeed, he grounds his philosophy on the presence and direct apprehensibility of this realm.

Leibniz's *Monadology* (1714) contains a well-known statement of the PSR, where we find it combined with the Law of Non-Contradiction:

31. Our reasonings are grounded upon two great *principles, that of contradiction,* in virtue of which we judge to be false, whatever involves a contradiction, and true, that which is opposed, or contradictory, to what is false.

32. *And that of sufficient reason,* in virtue of which we consider no fact to be true or existing, and no statement true, unless there is a sufficient reason why it should be such and not otherwise, although often we cannot know the reasons.

In his doctoral dissertation, Schopenhauer distinguishes the "root" of the PSR from four subordinate aspects in which that root is equally present. At the root of all explanation he recognizes a bipolar structure, namely, a *subject* of experience that seeks the explanation, and something that the subject seeks to explain, which is the *object* of the explanation. This subject–object distinction is not only at the root of all explanation; Schopenhauer claims that it underlies all "thinkability" itself, which makes the PSR very difficult to transcend. It infiltrates our entire awareness. In the first section of *WWR* (I), he writes:

> The division into object and subject . . . is the only form under which alone any representation of whatever kind it might be, abstract or intuitive, pure or empirical, is possible and thinkable at all. No truth is therefore more certain or more independent from all others, and less requisite of any proof than this: that everything that exists for knowledge – and therefore, the entire world – is only an object in relation to a subject, a perception of the perceiver, in a word, a representation.[3]

In union with the subject–object distinction, Schopenhauer identifies a complementary root to the PSR, which we met in the previous chapter's discussion of Hume and Kant. He states that if we are to have a genuine explanation of some fact or situation, the account must be necessary and not arbitrary. He consequently maintains, following Kant, that the idea of *necessary connection* is expressed in every form of the PSR. The kinds of subject matter can vary – and we will see this in the principle's fourfold division – but they equally involve necessary connections.

The PSR thus conveys a strong sense of rationality and provability, for whatever we aim to explain requires us to postulate that the things and relationships in question could not have been otherwise. It implies that all explanatory relationships are necessary, and yields a thoroughly deterministic outlook. If there is any free will, it consequently will not reside within the rational and explainable realm. As we shall see, when Schopenhauer characterizes the essence of the world as "Will," he consistently locates it inexplicably *outside* of the PSR.

In his description of the PSR's root, Schopenhauer introduces the form of logical judgment that we saw in Kant's analysis of causality, namely, "*if A, then B.*" He claims that every form of explanation embodies this style of thinking, whether it happens to be an explanation in mathematics or geometry, an explanation involving the definition of abstract concepts, an explanation about why some material object changed under certain conditions, or an explanation of why a person, given their character and situation, performed some action. In sum, then, the PSR's root has two main features: (1) the subject–object distinction, and (2) relationships of necessary connection.

ii the four basic forms of explanation

As the title of the *Fourfold Root* suggests, Schopenhauer believes that everything capable of explanation divides into four groups, each of which has its own self-contained explanatory style. These are (1) mathematical and geometrical objects, (2) abstract concepts, (3) physical objects or changes, and (4) motivations. These correspond to (1a) mathematical and geometric explanation, (2a) logical explanation, (3a) causal explanation and (4a) teleological (that is, "x for the sake of y" style) explanation.

Schopenhauer insists that we cannot combine two or more of the four principles of explanation (1a–4a) within a single explanation or argument and expect to have coherent results. It is rationally inappropriate, he believes, to begin an explanation with one type of object and a commitment to its associated style of explanation, and then conclude with objects associated with an alternative style of explanation. This is as if we could begin with a handful of apples and reasonably expect to extract orange juice from them.

Each kind of explanation involves necessary connection, but the types of necessary connections are different. It is one thing to say that a concept or judgment has logical implications, and another to say that a set of physical causes will have certain material effects. Geometrical and/or mathematical demonstrations differ from explaining why people act in light of their psychological motivations, although each style of explanation is grounded upon the basic "*if A, then B*" structure. Similarly, perfectly explaining how someone's brain works will not necessarily tell us what the person wants.

Schopenhauer draws some considerable philosophical implications from this prohibition against combining different modes of explanation. It violates his understanding of the PSR and its associated principles of explanation, for instance, to begin with a conceptual definition appropriate in the field of *logical explanation* and then use this to conclude that there are certain existing things for which *causal explanation* is appropriate. This is one reason why he rejects the argument for God's existence that begins by defining God as a perfect being. Assuming (controversially) that it is better to be than not to be, the argument is that if God has all positive qualities by definition, then God must exist.

Since this type of argument harbors incompatible styles of explanation, Schopenhauer unsympathetically dismisses all philosophies that ground themselves on it. He includes among them the German Idealist views of his contemporaries, Hegel and Schelling:

> The great extent to which Herr v. *Schelling* venerates the ontological proof can be seen from a long note on page 152 of the first volume of his

philosophical writings from 1809. But there is something even more instructive to be seen from this, namely, how an audacious assumption of fine airs and swagger is sufficient to throw sand into the eyes of the German people. That even such a thoroughly contemptible character as *Hegel* – whose entire sham-philosophy was actually a monstrous amplification of the ontological proof – tried to defend this proof against Kant's *Critique*, is an alliance of which the ontological proof itself would be ashamed, however little it might otherwise have reason to be embarrassed.[4]

Schopenhauer studied Aristotle in addition to Kant and Plato, and in confirmation of Kant's rejection of the ontological argument, he cites Aristotle, whom he believes refuted it definitively by stating centuries ago in his Posterior Analytics that the existence of any particular thing never belongs to its essence or definition. This is the very point Kant used to undermine the argument.[5]

When reading Schopenhauer's dissertation in abstraction from the history of philosophy, it is mysterious why he would identify four main aspects of the PSR, rather than two, five, seven, or some other number. If we recall Aristotle's own theory of explanation, though, the correspondence between Aristotle's doctrine of the four "causes" (or "becauses" or "reasons") and Schopenhauer's "fourfold root" of the PSR becomes evident. Their differences are also instructive.

In the explanation of any particular thing, Aristotle states that there are four basic questions to ask, the responses to which we can combine to form a full explanation of the thing. The questions are "What is it made of?" "What kind of thing is it?" "Where did it come from?" and "What is it for?" and they accordingly specify the material, formal, efficient, and final causes of the thing in question. In reference to a spoon, typical answers would be "it is made of metal," "it is an eating-utensil," "it was made by the eating-utensil craftsman," "its purpose is to help consume liquids or semi-solid food." In reference to a human being, the explanation would be that "it is made of flesh and blood," "it is a rational animal," "it came from its parent humans," and "its purpose is to act rationally."

In Aristotle's theory, the four answers jointly give an elementary explanation for the thing in question. Schopenhauer, within his own framework, contrastingly keeps separate the PSR's four modes of explanation and accordingly partitions the objects to be explained into separate aspects. A person, for instance, has a physical body subject to the laws of mechanics, a psychology subject to the laws of motivation, a bodily contour analyzable into geometrical configurations, and an intellect subject to assessments of logical integrity. These, however, remain four independent aspects of the person. As noted, Schopenhauerian would never admit that a person's complete brain-description could entail a motivational description for the person, even though they would parallel one another as two sides of the same coin.

We have seen that Schopenhauer's emphasis upon keeping separate the different objects of explanation, leads him to reject the ontological argument for God's existence and all philosophies that ground themselves upon it. These tend to start with a set of abstract conceptual forms, and proceed to derive the rest of existence, including the path of human history, as a matter of logical implication. Schopenhauer opposes such rationalism and self-consciously avoids starting his philosophy with abstract concepts, plans, or forms, such as to derive the spatio-temporal world from these abstractions in the manner of an ontological argument. He begins instead with concrete experience that can exceed what concepts can express, and remains focused upon it, developing his philosophy upon what he believes to be a truer, richer ground.

A point of tension arises in reference to Schopenhauer's admission that the PSR – the principle that he cannot but presuppose in the formulation of his philosophy – is not an absolute principle, but reflects only the basic form of human knowledge. If the PSR is so restricted, then it is puzzling how Schopenhauer's written philosophy could nonetheless assert that we can know how things absolutely are. He aims to transcend the PSR, but he must compose his philosophy in accord with it, simply to communicate his vision in publicly accessible terms. To intensify matters, the deepest levels of Schopenhauer's philosophy follow the structure of the PSR's root, for we can discern its bipolar structure in the title of his main text, *The World as Will* [subject] *and Representation* [object].

Throughout the exposition to follow, we will discern a tension between what Schopenhauer recognizes as knowable and expressible within the constraints of the PSR and what he wishes to indicate as the reality that underlies and to some extent transcends, everything that can be expressed within the PSR's scope. This expresses a philosophical predicament typical for anyone who begins their reflections with Kant's insights: if we are spatio-temporal beings who are attempting to develop a properly philosophical outlook, how can the spatio-temporal forms of language and meaning transcend themselves to indicate a mode of being that is independent of the PSR and its associated spatio-temporal forms? It is not clear how this can be achieved. Schopenhauer's solution, as we shall see, is to characterize as much as he can in terms of matters of degree, such as to indicate a mode of awareness that is almost, but not perfectly, PSR-independent. In the later chapter on Ludwig Wittgenstein's twentieth-century linguistic philosophy, we will see a related solution that is more explicitly mystical.

Recognizing the constraints that the PSR imposes, Schopenhauer states that he intends to provide the best "philosophical" expression of the world, while admitting that this expression is not absolutely descriptive of all that reality contains. He acknowledges open-mindedly that mystical, non-rational experiences – a position he calls "illuminism" – might reveal a higher reality, although philosophy and rational thought in general can have nothing positive to say about such hypothetical mystical dimensions. Everything Schopenhauer expresses philosophically, needs to be read in light of his recognition of inexplicable modes of awareness, even though the present interpretation will aim to diminish the metaphysically revelatory significance of these modes. The difficulty at the center of his philosophy is that although Schopenhauer believes wholeheartedly that his metaphysics of the Will is compatible with mystical awareness, the more he acknowledges the possibility of untold mystical dimensions of reality, the weaker his core assertion that the thing-in-itself is "Will" becomes.

Since the PSR operates within the parameters of space, time, logic, mathematics, geometry, and causality, Schopenhauer describes it as a principle of individuation. It applies to appearances or phenomena, but it does not apply to things in themselves. This has a wide-ranging impact in that a major part of our personal identity – the part constituted by how, for example, we physically look, where we were born, and what our particular experiences have been – does not consequently express what is essentially timeless and ultimately real within us.

Insofar as the PSR generates a spatio-temporal, historically grounded appearance that distracts us from the unchanging essentials, it can be seen as a principle of ignorance when we apply it without qualification. As a divisive principle of individuation, it produces a feeling of separation from other people and from reality as a whole; it is a principle of the "I" in the sense of "my ego" and my sense of finite individuality. The error lies in believing that such PSR-generated divisions are absolute and unbridgeable.

This all indicates that Schopenhauer's philosophy – a philosophy written within the constraints of the PSR and structured by it – as it directs us towards ways to transcend the PSR, will conclude by transcending itself as a philosophical construction. The associated change of consciousness will involve transcending our sense of separation from other people and from the physical world as a whole. It will direct us to see through the illusion, the *maya*, or living dream that the PSR generates in its crystallization of the world into a set of individual, separate things. In the end, we will apprehend ourselves as having been in a state of ignorance during our involvements with theoretical philosophy, ordinary routine, petty disagreements, selfish territoriality, and materialistic quests. We will see ourselves as having been like ice cubes floating in a basin of water, that failed to realize how they are constituted by the very water in which they were situated. This philosophy-transcending aspect of Schopenhauer's philosophy is nicely echoed in a concluding remark from Wittgenstein's *Tractatus Logico-Philosophicus* (1921):

> My propositions are elucidatory in this way: he who understands me finally recognizes them as senseless, when he has climbed out through them, on them, over them. (He must, so to speak, throw away the ladder, after he has climbed up on it.) He must transcend these propositions, and then he will see the world aright. (6.54)

notes

1 The English translation most commonly encountered is that of this longer second edition, and this creates some confusion in appreciating what Schopenhauer actually expected his readers to assume as necessary for understanding the first volume of *The World as Will and Representation* in 1818.
2 We can also formulate the Laws of Thought in reference to propositions. For instance, the Law of Non-Contradiction would deny that "this cat is red" and "this cat is not red" can both be true of this cat. Similarly, the Law of Excluded Middle would state that any given proposition must be either true or false, and that there is no third position between truth and falsity.
3 *WWR* (I), §1, P 3, HK 3, ZA 29.
4 *FFR*, P 16, ZA 24.
5 *WWR* (I), "Appendix: Criticism of the Kantian Philosophy," P 511, HK 129–30, ZA 623.

further reading

Hamlyn, D. W., *Schopenhauer: The Arguments of the Philosophers* (London: Routledge & Kegan Paul, 1980).

Pruss, Alexander, *The Principle of Sufficient Reason: A Reassessment* (Cambridge: Cambridge University Press, 2006).

Schopenhauer, Arthur, *On the Fourfold Root of the Principle of Sufficient Reason* [1813/1847], trans. E. J. F. Payne (La Salle, Illinois: Open Court, 1974).

White, F. C., *On Schopenhauer's* Fourfold Root of the Principle of Sufficient Reason (Leiden: Brill, 1992).

White, F. C. (ed.), *Schopenhauer's Early Fourfold Root: Translation and Commentary* (Aldershot: Avebury, Ashgate Publishing Ltd., 1997).

schopenhauer's idealism and his criticism of kant

i the rejection of a mind-independent reality

As we saw in Chapter 2, the Lockean theory of perception conceals the external world behind a screen of opaque mental imagery and gives a frustrating answer to the question "What causes the mental imagery that we do not seem to be causing ourselves?" The common assumption is that a satisfactory answer to this question will positively describe the mind-independent reality to which our shared experiences of the world seem to refer. That there *is* a mind-independent reality is a virtually unquestioned assumption for most philosophical theorists and most people. Schopenhauer, however, departs from the majority's opinion and denies that there is a mind-independent reality. This stems partly from conceptual difficulties he found in Kant's and Locke's theories of perception.

Granted, Kant's theory of perception solves some nagging Lockean problems by explaining more effectively how we can have direct knowledge of an external, spatio-temporal world. By regarding space, time, and logical relationships as humanly shared modes of organizing given sensory information, he adds a measure of transparency to the immediate flow of mental imagery before our minds. Since it is clear to Kant that the same mind-independent reality directly affects us all, and that everyone's experience is informed equally by space, time, and logic, he interprets space and time, in conjunction with our rational nature, as if they were a single lens through which we together apprehend what is independent of us. A mind-independent reality touches us directly, and through our spatio-temporal, logical modes of apprehension it presents itself to us publicly as a set of directly perceivable external objects. This retains the commonsense idea that our daily experience is the effect of a mind-independent reality that we apprehend in common. It is, however, not without a price, for Kant must consequently describe the mind-independent reality mysteriously as being timeless and spaceless in itself.

Kant explains how we can directly perceive external objects, but he leaves the question "What, then, is the nature of the mind-independent reality that causes the colors, sounds, odors, tastes, textures, shapes, and movements within our shared experience?" with a thin answer. Berkeley faces a similar difficulty within the context of the representative theory of perception, after having argued that an external, mind-independent material world could not exist, and could not therefore be the cause of the mental images that we do not imaginatively produce ourselves. As we know, Berkeley's answer is that God – a spaceless, timeless, spiritual, all-powerful, mind-independent reality – produces these objects.

Kant adopts a more careful attitude towards what he could prove, and soberly admits that he can demonstrate nothing positive about the world's mind-independent being as it is in itself. He adds, though, that we must refer to *something* foundational beyond possible human experience, for otherwise our experience will have no metaphysical ground. We can easily recognize Kant's rationale: it compares, for instance, to how we postulate some sort of determinate chemical substance that grounds or stimulates the experience of sweetness, knowing well that such experiences are not normally the mere product of a person's imagination, but issue from the contact of a certain type of material upon the tongue. The following excerpt reveals Kant's own argument, where he uses the concepts of "object" and "cause" to indicate the ground of our sensations:

> The capacity for sensory intuition is in fact only a receptivity for being affected by representations in a certain way . . . The non-sensory cause of these representations is completely unknown to us, and we cannot consequently intuit it as an object . . . Nonetheless, we can generally call the purely intelligible cause of appearances the transcendental object, but only to have something to which sensibility as a receptivity can correspond. To this transcendental object we can ascribe the entire extent and connection of all of our possible perceptions, and say that prior to all experience, it is given in itself.[1]

Since, for Kant, we never perceive objects as they are in themselves, there seems to be no choice but to postulate that however these objects are in themselves, their mind-independent condition – as unknowable as it may be – is what largely determines our experiences of them. This calls to mind how Locke refers to material substance as something, he knows not what, in which mind-independent qualities such as extension and solidity inhere.[2]

Schopenhauer wholly accepts the distinction between how things appear and how they are in themselves, claiming that Kant's philosophical use of it is one of his greatest achievements. He flatly rejects the use the term "cause," however, to characterize the relationship between our sensations and what metaphysically grounds them, taking the lead from Kant himself: Kant maintains that causal relationships express our own logical nature and that we cannot know whether they describe mind-independent connections within in the world as it is in itself. Furthermore, Kant often suggests that when a relationship or quality is mind-dependent, it cannot exist in the mind-independent sphere. Asserting otherwise is like maintaining nonsensically that we could discover the experience of sweetness within an untasted sugar cube.

Sometimes, however, Kant states more temperately that causality and other logically-grounded relationships cannot be proven to inhere in the world as it is in itself. This is as opposed to saying definitively that they are not there. Either way, Schopenhauer finds it inconsistent to say within the Kantian framework that the relationship between ourselves and the thing-in-itself – that is, between ourselves and the metaphysical ground of our sensations that is outside the bounds of human experience – can be characterized *knowingly* as a causal relationship. Kant himself holds that causal relationships apply with certainty only *within* the field of possible human experience and not beyond it. If we apply causal relationship outside of possible human experience, we merely speculate.

Schopenhauer concludes that Kant contradicts himself by stating that perceptual objects as they are in themselves *cause* our sensations. Imagining any other possibility is difficult for Kant, though, for he believes that if we do not employ the concept of causality to explain the source of our perceptions, the situation would be absurd.

His argument is that the very word, "appearance," implies a reference to something that appears, whose being is in excess of the specific way it appears.[3] Otherwise, an "appearance" will not be an appearance at all, but will be something that presents itself in its full being without hiding anything. In his effort to identify the source of our sensations, Kant cannot imagine any other relationship aside from the relationship of causality that can account for this difference. He consequently links the appearance/reality distinction to the cause/effect distinction:

> On the other hand, if appearances are not considered to be more than they are in fact – that is, if they are not considered to be things-in-themselves, but are considered to be merely representations connected together according to empirical laws – then they must have grounds that are not appearances. But such an intelligible cause, considered in terms of its causality, is not determined through appearances, although its effects appear and therefore can themselves be determined by other appearances. The intelligible cause along with its causality is therefore outside of the series of appearances, even though its effects are to be found within the series. The effect, considered in light of its intelligible cause, can therefore be considered to be free, while at the same time, when it is considered as an appearance, can

be considered to result from appearances according to the necessity of nature.[4]

Aside from the naturalness of this linkage and independently of the details of the above passage that concern human freedom, Kant is entrenched in a philosophical tradition that almost universally uses the concept of causality to answer foundational questions. This concept is used traditionally, for instance, to explain our perceptions within the context of a scientific description of the world, to explain our ordinary actions, as when we regard our motivations as the cause of our behavior, and to explain the very origins of the universe (as in the "first cause" [cosmological] argument for God's existence).

Moreover, we can appreciate Kant's use of the term "causality" if we recall the above example of the sugar crystals that, upon touching the tongue, contribute to causing the experience of sweetness. We can perceive the sugar visually as it is independently of our tongue and we can perceive the sugar when our tongue touches it, noting how the sugar is in its tongue-independent reality and in its tongue-dependent appearance. The same bit of sugar clearly causes both presentations. It is consequently reasonable to refer to the tongue-independent sugar as a contributing cause to the experience of sweetness, and it is natural to employ this relationship to elucidate the more general philosophical distinction between appearance and reality. It is particularly plausible when we are trying to explain perceptual experience.

Once we model the entirety of perceptual experience after the way we account for the sweetness of the sugar in the above example, the Kantian account leads us to refer to perceptual objects as they are imagined to be independently of space and time. Kant refers to these as "transcendental" objects, postulating them as a contributing causal condition to account for the presence of perceptual objects in our daily, shared experience. For him, perceptual objects are the appearances and effects of mind-independent transcendental objects.

Schopenhauer rejects this Kantian model, following one of his teachers at the University of Göttingen, G. E. Schulze, who claims that Kant's postulation of an unknowable, mind-independent reality as the *cause* of our perceptions, extends the concept of causality beyond its legitimate application. According to Schopenhauer, the problem is in assuming "that empirical perception, or more accurately, that the *sensation* in our sense organs from which it proceeds, must have an external [mind-independent] cause."[5] To ordinary ears, this sounds less like a problem, and more like a perfectly natural assumption.

It is perhaps reasonable enough to say in general, as did Locke, that our ordinary perceptual experiences have an external cause in publicly accessible objects located in space and time. It nonetheless remains incoherent for Kant to maintain that such experiences have a mind-independent cause outside of space and time. For, according to his own theory, causality cannot knowingly apply outside of space and time. Recognizing these constraints, Schopenhauer rejects the idea of a mind-independent, spaceless, and timeless reality (viz., the thing-in-itself) that is the *cause* our sensations as a matter of consistency. This yields a philosophically peculiar situation, for if we cannot say that a mind-independent reality causes our experience, it is unclear what plausible alternatives remain.

Moving towards a more definitively idealist position, Schopenhauer draws the radical conclusion that we must understand everything in our experience in reference to our own activity alone, without referring to a mind-independent reality:

> According to [Kant's] own and correct discovery, the law of causality is known to us *a priori*, and is consequently a function of our intellect, and is therefore of *subjective* origin. Furthermore, sensation itself, to which we here apply the causal law, is incontestably *subjective*; and finally, even space, in which we locate the cause of the sensation as object, is an *a priori* given form, and hence a *subjective* form of our intellect. Therefore the whole of empirical intuition thoroughly remains on a *subjective* ground and basis as a mere happening in us, and nothing from it that is completely different and independent can be brought in as a thing-in-itself, or demonstrated to be a necessary presupposition.[6]

Schopenhauer's objection to Kant's use of the term "causality" to characterize the alleged relationship between transcendental objects and our experience brings us a step closer to Schopenhauer's positive views. We have perceptual experiences (of the sun, moon, etc.) that we are unaware of consciously causing or willing, and the above arguments force us to admit that our perceptual experiences are not grounded in mind-independent entities, contrary to what common sense would say. Schopenhauer concludes that their grounds must be subjective in origin, but distinguishable from our conscious awareness. Again, this philosophical situation is comparable to the position at which Berkeley arrives after rejecting Locke's mind-independent material substance and considering whether God is the mind-independent spirit that causes the ideas we do not cause ourselves.

Schopenhauer's problem is more challenging than Berkeley's, for he can use neither the concept of causality nor the notion of a mind-independent reality to account for the qualities of our experience that we are unaware of causing ourselves. His solution is consequently that much more extreme. We will address it at the end of the present chapter and in the next chapter, but let us presently consider a second criticism that Schopenhauer levels at Kant's conception of a mind-independent reality to underscore the philosophical pressures to which Schopenhauer is responding.

ii kant's theory of perception

To appreciate Schopenhauer's second criticism of Kant, we can add a few words about Kant's theory of perception. Kant inherits the problem of justifying scientific inquiry as the result of a Humean critique that undermines all attempts to derive the concept of causality – understood as a necessary connection between events – from experience. Kant resolves this difficulty by deriving it from logical forms located within ourselves, rather than from the observation of the external world. With similar arguments, he argues that space and time are forms of our own perception, as opposed to the natural view that space and time are mind-independent forms of the world as it is in itself.

With this subjectivistic account of space, time, and causality, as we have seen, Kant resolved the Lockean problem of knowing the external world. For if space and time are our own projections, then the spatio-temporal "external world" need not be regarded as a mind-independent being, inaccessibly concealed behind a screen of mental imagery. The external world – the world of space, time, and scientifically analyzable perceptual objects – instead becomes in reference to its spatio-temporal qualities, a mind-*dependent* being of which we are directly aware.

Accordingly, for Kant, when we perceive the sun, a tree, or a round, brown table in ordinary circumstances, we are perceiving a mind-independent reality directly and undoubtedly. This reality is immediately present to us, but in itself, it lacks spatio-temporal dimensions. Through its contact with us, given the kind of beings that we are, it appears to us in the form of spatio-temporal perceptual objects. The result is that we perceive a set of objects that *seem* to be of themselves mind-independent. This "seeming" compares to how an ordinary object's color seems to be infused upon the object's very surface, when in fact, color qualities are more accurately located in us, like the taste of sugar. A mind-independent reality causes the entire spatio-temporal presentation of perceptual objects, and, owing to its own mind-independence, it fosters the illusion that the way it appears to us is also mind-independent, through and through.

The mind-independent appearance of ordinary perceptual objects, as is the case with the sun, tree, or round brown table mentioned above, includes for Kant, more exactly, only the spatio-temporal and logically derived qualities of the object (that is, what Locke called "primary qualities"). An object's circularity would be an example. The quality of circularity is publicly, scientifically, and measurably perceivable, since it is grounded on the a priori spatiality that we know all humans project identically. That we all perceive equally, universally, and necessarily according to these forms further supports the appearance that the spatio-temporal objects themselves are independent of this or that individual mind. In contrast, the brownness of the table is a more private matter, since this perceptual quality varies from person to person, as physiological sensitivities vary. It is like the sweet taste of sugar, which similarly varies.

The objects of ordinary perception thus partially *reveal* their mind-independent cause via the public accessibility (that is, intersubjectivity) of the object's spatio-temporal and logically-derived qualities. They also *obscure* this cause with the added presence of individually variable (that is, more privately determined) colors, tastes, sounds, textures, and odors. The mind-independent reality affects us all, and, insofar as we all think in concert, we apprehend a public world that contains objects that appear to be independent of each one of us.

At the same time, we never knowingly apprehend the mind-independent reality as it is in itself, since neither the spatio-temporal, nor the logically-derived, nor the more privately determined qualities allow us to apprehend the true being of things with total transparency. All perceptual qualities stand in relationship to mind-independent reality as colors and tastes stand to ordinary perceptual objects: such qualities reveal the immediate presence of a public reality, but they do not resemble it.

To understand this extraordinary situation through a further analogy, we can reflect that all flies have prismatic eyes and that any given fly's world is necessarily a prismatic world. If any fly happens to die, then the prismatic world of the remaining flies would nonetheless remain as the remaining flies' shared objective world. If all flies were to die, then the prismatic world of the flies would disappear, since the fly-independent cause of the flies' prismatic world is not in itself prismatic.

In this sense, Kant maintains that space and time (which are analogous here to the fly's prismatic eye) would vanish if there were no people. His theory of perception thus raises the question of whether, using the above analogy, a prismatic object in some individual fly's field of perception is a "fly-independent" object. The answer is that insofar as a fly-independent being causes and is itself present in the fly's prismatic perceptual object, the perceptual object is fly-independent. Insofar as the fly's perceptual object appears to be prismatic in itself, the object is not fly-independent.

Locke claims that we directly perceive only our mental images and that their spatio-temporal qualities resemble spatio-temporal, mind-independent qualities in external objects of which we can only be indirectly aware, adding that the colors, tastes, etc. within our mental imagery do not resemble qualities in the external objects. Kant stays close to this picture, except that he maintains that we directly, rather than indirectly, perceive the external objects. We perceive the external objects directly, with both their socially-constant qualities (for example, shapes) and individually-variable qualities (for example, colors) amalgamated in our perception. He writes:

> Colors, which are attached to the intuitions of bodies, are not qualities of the bodies themselves, but are only modifications of the sense of sight, which is affected by light in certain ways. In contrast to this, space, as the condition for external objects, belongs to the appearance or intuition in a necessary way. Tastes and colors are not at all necessary conditions under which objects can alone be objects of the senses. They are connected with appearances only as accidentally added effects due to the particular constitution of the sense organs . . . Through space is it alone possible that things can be external objects for us.[7]

Our *translucent* (as opposed to opaque or transparent) access to the apparently mind-independent spatio-temporal object according to this Kantian theory of perception will be of central importance in understanding Schopenhauer's views. According to Kant's theory, in ordinary perception we directly perceive an object that has empirically real qualities (viz., the intersubjectively invariant, public, spatio-temporal qualities) that are *perceptually blended* with empirically ideal qualities (viz., the subjectively variable tastes, colors, etc.), and we come into public contact with mind-independent reality via our awareness of the former, empirically real qualities. This epistemological translucency of the perceptual object is important not only for understanding Kant and for understanding Schopenhauer's criticism of Kant; it can serve as an illuminating model for understanding Schopenhauer's own account of how we can become of aware of things-in-themselves.

iii kant's use of the term "object"

Schopenhauer criticizes Kant's theory of perception on two counts, both of which concern Kant's use of the term "object." The first relies upon Schopenhauer's analysis of knowledge in the *Fourfold Root*, where he maintains that the subject–object distinction is at the root of the principle of sufficient reason (PSR). The second criticism maintains that external objects cannot be the appearances of transcendental, mind-independent objects that are in principle unknowable. Let us consider each in turn.

The first criticism extends the prohibition against using the concept of causality to characterize the relationship between things-in-themselves and the perceptions that we are not causing ourselves. Since the PSR (which contains the concept of causality) applies only within the field of possible human experience, and since things-in-themselves are located outside of this field, then the subject–object distinction at the PSR's root – a distinction that grounds the very concept of an object in general – cannot apply to things-in-themselves. Kant, according to Schopenhauer, therefore errs in referring to any mind-independent realities as "objects," transcendental or otherwise, in the first place:

> It is certainly striking that [Kant] did not derive this merely relative existence of the appearance from the simple, and so easily assessable and undeniable truth, *"No object without a subject"* in order to show that at the very root, the object – because it is in relationship to a subject in every instance – is dependent on the subject and conditioned through the subject. Therefore, the object exists not in itself unconditionally, but exists as a pure appearance.[8]

> . . . the being-of-an-object in general belongs to the form of appearances, and is conditioned by the being-of-the-subject in general, just as the object's manner of appearing is conditioned by the subject's forms of knowledge. Hence, if a thing-in-itself is to be assumed, it cannot be an object at all.[9]

Schopenhauer's second criticism is more technical, but it also questions Kant's reference to mind-independent "objects." It is that Kant's theory of perception involves three different sorts of entity and a corresponding triple distinction, but that one of these is actually a non-entity. We have on the face of things: (1) the presentation of some spatio-temporal perceptual object; (2) the non-experiencable, foundational dimension of that perceptual object (the "transcendental object")[10] that causes the perceptual representation to appear as it does; (3) the thing-in-itself that is the ultimate ground of the object's transcendental foundation.[11]

Included in (1) is the spatio-temporal form and the sensory qualities that constitute the perceptual object. Included in (2) – which Schopenhauer also refers to as the "object of experience" – is the projection beyond our sensations towards a mind-independent object that underlies and is correlated with the individual perceptual object. Whatever mind-independent reality is ultimately responsible for the mind-independent transcendental object that correlates with the perceptual object as the latter appears in space and time is represented by (3).

Schopenhauer claims that the transcendental object (2) is a non-entity, which reduces the true perceptual situation to (1) and (3). He cannot see how the idea of a transcendental object makes any sense, since all of the perceptual content is in (1) and since (3) is a totally sufficient, mind-independent reality:

[Kant's] "object of experience," of which he is constantly speaking, the true subject of the categories, is not the representation of perception. Neither is it the abstract concept. It is different from both, and is yet both at the same time, and is a complete non-entity and absurdity.[12]

. . . upon thinking clearly, there is nothing further to be found except representation [*Vorstellung*] and thing-in-itself [*Ding-an-sich*]. The unjustified insertion of that hybrid, the object of the representation, is the source of Kant's mistakes.[13]

A transcendental object is that which causes our sensations and is what a perceptual object is in itself mind-independently. In some excerpts, Kant also refers to the transcendental object as the ultimate object of all our particular representations. Schopenhauer questions the coherence of this notion because the transcendental object stands outside of all possible human experience and is ascribed causal efficacy nonetheless. Moreover, since PSR-related mental processes – ones that are legitimate only within the field of possible human experience – construct objects, it makes no sense to refer to objects that one cannot experience in principle.

These various criticisms of Kant's use of the term "object" indirectly illuminate Schopenhauer's own view, for they have the key effect of prohibiting the use of the term "object" in reference to whatever foundationally grounds our experience. This paves the way for Schopenhauer's alternative account of the thing-in-itself – one that denies that it is an object, denies that it is mind-independent, and asserts that it is directly apprehensible.

As a matter of terminological clarification, the above distinctions also allow us to identify three ways to refer to the non-phenomenal, spaceless, and timeless realm that arises within these discussions. Consider some perceptual object such as a table. The first usage draws our attention to the table as it is in itself, or the "transcendental table" that correlates with the perceptual table. This would be the table "in itself," or that thing "in itself," or the "thing in itself" within this context of perceiving the individual table. The second refers to the unknowable collection of all transcendental objects as "things-in-themselves." The third usage is the "thing-in-itself" that refers to the single unknowable being that is non-spatial, non-temporal, and is "reality" as it is in itself. Owing to his critique of Kant's notion of the transcendental object, Schopenhauer typically uses the phase, "thing-in-itself" in the third, universalistic sense. The emerging question is whether we can apprehend the nature of reality as a whole – the "thing-in-itself" – in the absence of illusion or distortion.

iv the logic of manifestation

A leading feature of Kant's philosophy is the assumption that in daily life we experience the appearance of an unknowable mind-independent reality that is in itself different from the way it appears. He accordingly states, "the things that we intuit are not in themselves what we intuit them as being,"[14] suggesting that the things in our experience somehow retain their individuality and integrity mind-independently as things *per se*. He adds that between the mind-independent objects and their respective spatio-temporal appearances, the relationship of causality applies, if mysteriously.

If Schopenhauer's criticisms of Kant are plausible – especially if we accept that it is illegitimate to say knowingly that transcendental objects cause anything in our experience – then if we distinguish between reality as it is in itself as opposed to how it otherwise appears to us, we must define some relationship between appearance and reality that is not causal. We also need to avoid referring to reality in itself as some sort of object.

One of the more subtle and penetrating difficulties Schopenhauer has with the concept of causality is that it introduces sharp divisions within any subject matter into which it is projected. We can see this by noting how it makes no obvious sense to assert that anything is self-caused. If it were, then it would incoherently need to be before it came into being. So if one asserts "*A* causes *B*," then *A* and *B* cannot be identical. Applying the relationship of causality within any situation or subject matter thus divides that situation or subject matter from the very start. The idea that "all is seamlessly one" contradicts the very logic and application of causal relationships.

The statement that "reality as it is in itself" *causes* our sensations consequently makes it seem as if we are different from this reality, and that it could continue to exist when we no longer exist. The introduction of the causal relationship to describe our relationship with how things are in themselves consequently alienates us from this fundamental being, as if we could be divorced absolutely from reality itself, as if we were not an essential part of it, and as if it did not itself flow through us all equally as well.

This alienation from metaphysical truth gives a false ring to post-Kantian philosophers such as Schopenhauer, and it motivates them to criticize Kant's theory of knowledge. Arguably, the root of the problem involves using the concept of causality to characterize our metaphysical relationship to what fundamentally is. As noted above, the philosophical challenge facing Schopenhauer was to find a way to preserve the appearance–reality distinction while rejecting the causal relationship as a way to account for this distinction.

To replace the causal relationship, Schopenhauer introduces an alternative that when applied to two apparently different things, A and B, allows A and B to be substantially identical despite their apparent difference. This relationship can be variously expressed and Schopenhauer famously uses terms such as "objectification" and "manifestation" for this purpose. For instance, ice cubes are a manifestation of the chemical substance, H_2O, lightning is a manifestation of electricity, and X-rays are a manifestation of electromagnetic energy. In each case, the basic substance or form of energy remains the same, while the appearances of the basic substance or energy vary. Ice cubes *are* water; lightning *is* electricity; X-rays *are* electromagnetic energy.

Sometimes the differences between an underlying reality and its manifestations are sharp, as in the case where the substance, carbon, manifests itself as either black charcoal or as crystalline diamond, or where the substance, H_2O, which has a microscopic configuration, manifests itself either as solid ice, liquid water, or gaseous water vapor.

Sometimes the differences between some underlying reality and its manifestations express matters of degree. We see this in how glass manifests itself in forms that range from purely transparent glass to translucent glass to opaque glass. Similarly, tea manifests itself as a leaf on a plant, as a semi-dried leaf, as crispy dried leaf or as a fine powder.

Another example would be an insect that slowly changes from a caterpillar to a butterfly through metamorphosis, where the various stages are manifestations or objectifications of the same individual insect's life. Yet another would be consciousness, which manifests itself in a continuum ranging from thoroughly unconscious states to deep sleep states to active dreaming states to semi-awake states to normal conscious states to super-aware states. Consciousness is the prime example here, for Schopenhauer asserts that reality itself has a foundationally subjective character akin to a deeply sleeping, or blind and unconscious, state of mind.

Independently of whether the relationship between some underlying reality and its manifestation is sharp or continuous, when we speak of A being a manifestation of B we assume that A and B are identical in some substantial sense. Schopenhauer uses this sort of logic to characterize the relationship between appearances and the way things are in themselves. When he refers to "the world as representation" and of "the world as will," he always does so with the understanding that they are metaphysically identical, and that the former is a manifestation of the latter.

The logic of manifestation is typically asymmetrical: if B is a manifestation of A, then it does not follow that A is a manifestation of B. Ice cubes are a manifestation of water, but water is not a manifestation of ice cubes. So when Schopenhauer states, "no object without a subject" upon the assumption that objectivity is a manifestation of subjectivity, it would follow that there can be no objects without subjects. It would not follow that there can be no subjects without objects. This makes it possible to refer to an energy or mode of being that is in itself purely subjective. Schopenhauer will call this "Will."

In sum, Schopenhauer's critique of Kant leads us negatively to understand the thing-in-itself as not being an object of any sort, and positively as bearing a manifestational or objectificational relationship to individual selves and to our world of daily experience. The substance of reality does not "cause" an additional and separate layer of appearance that is metaphysically independent and distinct from it. Rather, the substance of reality constitutes the things that appear to us. The problem that Schopenhauer will be addressing is how there can be an experience of perceptual objects that we are unaware of producing ourselves, when his theory entails that there is a sense in which we *are* indeed producing them. As we shall see, he accounts for this in a manner analogous to how dream contents are explained: while we are dreaming, we are not conscious of producing the dream contents ourselves, but it remains that the dream products are a manifestation of our own minds. At bottom, with the world's pain and suffering in mind, he believes that we are the manifestations of reality's nightmare.

notes

1 *CPR*, A494/B522.
2 See Locke's *An Essay Concerning Human Understanding*, Book II, Chapter XXIII, Section 2.
3 *CPR*, Bxxvi.
4 *CPR*, A537/B565.
5 *WWR* (I), "Appendix: Criticism of the Kantian Philosophy," P 436, HK 30, ZA 535.
6 *WWR* (I), "Appendix: Criticism of the Kantian Philosophy," P 436, HK 30–1, ZA 535–6.
7 *CPR*, A 28–9.
8 *WWR* (I), "Appendix: Criticism of the Kantian Philosophy," P 434, HK 28, ZA 533.
9 *WWR* (I), "Appendix: Criticism of the Kantian Philosophy," P 503, HK 119, ZA 614.
10 *WWR* (I), "Appendix: Criticism of the Kantian Philosophy," P 444, HK 41, ZA 545.
11 *WWR* (I), "Appendix: Criticism of the Kantian Philosophy," P 444, HK 41, ZA 545.

12 *WWR* (I), "Appendix: Criticism of the Kantian Philosophy," P 437, HK 32, ZA 537.
13 *WWR* (I), "Appendix: Criticism of the Kantian Philosophy," P 444, HK 41, ZA 545.
14 *CPR*, A42/B59.

further reading

Schopenhauer, Arthur, "Appendix: Criticism of the Kantian Philosophy" in *The World as Will and Representation*, Vol. I, trans. E. F. J. Payne (New York: Dover Publications, 1969).

Schulze, G. E., "Anesidemus" (excerpt) in *Between Kant and Hegel: Texts in the Development of Post-Kantian Idealism*, translated and annotated by George di Giovanni and H. S. Harris (Albany: SUNY Press, 1985).

Young, Julian, *Willing and Unwilling: A Study in the Philosophy of Arthur Schopenhauer* (Dordrecht: Martinus Nijhoff, 1987).

the world in itself as a meaningless and almighty will

i universal subjectivity

We have just seen how Schopenhauer conceives of the relationship between reality and appearance as one where reality *manifests*, rather than causes, a certain appearance. When "*A* manifests itself as *B*," *A* and *B* can be identical; when "A causes B," they cannot. The manifestational relationship preserves a fundamental unity between the items in relation; the causal relationship sharply separates them. The former is appropriate for a monistic metaphysics that asserts, "all is essentially one"; the latter fits the spirit of a dualistic or pluralistic metaphysics that asserts, "all is essentially two" or "all is essentially many."

This brings us to Schopenhauer's conception of the universal being that manifests itself as the world we perceptually experience. To formulate this conception, he reflects upon his own inner being, hoping to plumb its depths to a point where he touches upon his most basic subjective dimension. His reflective method is like Descartes's, except that Schopenhauer does not radically doubt his bodily presence to the point where he ends up philosophizing from the standpoint of a disembodied spirit. For Schopenhauer, his bodily awareness remains central, and his philosophy rests upon an analysis of this awareness.

If each of us places our hand on the table and observes it visually, as far as concerns the generally perceived quality of the items within our visual field, our hand is exactly like the rest of the items; it has a color, weight, texture, and so on. When we observe someone else's hand, the other person's hand appears the same as ours, as a physical object like the other perceivable objects on the table.

In Schopenhauer's language, one's hand or body, as a representation *qua* representation, is essentially no different from any other representation.

Indeed, his *principal* contention is that when we perceive the world, *all* representations are on a metaphysical par. They thoroughly constitute perceptual experience, and as *objects* (as opposed to conscious subjects), their basic phenomenological and metaphysical quality is uniform.

Schopenhauer notes that he has an additional and privileged access to his own body – one that is of decisive philosophical significance:

> To the subject of knowing – which appears as an individual through his identity with the body – this body is given in two completely different ways: first as representation in intelligent perception as an object among objects and as prone to the laws of these objects. It is also simultaneously given in an altogether different way, namely, as that which is immediately known to every one of us, which the word *will* indicates.[1]

Before we reflect upon Schopenhauer's meaning of the term "will," we can say that for each of us, and for a simple reason, the representation of our body is special among all of our perceptual representations. Unlike the bulk of our perceptual experience, we experience as intrinsic to our body's objective or "outer" aspect, a subjective or "inner" aspect as well. We can feel the inside of our own hand as we look at it resting upon the table. We cannot feel the inside of another person's hand, nor can we feel the inside of the fork, knife, plate, or table upon which our hand rests. Like the two poles of a magnet, we experience our hand as having two aspects, closely connected and basic, whereas the other objects appear to have only one aspect, namely, their objective side. They appear to be nothing more than objects.

This asymmetry between the dual-aspected, or polar, representation of our bodies and the single-aspected quality of all other representations presents a puzzling picture for Schopenhauer, since he observes that *all* representations look, sound, taste, smell, or feel exactly alike in their objective qualities. The brown color of one's eye is exactly the same brown as can appear in a blotch of paint. So we need to accept either that the representation of our body is the only representation within our experience that has a subjective side and a polar structure – and this amounts to solipsism, the view that "only I exist" – or that some other representations, and maybe all other representations, have a subjective side and a polar structure as well.

Solipsism is not a viable option, but the way Schopenhauer argues for the alternative is novel. An unexpected aspect of his argument is that he does not claim that representations other than that of one's body have a subjective side owing to peculiarities of their appearance (for example, because they have a human form). He argues more radically, and in-dependently of behavioral and evolutionary considerations, that since all representations have the same objective quality no matter what they look like, and that – recalling the root of the PSR – since subjectivity is the philosophical correlate of objectivity, then every representation must have a subjective aspect. This yields more than the presence of other people. It entails that *everything* we experience – the rivers, trees, sun, moon, clouds – has a subjective reality behind it. There are no dead spots, for not only does a subjective reality underlie other human and animal bodies, it underlies plant and inanimate material bodies as well. Schopenhauer refers to this universal subjectivity as "Will," and claims that this is the ultimate ground of things.

His argument to the conclusion that "all is Will" appears misleadingly to be an argument from analogy. It seems as if Schopenhauer is arguing that if a set of items (representations) share a single essential aspect (objectivity) and if one of them (my body) has a second essential aspect (subjectivity), then it is reasonable to suppose that the entire set has both aspects (objectivity and subjectivity). Aside from the question of whether the second aspect is truly essential, the argument is unconvincing. Arguments from analogy typically run in the reverse direction. If we have a large set of items that are identical in many key aspects, and if we are sure that a newly encountered item has all those key aspects, except for one, about which there remains some uncertainty, then it is reasonable to suppose that it has the remaining aspect. Schopenhauer uses the term "analogy" in characterizing his argument, but his unfortunate wording distracts us from the argument's actual structure.

The leading ideas for Schopenhauer's argument are that the subject–object distinction (or better, the subject–object polarity) is at the PSR's root, and that all representations are objects of one kind or another. He also assumes that it is impossible to conceive of a representation without there being a subject who has it. To think otherwise would be like trying to imagine the experience of sweetness without there being anyone who has the experience.

Suppose then, I (or anyone) am experiencing a field of representations. Within this field, I notice that a section of it, namely, my body, has a subjective aspect that is congruent with the very mind (that is, my mind) that contains the *entire* field of representations in which that body is located. Since my body is a representation, it is in my mind, but my mind also permeates and enlivens that very body from the inside. It does not, however, permeate and enliven the remaining representations in my perceptual field. Within this knotted context, Schopenhauer is struck by how incomprehensible it would be if the remaining representations in my perceptual field – the chair, table, knives, forks, etc. – were not also backed by a mentality similar to what I apprehend directly as underlying the representation of my body.

Here is the same argument, formulated from a slightly different angle. From the subjective standpoint, every representation in my experience is "my" representation and is a mental entity. The representations are identical in this respect. From the objective standpoint, the representation of my body has a subjective backing, but since the other representations in my perceptual field do not display one, it is difficult to know whether they have one or not. The subjective backing to my body is my consciousness, and if – and this is the crucial point – there is to be a perfect parallel and consistency between the subjective and objective standpoints in general, as the root of the PSR would dictate, then the remaining representations in my perceptual field must have a subjective backing as well.

Schopenhauer accordingly ascribes an underlying subjectivity to every representation, such that each object becomes the manifestation of some sort of subjectivity. The presence of subjectivity in the world does not consequently find its explanation in reference to the historical or evolutionary workings of matter and energy, as materialists would claim. To the contrary, the physical world is explained as the objectification of a universal subjectivity – one that bears a relationship to the entire world as representation in the way we, as individual subjects of experience, bear a relationship to each of our bodies. One's body and its consciousness is a microcosm, for just as *it* has a subjective aspect, the "world as representation" has a subjective aspect of a wider and more universal quality – one that seamlessly includes within it one's own individual subjectivity, along with the subjectivities of everyone and everything else.

Not resting with the postulation of many subjective conditions that would correspond to the various types of representation in any perceptual field, Schopenhauer recalls that multiplicity itself is an appearance that arises from the principle of sufficient reason (PSR), and that in particular, arises from the notions of space, time, and causality. This implies dramatically that at the level of things in themselves, the inner reality associated with all representations is unitary: a single, universal subjectivity underlies the diversity of the representations within all human experience, whenever or wherever the experiences take place.

In a metaphysical sense, then, your subjectivity, my subjectivity, along with the billions of other human subjectivities, are manifestations of a single, universal subjectivity – the same one that enlivens every animal, plant, and form of inorganic matter. This subjectivity can be described in various ways. It is a "single eye" that timelessly looks out from everything and that constitutes the subjectivity of the world as a whole; it is the "world as will" that manifests itself as the "world as representation"; it is a single, infinite, and active subjectivity, although active in a predominantly dreamlike and unreflective manner; it is the universe's unconscious psyche.

This philosophical vision may sound fantastic, but it is similar to the metaphysics of the Upanishads that ascribes a subjective and objective side to the universe as a whole, namely and respectively, as *Atman* and *Brahman*. Among the core teachings of the Upanishads is "*tat tvam asi*," which translates as "that, you are" or "thou art that": you, the subject of experience, are of the very same being as that, or indeed any, object that is perceived. One's sense of historical and finite individuality (that is, ego) conditioned by space and time, accordingly, is an illusion that obscures the undivided nature of us all.

Here, "subject" is identical with "object," and this general and metaphysical identification of subject and object implies that anyone can apprehend the innermost essence of the universe by apprehending the innermost essence of himself or herself. The phrase "know thyself" assumes a profound metaphysical significance within this context. In the Upanishadic tradition, this knowledge is believed to be attainable through the practice of introspective meditation, and in particular, through the practice of yoga.

ii the world as will

To disclose the timeless subjectivity that all representations manifest, Schopenhauer proceeds along a philosophical rather than a meditative and mystical path. He reflects upon the world using logic, commonsense observation, and the need to postulate a kind of subjectivity that could fit equally the inner nature of an inanimate rock as well as that of a highly reflective human being. With this criterion, he explores the depths of his mind in the search for the *lowest common denominator* of all his representations, stripping away layer upon layer of qualities that would distinguish human beings from animals, animals from plants, and plants from inorganic matter.

At his subjective core, Schopenhauer does not experience an absolute act of self-conscious reflection – he does not hit bedrock with an "I think, I exist" that accompanies all of his representations – but instead apprehends an irrational, unreflective, unarticulated, directionless, and meaningless urge. In human beings, this is sheer will or raw (and ultimately sexual and reproductive) desire. He maintains that this untamed urge is the "thing-in-itself" that remains an unknowable mystery within Kant's philosophy:

> *Thing-in-itself*, however, is only the *will*: as such it is not at all representation, but is *toto genere* different from it. It is that of which all representation, all object, is the appearance, the visibility, the *objectivity*. It is that which is innermost, the core of every individual and also of the whole. It appears

in each blindly acting natural force and also in the deliberate actions of people. The great difference between the two concerns only a difference in the degree of appearance, not in the essence of that which appears.[2]

> If this *thing-in-itself* . . . which as such is never an object, because all object is its mere appearance . . . is to be thought of objectively, it must borrow its name and concept from an object, from something that is somehow given objectively, and therefore from one of its appearances. But to serve as a point of explanation, this can be nothing other than the most perfect of all its appearances, i.e., the clearest, the most developed, the most directly enlightened by knowledge. This, however, is the human *will*.[3]

Schopenhauer acknowledges that the human being is the highest manifestation of the universal and subjective reality that underlies all things. This is mainly because we can understand this essential nature, unlike animals, plants, and rocks, which have either limited or no reflective capacities. Despite our potential for insight, he maintains that what foundationally is, and what we self-consciously realize, is in itself a senseless and irrational urge. We can appreciate the distinctiveness of this position by contrasting it with a closely related philosophical alternative. This focuses more substantially and specifically on the human being as the most highly developed presence in the world, as opposed to attending generally to the primordial, rudimentary, and unarticulated condition of everything that is, as Schopenhauer prefers.

One could maintain alternatively that non-human forms (such as what characterizes the subjectivity and behavior of animals, plants, and inanimate matter) are only dim and undeveloped expressions of the universe's essence, and that universe has been slowly developing and struggling to realize this essence – an essence whose mature presentation we encounter in the structure of human self-consciousness.

The rationale behind this alternative is easy to appreciate. To understand what an oak tree essentially is, it reveals less to examine an acorn, and more to examine a mature oak tree. Similarly, to appreciate what the universe essentially is, it reveals less to examine its undeveloped rudimentary forms such as blind urges, and more to examine its mature and articulate products, such as the human being.

Instead of philosophizing along the above path – the one, in fact, taken by German Idealists such as Fichte, Schelling, and Hegel – Schopenhauer adopts an immediate approach that strips away from representations in general, layer upon layer of human quality to arrive at a discernable metaphysical core. To him, this core is not an immature, abstract, seed-like, or undeveloped potential. It is a basic, primordial reality that remains timelessly as it is, and that manifests itself in various forms without reason. The rationale behind his approach is also readily understandable: it matches how physicists and chemists search for basic elements and compounds. To appreciate what water essentially is, for example, we would aim to discern the common essence of all its diverse appearances, disregarding the differences in appearance that steam, liquid water, and ice present.

Schopenhauer's "Will" is a universal subjectivity that manifests itself objectively, but without ever knowing while in its primal condition that it is even objectifying itself. It compares to the subjectivity of a lower animal or plant, insofar as animals and plants are unaware that they exist. It also compares to one's unconscious or subconscious psyche that produces dreams, while remaining unaware that it is dreaming.

The resulting characterization of the thing-in-itself is exceedingly remote from some of the more friendly conceptions of humanity. The thing-in-itself is one, almighty, self-determining, timeless, and absolutely free, but it is unconscious and devoid of knowledge. It is a blind, irrational, meaningless, and aimless striving. It is pandemonic rather than pantheistic, and, more exactly, beyond good and evil. It is raw free will, without any direction, either moral, rational or otherwise. Such is the universe's meaningless core according to Schopenhauer, insofar as we can apprehend ourselves immediately and express the contents of this primordial experience philosophically.

A single eye looks out from all of us, but this eye is senseless, insensitive, and morally blind. Nonetheless, we are all expressions of this selfsame being and, as such, we each bear an intrinsic relation to the universe as a whole:

> The will reveals itself just as completely and as much in *one* oak, as in millions: their number, their manifoldness in space and time, has no meaning at all in relation to the will, but only in relation to the knowing individuals in space and time, which are themselves multiplied and spread throughout it, whose multiplicity is itself again only their appearance and does not concern the will. From this one can maintain, that if, *per impossibile*, a single being – even if it were the most insignificant – were completely annihilated, then the entire world have to go down with it. In light of such a feeling, the great mystic Angelus Silesius said:
>
>> "I know that without me,
>> God could not a moment live;
>> Were I to cease to be,
>> Must he also his spirit to nothingness give."
>> [*Cherubinischer Wandersmann*, i, 8][4]

Schopenhauer asserts the above in light of his view that although our fundamental principle of knowledge and explanation, the PSR, generates the appearance of a plurality of individuals, the world in itself remains a seamless unity. As he states many times, the PSR is like a kaleidoscope that breaks the universal and subjective aspect of the world into an array of individuals dispersed throughout space and time. With this in mind, we can now proceed to Schopenhauer's account of the twofold structure of appearance, or what he refers to as "the world as representation," recalling the basic structure of the PSR.

iii the two-tiered objectification of the will: platonic ideas and spatio-temporal individuals

The PSR has a basic root and four specifications, each one of which determines a unique style of explanation and an associated type of object. The root of the PSR is the subject–object distinction in conjunction with the idea of necessary connection; its fourfold specification is comprised of logical explanation, mathematical and geometrical explanation, causal explanation, and motive-related explanation, all considered as parallel, non-intersecting explanatory modes.

Owing to the application of this two-tiered structure (viz., the general root and the PSR's four aspects) in every moment of human awareness, the world as representation, which is the very product of the PSR, appears accordingly with a two-tiered form. In this respect, the subject–object distinction manifests itself in both general and specific ways that correspond to the PSR's general root and its fourfold division. Corresponding to the root of the PSR, the subject–object distinction manifests itself with *universalistic* contents. At this level, universal subjects become aware of universal objects. Corresponding to the specific forms of the PSR, the subject–object distinction manifests itself with more *individuated* contents: individual subjects become aware of individual objects in space and time.

Within the first layer of the will's manifestation, or what Schopenhauer refers to as the "immediate" or "direct" objectification of the will, ideally timeless, will-less, and painless universal subjects become aware of universal objects, viz., the Platonic Ideas, or the perfect forms of things. Within the second layer of the will's manifestation, or what Schopenhauer refers to as "indirect" objectifications of the will, individual subjects as historical people with specific personalities become aware of individual material objects, stimuli, and psychological motives. We can refer generally to this two-tiered model as Schopenhauer's account of the a priori forms of human experience, for these layers are generated by the presence of the PSR. The "world as representation" is of our own making to this extent.

One important feature of this activity is that both sorts of object, universal and individual, issue from our projection of the PSR. The universal objects or Platonic Ideas issue from our projection of the PSR's root, and are not mind-independent entities in the manner that Plato conceived of them.[5] The individual objects in space and time issue from our projection of the causal relationship (with which Schopenhauer associates matter and material objects) in conjunction with temporal (for example, mathematical) and spatial (for instance, geometrical) projections.

If we combine with our projection of the PSR, Schopenhauer's hypothesis of a single, timeless, subjective, and universal activity at reality's core, his more complete vision of the world emerges. At the foundation of everything, a single, subjective, universal activity manifests itself in, and as, our own conscious being, and it appears to us as an objective world. This "world as representation" has two levels, namely, a realm of universal objects or essences and a realm of individuated objects that kaleidoscopically reflects those essences.

As described here, Schopenhauer's vision recalls – despite one crucial difference that we will mention below – the Neoplatonistic vision of Plotinus (204–70 CE), who also amalgamated Greek philosophy with Asian religion. According to Plotinus, a single metaphysical activity called the "One" [τὸ ἕν] emanates as if it were a fountain or sun, a great chain of being that begins with a level of universal essences and then coalesces into a layer of concrete individual things that range from the animate to the inorganic.

A bit surprisingly, Schopenhauer's philosophical vision also compares structurally and coincidentally with the Three-Body doctrine that is central to Mahayana Buddhism.[6] This is a philosophical and metaphysical doctrine where a universal Buddha-principle that is said to be reality in itself, resides at the core of things. This principle subsequently specifies itself into a series of Buddha-manifestations, viz., deities such as Vairocana, Ratnasambhava, Amitabha, Amoghasiddhi, and Aksobhya, representative of virtues such as wisdom, equanimity, clarity of thought, accomplishment, detachment, and compassion. These compare to the Platonic forms of wisdom, beauty, strength, and so on, as embodied by Greek gods such as Athena, Aphrodite, and Apollo. Finally, the Buddha-principle further specifies itself into historical individuals, among whom is the historical Buddha.

Given such cross-cultural associations, we can categorize Schopenhauer's metaphysics as an intriguing variant upon a general and universal style of philosophical speculation. This involves postulating an all-permeating oneness as the ground of all being, and interpreting the rest of existence as manifestations or particularizations of this foundational force or activity. As the characterizations of this foundational activity vary, so do the resulting metaphysical views. Some characterize it in a conceptually-rich manner, ascribing to it many wisdom-and-intelligence-related qualities. Others characterize it minimalistically, ascribing to it relatively little. Schopenhauer adopts the latter style.

We have said nothing so far about the origin of the particular qualities of either the universal objects or spatio-temporal objects that appear within Schopenhauer's metaphysical construction, and have been speaking generally about the a priori form of the world as representation as it stands as a manifestation of the world as will. Perhaps, needless to say, it might be expecting too much of any philosopher to explain exactly why the world has the particular sorts of things and qualities that it does. Kant finds himself in this difficult position when he argues well for the subjective origins of space, time, and causality but cannot provide a comparably convincing account of why the specific laws of nature assume the forms that they do. Schopenhauer defines the field of possible explanation only as far as the PSR can extend, so he self-consciously does not explain why the universal Will manifests itself in the particular Platonic forms that appear.

He consequently accepts as a given fact the commonly recognized set of natural kinds such as metals, minerals, physical energies, animal, and plant kinds, and attempts to coordinate these types with a general meta-physical presentation that respects the a priori necessities associated with the PSR:

> ... there is a higher degree of this visibility or objectification [of the will] in the plant than in the stone; a higher degree in the animal than in the plant; indeed, its coming forth into visibility, its objectification, has endless gradations, just as there are between the dimmest twilight and the brightest sunlight, and between the loudest tone and the softest echo.[7]

This excerpt illuminates how Schopenhauer conceives of nature in terms of fine and subtle gradations of the Will's objectification, and how he tends not to recognize sharp breaks between species. Within the world of representation, the Neoplatonistic principle of emanation and continuity closely represents how he conceives of the natural world, at least insofar as we can recognize a metaphysical continuity that resides beneath our discrete divisions of nature.

With respect to this Neoplatonistic comparison (as well as to the Buddhistic Three-Body doctrine), two qualifying points should be made. The first is to reiterate that Schopenhauer does not conceive of the objectifications of the Will realistically, as if the Will objectifies itself in space and in time, independently of human conceptions and human presence. He accepts Kant's account of the subjectivity of space and time, and is antagonistic to any "historical philosophizing" (such as he finds in Plotinus) that ascribes space and time to things in themselves.[8] He maintains alternatively that the manifestation of the Will in its various grades of appearance requires our own presence and the activity of the PSR.

The second point is that within Schopenhauer's framework, although the grades of the Will's objectification are on a continuum, and although the contents of one's own mind are on a continuum ranging from conscious to subconscious to unconscious states, the timeless act of the Will's objectification does not itself operate as a matter of continuity. There is a sharp transition between the world's inner, continuous, subjective reality and its outer, continuous, objective appearance. This discontinuity is evident in Schopenhauer's many characterizations of the relationship between the Will in itself and the world as representation where he states that the Will is *toto genere* different (viz., completely different in kind) from the world as representation. The following is an example:

> The truth is, that on the path of the representation, one can never get beyond the representation. It is a closed whole and has within itself no thread that leads to the *toto genere* different essence of the thing-in-itself. If we were beings capable of only having representations, the way to the thing-in-itself would be completely closed off for us. Only the other side of our own essence can reveal the other side of the essence in-itself of things.[9]

The above considerations yield a metaphysics that postulates a core subjective force called "Will," which manifests itself as human consciousnesses that have representations. The representations are different in kind from the Will as it is in itself, and they exhibit a set of smooth gradations that divide further into discrete conceptions of natural kinds and species. This gives us a double-aspected theory, where one aspect is metaphysically primary and manifests itself in a second, self-alienated, and objectified form.

The basic structure of Schopenhauer's philosophical vision compares to an act of frustrated self-conscious reflection, where a subject thinks about an object that is indeed that subject in an objectified form, but where it fails to recognize the object as its own reflection. There are many examples of this sort of phenomenon. It is like falling in love with someone who looks and thinks exactly like oneself, without realizing that one has only narcissistically fallen in love with oneself. It is like trying to annihilate an enemy, without realizing that the person is another human being, and that one is trying to annihilate only oneself. It is also like being afraid of monsters in a nightmare without realizing that the monsters are of one's own psychological making. With the exception of a few people who realize what is actually happening, Schopenhauer maintains that the Will is likewise benighted.

Neoplatonism was less inspirational to the formulation of Schopenhauer's metaphysics than was Kant's account of the distinction between timeless human freedom and human activity in space and time. This distinction significantly motivates Schopenhauer's contrast between the world as will and the world as representation. Kant argues that if we are to know and comprehend the spatio-temporal world in a scientific manner, then we must regard it as a predictable mechanism. One consequently asks how human freedom is possible, and Kant replies that nature's mechanism is merely an appearance of the world in itself, and that nature does not reflect how things are in themselves. He consequently locates human freedom speculatively at the level of the thing-in-itself, rather than at the level of natural appearances. Each human action thus becomes interpretable in two ways, as resulting either from mechanical causes, or more truly from an act of freedom whose incomprehensible origin is independent of space and time.

Schopenhauer extends Kant's account of timeless human volition to develop a wider metaphysical picture of the world, citing Kant's influence in the following:

> What, then, Kant teaches about the appearances of people and their actions, my teaching extends to *all* appearances in nature, since it grounds them in the *will* as thing-in-itself. This procedure is justified above all in that it ought not to be assumed that people are specifically, *toto genere*, and fundamentally different from the other beings and things in nature, but on the contrary, that people are different only in degree.[10]

By eliminating the Cartesian, classical, and biblical idea that human beings are of a special and higher order than all other natural beings,[11] Schopenhauer is able to generalize the Kantian theory of freedom to cover the rest of nature. To achieve this, he thins-down and broadens the Kantian conception of a rational will to that of merely a blind, irrational, and rudimentary will – the sort that is more appropriate for characterizing the inner subjective nature of rocks, plants, and animals.

We accordingly find Schopenhauer stating that in the cases of human action, we do not cause our bodies to move through an act of will. The act of will and the movement of one's body are two sides of the same action:

> Every true act of his will is immediately and without exception also a movement of his body: he can not in fact will the act, without simultaneously perceiving that it appears as a movement of his body. The act of will and the action of the body are not two different conditions that are objectively known, connected by the causal bond; they do not stand in the relationship of cause and effect. They are rather one and the same, although given in two completely different ways: one is given immediately and one

is given in perception for the understanding. The action of the body is nothing different than the objectified, i.e., brought into visibility, act of the will. It will later be shown to us that this applies to every movement of the body, not merely from those related to motives, but also to involuntary movements that follow from mere stimuli. Indeed, the entire body is nothing other than the objectified will, i.e., will that has become representation.[12]

This excerpt encapsulates Schopenhauer's double-aspect theory, and we can see more explicitly how the root of the PSR – the subject–object distinction – is expressed with the addendum that not only are there no objects without subjects, the two are essentially the same. This coordinates the Upanishadic *tat tvam asi*, "thou are that," unifying principle with the "subject vs. object" differentiating principle to produce a double-sided message: in general, the PSR explicitly expresses dividedness and at its root level it expresses the division and opposition between subject and object. Implicitly, however, the Upanishadic formula prevails implicitly and foundationally, reminding us that all is one and that subjects and objects are essentially the same. This tension in the root of the PSR is embodied in the metaphysical relationship between the world as will and the world as representation: epistemologically, superficially, and explicitly they are opposed, whereas metaphysically, foundationally, and implicitly they are the same.

notes

1   *WWR* (I), Book II, §18, P 100, HK 129–30, ZA 143.
2   *WWR* (I), Book II, §21, P 110, HK 142–3, ZA 155.
3   *WWR* (I), Book II, §22, P 110, HK 143, ZA 155.
4   *WWR* (I), Book II, §25, P 128–9, HK 167, ZA 176.
5   See, for example, *WWR* (II), Chapter I, "On the Fundamental View of Idealism," P 5, HK 166, ZA 11–12.
6   This doctrine appears primarily in the Lotus Sutra (c. second century CE).
7   *WWR* (I), Book II, §25, P 128, HK 166–7, ZA 175–6.
8   *WWR* (I), Book IV, §53, P 274, HK 253, ZA 346.
9   *WWR* (I), "Appendix: Criticism of the Kantian Philosophy," P 502, HK 118, ZA 613.
10 *WWR* (II), Chapter XVII, "On Man's Need for Metaphysics," P 174, HK 377, ZA 203.
11 This is yet another reason why Schopenhauer does not follow the Fichtean, Schellingian, and Hegelian German Idealist picture of things, even though such views also stemmed from a metaphysical expansion of Kant's theory of freedom.
12 *WWR* (I), Book II, §18, P 100, HK 130, ZA 143.

further reading

Jacquette, Dale, *The Philosophy of Schopenhauer* (Chesham, UK: Acumen, 2005).

Magee, Bryan, *The Philosophy of Schopenhauer* (Oxford: Clarendon Press, 1983).

Young, Julian, *Schopenhauer* (London & New York: Routledge, 2005).

critical interpretations
of the world as will

i scientific knowledge, philosophical knowledge, and mystical knowledge

When Schopenhauer claims that the thing-in-itself is Will, it seems to be an absolute and exhaustive characterization of the basis of things. This would locate him squarely among the more optimistic post-Kantian philosophers who maintain that since the thing-in-itself is knowable, traditional metaphysics is possible and achievable. Hegel is the most famous of these ambitious philosophers, and he argues in considerable detail that the structure of self-consciousness is nothing less than the very structure of the universe.

If we associate Schopenhauer's philosophical style with Hegel and post-Kantian metaphysics, it requires us, as Kant would say, to characterize Schopenhauer as a dogmatic philosopher who believes that we can know the absolute truth and explain what this truth happens to be. Schopenhauer is usually interpreted in this manner – correctly, in this writer's view – since his repeated assertions that the thing-in-itself is Will irresistibly convey the impression that he is a traditional metaphysician. This is not the only way to interpret Schopenhauer's claims about the thing-in-itself, however.

It is possible to read Schopenhauer in a more Kantian way, as someone who denies that we can know anything absolutely about the thing-in-itself. By these lights, his claim that the thing-in-itself is Will requires some considerable softening, but some of Schopenhauer's passages indeed sound very Kantian. One of the most suggestive is in the second volume of *The World as Will and Representation*, published some 26 years after the publication of the first volume. The dating suggests that although Schopenhauer might have been a dogmatic metaphysician in 1818, he was a Kantian by 1844.

It is, though, probably a mistake to refer to an "earlier" and "later" Schopenhauer to explain whether Schopenhauer's philosophy stands closer to Kant or to Hegel, since the fact is that Schopenhauer simply offers what appear to be conflicting remarks, often in the same texts. We have seen some of the traditional metaphysical excerpts in the previous chapter. Some of the contrasting Kantian passages, as noted above, are as follows:

> . . . we consequently have to trace back the entire world of appearances to that in which the thing-in-itself is exhibited through the thinnest of veils and still remains appearance – only insofar as my intellect, which is alone capable of knowledge, is distinguished from me as the one who wills, and which even in *internal* perception does not set aside the cognitive form of *time*.
>
> Accordingly, even after this last and most extreme step, one can still ask what that will – which represents itself in the world and as the world – is ultimately and absolutely in itself. That is, what it would be quite independently of the fact that it represents itself as *will*, or generally *appears*, i.e., *is known* in general. This question can *never* be answered because, as already said, the being-of-knowledge itself contradicts being-in-itself, for every act of knowledge is as such only an appearance. But the possibility of this question indicates that **the thing-in-itself, which we recognize immediately in the will, completely outside all possible appearances, may have [*mag haben*] determinations, qualities, modes of existence which are for us absolutely unknowable and incomprehensible** [emphasis added]. These are such as remain as the essence of the thing in itself, when this, as was set out in the fourth book, has freely sublimated [*aufgehoben*] itself as *will*, has therefore stepped completely out from appearances, and as far as our knowledge is concerned, i.e., with reference to the world as appearance, has passed over into empty nothingness. This nothingness would be *absolute*, if the will were simply and absolutely the thing-in-itself; instead it is given to us expressly only as a *relative* nothingness.[1]

> Lastly, although it is immediate knowledge, the knowledge that I have of my will is incapable of being separated from the knowledge of my body. I know my will not as a whole, not as a unity, not perfectly according to its essence, but I know it only in its individual acts, therefore in time, which is the form of the appearance of my body, as is the case for every object. Therefore the body is a condition of the knowledge of my will. I cannot therefore in fact represent this will without my body.[2]

The first excerpt, from 1844, appears almost verbatim over twenty years earlier in Schopenhauer's 1818–22 notebooks, casting doubt on the idea that we are dealing with two "Schopenhauers," an "earlier" and a "later" one.[3] In both excerpts, he is concerned with the validity of the extraordinary states of mystical consciousness. This context is notoriously problematic, for we cannot say that the mystic knows anything in the technical and scientific sense of the term, since mystical experiences fail to fit words. It also seems foolish, however, to dismiss mysticism out of hand.

With an appropriately open mind, Schopenhauer recognizes mystical experience as a possible way to apprehend metaphysical realities. He concludes that if a positive content is ascribed to mystical experience, then we must – so he believes – speculate that there are aspects to the thing-in-itself that are mystically apprehensible, but not knowable in either the technical (that is, scientific) or philosophical sense of the word "knowledge." Most of the time, he uses the terms "know" and "knowledge" in the technical, PSR-related sense, following Kant's view that, strictly speaking, empirical knowledge exclusively concerns appearances, representations, and the notion of being an object for a subject. Beyond the principle of sufficient reason (PSR), consequently, nothing would be knowable in the technical sense, thus setting mystical experience outside of the bounds of reasonable discussion.

These reflections yield a general point concerning Schopenhauer's use of the term "know" in relationship to the prevailing question of whether the thing-in-itself is knowable. He states that the thing-in-itself is not an "object," so it follows that any sense of the term "know" that requires our being aware of some object, cannot apply to the thing-in-itself. This precludes knowing it either as a form of conceptual knowledge or as ordinary empirical knowledge, since these are both restricted to the PSR-determined realm of appearances. Any reference to PSR-related knowledge would tell us only how the thing-in-itself appears, and not how it is in itself. If the only sort of legitimate knowledge is PSR-related knowledge, as Kant would maintain, then absolute knowledge of the thing-in-itself would be impossible.

Such considerations put Schopenhauer in a delicate philosophical position, because he is disposed to use the term "knowledge" in the standardly Kantian PSR-related way. When he adds that the thing-in-itself is not an object, he creates some philosophical tension within his view: insofar as the thing-in-itself is not an object, it cannot be PSR-knowable, and yet he admits that not everything of which we are aware is an object. This opens a door through which we can be aware of the thing-in-itself in a manner less tied to the PSR, although we might hesitate to refer to this awareness as "knowledge" in the strict sense. Our experience contains subjects as well as objects, and as it is in itself, the thing-in-itself for Schopenhauer resides wholly on the subjective, but nonetheless apprehensible, side of things. This introduces a pivotal non-Kantian dimension into Schopenhauer's view.

If we focus on the subjective side of things, and if it is possible to discern the essence of this subjective side, then we would have a mode of awareness that might absolutely reveal the thing-in-itself, and that we would *not* describe as knowledge in the objective PSR-related sense of the word. This special awareness could take one of two forms: either it would be an indescribable mystical awareness, or it would be an awareness that we can intersubjectively describe. Schopenhauer acknowledges both, claiming that the intersubjectively describable awareness provides philosophical knowledge. This is, namely, our awareness of the subjective aspect of the representation of our body as Will. Philosophical knowledge consequently stands between scientific, PSR-related knowledge and mystical knowledge.

What complicates Schopenhauer's position is that although he allows for a purely subjective mode of awareness that does not refer to objects, his theory does not have room for an intersubjective mode of awareness that is independent of *all* forms of the PSR. Schopenhauer is aware that in his key argument where we become introspectively aware of the thing-in-itself as Will, we do so only by means of a temporal experience. Since time is an a priori form of our experience that does not reflect how things are in themselves, our introspective awareness of the thing-in-itself as Will is not PSR-independent.

When examining our body, for instance, we notice that we have a subjective access to it and that the representation of our body has a dual aspect, namely, a subjective temporal aspect and an objective spatio-temporal aspect. Once we isolate the subjective aspect for scrutiny and set aside our body's external spatio-temporal aspect, time as a form of inner experience remains present in our apprehension of the body's subjective aspect. We therefore experience it through the form of time, for time is necessarily present in both inner and outer experience. Within this context, Schopenhauer identifies three main forms – time, space, and causality – noting that although space and causality are absent in the apprehension of the Will as thing-in-itself, the form of time persists as "the thinnest of veils."

With respect to determining whether Schopenhauer is metaphysically closer to Hegel or Kant, the bump in the road is this: within an orthodox Kantian framework, if we apprehend something in time, then we apprehend it as an appearance and as being for us in a manner that is *not* how it is in itself. The situation is "all or nothing," where the presence of any a priori form of sensibility (viz., space or time) or any a priori category of the understanding (for example, causality) flatly rules out the knowledge of things as they are in themselves.

If we ascribe to Schopenhauer an orthodox Kantian theory of knowledge, then the presence of time in the experience of one's inner subjective nature would entail that absolute knowledge of the thing-in-itself is impossible. Time defines the form of both inner and outer experience, so even if the thing-in-itself is not an object and even if we avoid looking outwards to discover the nature of reality, the presence of time remains an impediment within us.

This seems to draw Schopenhauer very close to Kantian skepticism, but we know that he does *not* conceive of himself as a strict Kantian. It is essential, then, to explain how Schopenhauer can assert that the thing-in-itself is Will while also admitting that when we attend to our own subjectivity to discern the nature of the world, the form of time clouds the waters of our clear self-apprehension. In *Parerga and Paralipomena* (1851) and in the second volume of *WWR* (1844), Schopenhauer distinguishes his own position from Kant's, as we can see in the following two excerpts. The first, from 1851, also appears earlier in Schopenhauer's 1825 notebooks:

> *Thing-in-itself* signifies that which is independent of anything that is available to us via perception, and therefore signifies that which actually is. For Democritus this was formed material, and for Locke it was essentially the same. For Kant, it was an *x*; for me, it is *will*. [4,5]

> . . . we call this the *will*, by which word we accordingly indicate hardly an unknown *x*, but on the contrary that, at least from one side, is to us infinitely more familiar and more intimate than anything else. [6]

Schopenhauer is obviously trying to make some room for apprehending the world in a more revealing metaphysical manner. We see this again in his reference below to how the apprehension of the identity between one's objective body and one's subjective will is independent of the fourfold aspects of the PSR. This reveals a broader conception of knowledge that includes modes that the PSR does not encompass:

> [The identity of the will and of the body] is a knowledge of a very peculiar kind whose truth cannot in fact be brought under one of the four headings . . . by which I have partitioned all truth, namely, logical, empirical, metaphysical and metalogical. This is because it is not, like all these, either the reference of an abstract representation to another representation, or to a necessary form of intuition, or to an abstract representation. It is rather the reference of a judgment to the relation that a perceptual representation of the body has to that which is not representation at all, but which is *toto genere* different from representation, namely, will. I would therefore like to distinguish this truth from all others, and call it *philosophical truth par excellence* [κατ' ἐξοχην; *kata exochēn*]. [7]

We have here a PSR-independent kind of knowledge, namely, philosophical knowledge. This signals loudly that when Schopenhauer uses the term "knowledge," it is crucial to reflect upon whether he is referring to the standard PSR-related knowledge (scientific knowledge), as is usually the case, or to the special, non-PSR-related knowledge (philosophical knowledge), or to both sorts at once, or to something else altogether (mystical knowledge).

In light of these distinctions, when Schopenhauer claims in a Kantian-sounding manner that the thing-in-itself can have modes of existence which for us are absolutely unknowable and incomprehensible, he can be understood in at least two ways. The first is innocuous, where he would be using the term "know" in the standard, scientific, PSR-related sense. It amounts to saying only that when the Will is apprehended, it is apprehended in a way that is not categorizable within the fourfold forms of the PSR, that the Will is not an object, and that this apprehension provides a philosophical truth as opposed to a scientific truth. Knowledge of the world as Will is not scientific, but as philosophical knowledge, neither is it purely speculative and unrelated to direct experience.

The second sense is more problematic and philosophically challenging, and we can interpret Schopenhauer as saying that although the thing-in-itself is philosophically knowable, it remains knowable only to a certain degree. Insofar as the knowledge of the thing-in-itself is not complete or absolute, inscrutable mystical aspects of the thing-in-itself could remain, unknowable and incomprehensible in either a scientific or a philosophic sense. Therefore, we need to ask whether Schopenhauer's acknowledgement of mystical knowledge transforms him into a strict Kantian nonetheless.

To clarify this issue, we should distinguish two questions. The first is whether absolute knowledge of the thing-in-itself is attainable, given that we must become aware of the thing-in-itself through the form of time. Schopenhauer usually speaks as if this knowledge is attainable, but if time is required for our awareness of the thing-in-itself as Will, then contrary to these remarks, he seems to end up as a Kantian who must admit that metaphysical knowledge is impossible. The second question is: if philosophic or mystical knowledge of the thing-in-itself is attainable, then is this absolute knowledge, or is it somehow limited?

If scientific and philosophical knowledge of the thing-in-itself is not absolute and if mystical aspects of the thing-in-itself remain forever outside of either scientific or philosophical knowledge, this would not imply that the thing-in-itself is an unknowable "x" in the broadest sense of "know." To admit that knowledge of something is not absolute, is not the same as asserting that we know nothing about it. Also, to admit that absolute knowledge is attainable via mysticism is not the same as asserting that metaphysical knowledge is impossible. Schopenhauer acknowledges mysticism, and this is sufficient to reject interpretations that portray him immediately as a strict Kantian.

With respect to the first question of whether knowledge of the thing-in-itself is attainable – and this question motivates the Schopenhauer-as-strict-Kantian interpretation – the main problem is whether an experience can be in time and yet involve an apprehension of the thing-in-itself as it is in itself, either absolutely or to some significant degree.

As we know, the Kantian theory of knowledge precludes absolute knowledge of the thing-in-itself. To resolve whether some sort of non-mystical knowledge of the thing-in-itself remains possible within Schopenhauer's view, we can consider more closely his discussions of time, since Kant regards time as an impediment to the knowledge of the thing-in-itself.

ii regular time versus the eternal present

Time is a form of human awareness according to Kant, and he claims that we experience it as an infinite magnitude stretching endlessly into the future and past. It is a necessary, exclusive, and universal format of both inner and outer experience, and as such, Kant believes that if there were no people, then time would vanish.

Schopenhauer accepts this, and, agreeing that time is mind-dependent, he maintains that the past and the future "are as empty as a dream."[8] In this regard, he associates the perception of the world in time with the Vedic conception of "the veil of Maya," which conceives of the daily world as a sort of play or illusion. Given Schopenhauer's advocacy of Kant's account of space and time, it is easy to conclude that the apprehension of the thing-in-itself as Will must be an illusion or mere phenomenon, since it appears only through one's body in time.

This reduces Schopenhauer's position to Kant's, where all apprehensions that take place in time tell us nothing about how things are in themselves, and it supports the view that we should interpret Schopenhauer as a Kantian, despite his own statements to the contrary. Schopenhauer admits that we temporally apprehend the thing-in-itself as Will, but this admission seems self-defeating, for if the foundational apprehension of the thing-in-itself as Will is merely phenomenal and illusory, it is unsuitable for asserting how the thing-in-itself is *in itself*.

One good reason to doubt the above line of reasoning is this: the conception of time that problematically generates experiential illusion is not the only one available. So far, we have been referring to a conception of time that locates the past, present, and future on an *equal* par. When Kant states that time is given to us as an infinite magnitude, he implies that past, present, and future follow the pattern of a line that extends infinitely forward and backward, where all points are of the same qualitative value.

In contrast to this linear, regular, mathematical, scientific conception of time, Schopenhauer sometimes refers to time in a non-Kantian manner. This alternative renders it more plausible to apprehend the thing-in-itself as Will through the form of time and not be subject to the constraints that Kant's theory of knowledge imposes.

Specifically, Schopenhauer states in contrast to the Kantian conception of time, that *only the present* is the true temporal reality, and that the past and future are illusions. He does not ascribe an equal status to past, present, and future, and implies importantly that the *strongest* illusion results from the Kantian belief that the past and future are equally as real as the present:

> Now all object is but the will, insofar as the will has become representation, and the subject is the necessary correlate to the object. However, real objects are given only in the present: past and future contain mere concepts and phantasms. Therefore the present is the essential form of the appearance of the will and is inseparable from this; the present alone is that which is always there and is immovably steadfast. To the metaphysical eye – one that sees beyond the forms of empirical intuition – that which is empirically apprehended as the most transitory of all, presents itself as that which alone endures, as the *nunc stans* [the permanent Now] of the scholastics. The source and support of its content is the will-to-live, or the thing-in-itself – which we are.[9]

This excerpt states that "the present" is the essential form of the phenomenon of the Will, as opposed to saying more generally that "time" is its essential form. If we focus upon the experience of the present, noting that "the present alone is that which is always there and immovably steadfast," we can have a more purified perception that is mostly independent from considerations of the future and the past. This involves a minimization of one's personal willing, or a lessening of the projection of one's consciousness towards a future goal, and a more universalistic and ever-present mode of consciousness. One apprehends things in a manner that attends to how they simply present themselves right here and now, without excessive categorization, interpretation, and reflection upon the thing's practical use. In short, focusing on the present generates a more aesthetically-aware mode of disinterested consciousness.[10]

If we apply this aesthetic mode of consciousness to the awareness of the double aspect of one's bodily representation, we can apprehend the "inside" of one's hand (for instance) as having a goal-orientation or "will," but without any specific goal, since the future in reference to which such a goal would be defined would drop significantly out of the experience. We would be apprehending the inside and outside of our hand as being two sides of the same coin, but without the distractions that issue from attending significantly to the future and past. The present would move into the foreground, and the past and future would fade into the background, with the latter remaining in awareness only to the extent needed to render the experience comprehensible. Schopenhauer describes this mode of awareness in the following:

There is no greater contrast than that between the unceasing flight of time, which drags its complete content away with it, and the rigid immovability of what is actually present, which is always one and the same. And if one adopts this latter standpoint with the events of life genuinely and object-ively before one's eyes, then the *Nunc stans* at the center of the wheel of time will become clear and visible.[11]

The "phenomenon" of the Will is thus understandable either as the Will experienced in time with an equal emphasis on past, present, and future, or as the Will experienced almost wholly in the present. The for-mer defines a regular, practical, goal-oriented experience where the Will generates desires; the latter characterizes a detached, aesthetic experi-ence of the Will, where we regard it for its own sake, or as it is in itself, in isolation from practical concerns. The latter is more suitable for identi-fying the inner quality of a representation, insofar as we are trying to apprehend what the representation is like on the inside in a neutral and descriptive manner appropriate for all people and for all representations, independently of our particular interests.

To characterize the situation in more Schopenhauerian terms, the aes-thetic mode of consciousness where we experience time as an "eternal now" is the most appropriate mode for discerning the eternal presence of the Will. The distinction between the illusory time of "past, present, and future" versus the less illusory time of the "eternal now," thus helps explain how the presence of time in one's inner experience (that is, the experience of the "inner" or "subjective" side of a representation) need not be construed in a regular, scientific, knowledge-precluding, Kantian sense of time.

Schopenhauer does not explicitly distinguish between these two forms of time as we are doing here, and he seems to have had the Kantian conception of time in mind when he addresses the question of whether or not we can know the thing-in-itself absolutely. In the following excerpt, the resulting tension in his view is evident. On the one hand, his position is that we can experience the thing-in-itself directly, because we *are* the thing-in-itself; on the other hand, he acknowledges that all experience is in time, which implies that no temporal experience can tell us anything absolutely about how things are in themselves.

To resolve these tensions, Schopenhauer accepts as much of the Kantian theory as he can, while he develops an interpretation that allows him to speak – in a manner quite unlike Kant – in terms of *mat-ters of degree* with respect to the knowledge of the thing-in-itself. Schopenhauer believes that it makes a world of difference whether space, time, and causality are involved in an experience, or whether time alone is involved. He regards each a priori form of experience as a translucent "veil" that in some cases (viz., space and causality) can be removed to provide us with a clearer knowledge of the thing-in-itself:

In the meantime it is well to observe, and I have always adhered to this, that even the inner perception we have of our own will, in no way delivers an exhaustive and adequate knowledge of the thing-in-itself. This would be the case only if it were completely unmediated . . . but our knowledge of the thing-in-itself is not perfectly adequate. Firstly, it is connected to the form of representation, it is perception, and it consequently divides itself into subject and object. Even in self-consciousness, the I is not absolutely simple, but consists of a knower, an intellect, and a known, the will. The former is not known and the latter is not knowing, although both flow together in the consciousness of an I. But for this reason this I is not thoroughly *intimate* with itself, is not thoroughly illuminated so to speak, but is opaque and remains a riddle to itself. Therefore in inner knowledge we still find a distinction between the being-in-itself of its object and the perception of this object by the knowing subject. This inner knowledge is, however, free from two forms upon which outer appearance depend, namely, that of *space*, and the form of *causality* that brings about all sensory perception. On the other hand, the form of *time* remains, as well as that of being-known and knowing in general. In this inner knowledge, the thing-in-itself has consequently gotten rid of its veils **for the most part** [emphasis added], but it still does not present itself as being completely naked.[12]

Insofar as it remains difficult to see how metaphysical knowledge could be possible if the form of time is present, the temptation to reduce Schopenhauer's view to a strict Kantianism poses a nagging problem that needs to be resolved. If the veil is opaque, then one veil over the thing-in-itself is sufficient to bar metaphysical knowledge. Having several opaque veils is unimportant, since the knowledge we were seeking is already lost with the first veil's presence. It is therefore essential to explain how it makes more Schopenhauerian sense to construe the epistemological access to the thing-in-itself in terms of degrees of translucency, as opposed to discrete segments, layers, partitions, and opaque veils.

We have seen that we can experience time in two different ways, and that one of these – where we attend to the eternal now – is more appropriate for apprehending the thing-in-itself in an absolute manner, since it is more detached from specific desires. In the above excerpt, Schopenhauer states that since the awareness of the inner nature of the representation of one's body is tied to that representation, the form of the phenomena must somehow enter distortingly into the experience and into the resulting knowledge. Nonetheless, it can be argued that apprehending the thing-in-itself as Will independently of space and causality helps allow the Will itself to shine through, which is in fact how Schopenhauer argues. He rejects the "all or nothing" Kantian view of time and believes that the knowledge of the thing-in-itself is a matter of degree, measuring this degree of translucency in reference to the number of veils that cover the thing-in-itself. He repeatedly refers to time as the "thinnest" of veils, which implies that the veil is diaphanous, not opaque.

As we can now see, the "veil" metaphor is itself ambiguous between a series of opaque covers and a series of (for example) thin sheets of transparent, but colored cellophane, which when layered upon each other, finally result in an opaque barrier. The logic of the term "manifestation," which admits of degrees, suggests that the cellophane sheet metaphor is more apt. The opaque veils metaphor is also useless for capturing the spirit of Schopenhauer's claim about the successive removal of space and causality, for we have seen that if each veil is opaque, the presence of one opaque veil does the same damage as do several. The main point is that since Schopenhauer's underlying logic is a logic of manifestation, as opposed to a logic of causality, then access to the thing-in-itself in terms of degrees of translucency is not only possible, it is consistent with his description of the veil of time as the "thinnest of veils."

Beyond the basic claim that Schopenhauer's logic is manifestational, as opposed to causal, we can reinforce this translucent-access model by referring to Kant's theory of perception – a view discussed in the opening chapter on British empiricism. We noticed earlier how Locke's representative theory of perception presents an opaque "veil of perception" that prevents the direct awareness of external material objects, and that allows knowledge of these objects only indirectly by means of drawing inferences from our immediately presented ideas.

In reaction to this, we also saw how Kant subjectivizes space and time and reveals a way to reinterpret our experience that allows for the direct perception of external objects, since their externality itself becomes a feature and function of our own minds. Within this theory of direct perception, the presentation of every external object contains amalgamated together, both subjectively variable qualities (for example, colors) and intersubjectively invariant qualities (for example, shapes). We perceive the two simultaneously and in conjunction with one another. Through a process of abstraction, in which we mentally separate subjectively variable qualities (that is, secondary qualities) from intersubjectively invariant qualities (that is, primary qualities), we can identify, isolate, and apprehend the latter.

This Kantian model of perception applies analogously to the Schopenhauerian apprehension of the Will as thing-in-itself. Just as space and time are inherent in us on the Kantian view, the thing-in-itself as Will is inherent in us on the Schopenhauerian view. We do experience the Will in time, and the temporal quality of this experience – whether it is the regular, past–present–future quality or the eternally present quality – compares analogously to the secondary qualities of a perceived material object, such as the object's color. Similarly, the Will-in-itself is comparable to the object's primary qualities. One can say, then, that in the apprehension of the Will-in-time, there is a timeless aspect, but that this is always present in conjunction with a temporal dimension. This compares to saying that in the apprehension of a perceptual object, a dimension that does not vary from person to person (the primary qualities) is always present in conjunction with a dimension that does vary (the secondary qualities).

To display the systematic power of this interpretation across Schopenhauer's view as a whole, we can note that the above situation fits how Schopenhauer describes the apprehension of the timeless Platonic Ideas – an apprehension that can only take place within a person who has an actual, spatio-temporal existence:

> . . . the particular can also be apprehended as a universal, namely, when it is raised to the (Platonic) idea; but in this event, which I have analyzed in the Third Book, the intellect steps beyond the constraints of individuality and consequently, the constraints of time . . .[13]

In the case of the apprehension of the Will-in-time in its individuated acts, we do not apprehend a Platonic Idea, but apprehend the timeless dimension of the Will itself, which we have seen Schopenhauer model on Kant's account of freedom. This is a spontaneous act whose ground is outside of time and space – an act, we should add, that is inspired by the cosmological argument for God's existence, where an uncaused cause, or timeless act, is postulated as the universe's cause. In Schopenhauer's account, this act is not God's, but is the creative and timeless act of an almighty, universal, and blind Will. So if we combine Kant's theories of perception and freedom, noting also Schopenhauer's account of the perception of Platonic Ideas, we can derive models for understanding how the apprehension of the Will-in-time need not be an exclusively a phenomenal experience, and how this apprehension can be interpreted as providing a positive awareness of the Will-in-itself, conceived of as the thing-in-itself.

A further consideration supports the idea that we can remove various translucent "veils" from our PSR-conditioned perception to reveal the thing-in-itself clearly. This concerns the thing-in-itself's subjective nature. Quite independently of specifying the thing-in-itself as Will, Schopenhauer argues that it is not an object, but is a subjective being. If we reflect upon our own minds as expressions of this subjective being – for example, as we experience ourselves slowly becoming tired or slowly waking up – we notice that continuity prevails. We are more like a body of water that becomes indistinct as we perceive further into its depths, and less like a building with a discrete series of floors, basements, and sub-basements. Our consciousness has both continuous and discrete aspects, but, in its natural and healthy forms, it tends fundamentally to be more integrated, continuous, and free-flowing, than fragmented and robotic.

These reflections indicate the following: transparently and absolutely, we cannot apprehend the thing-in-itself as it is in itself, but it is reasonable to say that our apprehension of the Will-in-time, especially in its form within an eternal present, provides us with a translucent apprehension of the thing-in-itself that approaches transparency. This apprehension reveals clearly how the thing-in-itself is in itself, as if one were seeing it through colored cellophane. As far as we can discern introspectively and philosophically, we can describe the thing-in-itself as Will – a Will whose timeless act compares to the act of divine creation, with the qualification that this act lacks self-consciousness, intelligence, and morality.

We can also express Schopenhauer's insight by saying that the thing-in-itself is *essentially* Will, and that this essence appears in human experience in conjunction with other non-essential qualities, the most salient of which is a temporal quality. An important question remaining will be what implications we should draw from the fact that the thing-in-itself, although it may be knowable translucently to a high degree of clarity, is still not absolutely and transparently knowable.

notes

1   *WWR* (II), Chapter XVIII, "On the Possibility of Knowing the Thing-in-Itself," P 197–8, HK 408, ZA 231. At the end of this paragraph, Schopenhauer is referring to the last lines of the first volume of *WWR*, quoted above (§71, P 412, HK 532, ZA 508).

2   *WWR* (I), Book II, §18, P 101–2, HK 132, ZA 145.

3   *MSR* (III), Reisebuch 1818, p. 41.

4   *MSR* (III), Berlin 1825, p. 247.

5   *PP* (II), Chapter IV, "Some Observations on the Antithesis of the Thing-in-Itself and the Phenomenon," §61, P 90, ZA 102.

6   *WWR* (II), Chapter XXV, "Transcendent Considerations on the Will as Thing-in-Itself," P 318, HK 66, ZA 372.

7   *WWR* (I), Book II, §18, P 102, HK 133, ZA 146.

8   *WWR* (I), Book I, §3, P 7, HK 8, ZA 34.

9   *WWR* (I), Book IV, §54, P 279, HK 359–60, ZA 352.

10 In *PP* (II), Chapter VI, "On Philosophy and Natural Science," §153, P 296–7, ZA 322, Schopenhauer states:

> It is just this *complete absorption in the present* that adds so much to the joy that we have in our housepets. They are the personified present and to a certain extent, make us feel the value of every unburdened and unclouded hour, which we usually pass over with our thoughts and leave unnoticed.

11　*WWR* (II), Chapter XLI, "On Death and Its Relation to the Indestructibility of Our Inner Nature," P 481, HK 272, ZA 564.
12　*WWR* (II), Chapter XVIII, "On the Possibility of Knowing the Thing-in-Itself," P 196–7, HK 406, ZA 229–30.
13　*WWR* (II), Chapter XV, "On the Essential Imperfections of the Intellect," P 141, HK 336, ZA 164.

further reading

Janaway, Christopher, *Self and World in Schopenhauer's Philosophy* (Oxford: Clarendon Press, 1989).
Young, Julian, *Willing and Unwilling: A Study in the Philosophy of Arthur Schopenhauer* (Dordrecht: Martinus Nijhoff, 1987).

schopenhauer's practical philosophy

endless suffering in the daily world

i a universal will without purpose

If the principle of sufficient reason (PSR) renders our experience rational, and if ultimate reality is a senseless, directionless, timeless, undivided "Will," then many practical consequences follow. As we have seen, space, time, and causality – all of which are the PSR's expressions – are individuating principles that produce an experience whose parts stand in a systematic connection with one another. They act like a prism, separating into fragments the undivided Will, and with kaleidoscopic patterning organize the shards into a comprehensible pattern. At the same time, paradoxically, our PSR also produces the world's strife. In rendering the Will comprehensible, we also render it violent.

By itself, the PSR's divisive activity does not produce conflict, disconnectedness, and disruption. The nature of what it fragments is also a factor. If, for example, ultimate reality were a harmonious being in which a principle of the unity of opposites inheres, then the fragmentation of this type of being would produce a set of individuals whose inner nature would eventually reconcile their differences.

Since the Schopenhauerian thing-in-itself is a raw urge or blind Will, it has no principle of unity except for its own oneness and singularity. When the PSR fragments this blind Will – and this is also to say that since the PSR is an aspect of ourselves, that *we* are fragmenting the Will, and that, since we are manifestations of the Will, that the Will is actually fragmenting *itself* – the result is a multiplicity of driving, senseless, continually combative individuals. If we begin philosophically with this type of thing-in-itself, the PSR's activity may introduce rationality, but it also produces an amoral world filled inexhaustibly with selfish and aggressive individuals.

Within this mixed-up Schopenhauerian jungle, the thing-in-itself "feasts on itself" creatively, self-destructively, and endlessly. In a memorable example – one that serves well as a microcosm of his vision of the daily world – Schopenhauer describes the bulldog-ant of Australia:

> The bulldog-ant of Australia offers the most glaring example along such lines, for when one cuts it in half, a struggle begins between the head and the tail. The head catches hold of the tail with its teeth, and the tail fearlessly defends itself by stinging the head. The struggle lasts usually for a half an hour, until they die or are dragged away by other ants. This happens every time.[1]

> And it is in reference to this world, to this playground of tortured and anguish-ridden beings that endure only by eating one another, where consequently every vicious animal is the living grave of thousands of others, and where its self-sustenance is a chain of torturing deaths . . . that people have [absurdly] associated the system of *optimism*, and wanted to demonstrate that it is the best of all possible worlds.[2]

The human being is a party to this violent scene, since our quest for knowledge requires the PSR, and this principle divides the thing-in-itself into antagonistic parts. The thing-in-itself is essentially a single, blind, and timeless Will, so when the PSR divides it, a living theater of death and destruction shockingly results. Human cognition is mainly responsible for this nightmare: without the quest for knowledge, space and time would not exist, and without space and time, there would be no divisions, no individuals, and no violence. We are thereby an essential ingredient for producing a world of violent individuals, all of whom exhibit the phenomenon of the Will feasting on itself. Why the Will manifests itself as human beings whose thirst for knowledge creates such a violent world, is a question beyond the PSR, and is hence a question that has no possible answer.

We also feast on *ourselves* at a reflective level, for our moral sensibilities recoil at the brutal, aggression-filled world that our cognition generates. Morality and knowledge, practice and theory, are here opposed within the human being, antagonistically and self-destructively. People are essentially at odds with themselves, and as our will feasts on itself both inwardly and outwardly, it becomes evident that the negation of the Will by the Will itself is of our very essence.

Schopenhauer's account of human nature resonates revealingly with the story of Adam and Eve, viz., the pair of original humans in the Judeo-Christian religions, who, owing to their thirst for knowledge of good and evil, were cast out of a perfect and virtually timeless world into a life of hard work, suffering and death. The human condition is the same within Schopenhauer's philosophy, except that he expresses it in reference to the metaphysics of the Will in conjunction with the PSR. His formulation is intellectually sophisticated, but within it, we still share the plight of Adam and Eve: the quest for knowledge plunges us responsibly into a morally repugnant world of violence, pain, and downfall. This penitential consequence of the Kantian theory of knowledge is uniquely Schopenhauerian: Kant never imagined it, since he did not characterize the thing-in-itself as having qualities that, once it is cognitively divided, would generate endless aggression.

In tune with this, Schopenhauer describes the thing-in-itself as a fundamental "lack": it is an aim to be satisfied in general, without reason or specific object. One could say here that reality is an unexplainable emptiness that aims for satisfaction, but has absolutely no direction. It is easy to imagine a person feeling this way, when spiritually lost or nihilistic. More broadly, such a description can also describe the human condition, as we continually reproduce ourselves and strive for an endless variety of goals, while knowing nothing about what our ultimate point might be, or whether we even have one.

The idea of an utterly aimless Will nonetheless remains puzzling from a theoretical standpoint, since it is difficult to comprehend a Will that wills nothing specific, or wants, but wants nothing in particular, or is goal-oriented, but has no specific aim or point to it. One expects some specification of that towards which the Will intrinsically aims (for example, that it aims to become self-consciousness, or that it aims for more power). Let us then, consider a few ways to make more sense of this rarefied idea.

ii the purposelessness of schopenhauer's thing-in-itself

An initial way to appreciate Schopenhauer's conception of the thing-in-itself as blind Will is to observe how it is an artifact of Kant's style of philosophical thinking. The latter typically involves taking some concrete individuals and intellectually separating out their different constituents, like an analytical chemist. One of the more well-known examples is Kant's analysis of a perceptual object into its sensory, conceptual, and formally-intuitive aspects:

> In the transcendental aesthetic we will therefore first isolate sensibility, such as to remove everything that the understanding thinks through its concepts, so as to leave nothing more than empirical intuition. Second, we will also separate from this everything that belongs to sensation, so as to leave remaining nothing more than pure intuition and the mere form of appearances, which is exclusively what sensibility can provide *a priori*. From this investigation it will be found that there are two pure forms of sensible intuition as principles of *a priori* cognition, namely space and time . . .[3]

Similarly, Schopenhauer strips away layer upon layer of what he takes to be his body's accidental qualities, and identifies "Will" as the basic subjective aspect of his body. This reveals to him a notion of Will that lacks rationality or any specific goal. In Kantian terms, Schopenhauer arrives at the universal *form* of Will that all willing has necessarily. This is also the abstract form of suffering, as we shall see.

As a general goal-orientedness that lacks any specific goal, Schopenhauer's Will has a curious affinity to the notion of "purposiveness without a purpose" (*Zweckmässigkeit ohne Zweck*) that figures centrally in Kant's theory of beauty. Kant maintains that when we properly call an object "beautiful," we disinterestedly contemplate its systematic structure, and in view of it, feel intellectually compelled to regard the object as the product of an intelligent design, independently of considering what the object's purpose happens to be. For Kant, the object's "purposiveness without a purpose" rests on our perception of its systematic structure and therefore always has a rational quality, and this link to rationality is what makes the label "beautiful" appropriate.

Schopenhauer's thing-in-itself as Will also exhibits a purposiveness without a purpose, but it is non-rational. The Will aims, and in this sense, it is purposive. It also aims for nothing specific, and in this sense, it is without a purpose. Since it lacks a rational dimension, however, its purposiveness is foreign to systematicity, reason, and morality – all of which Kant associates with beauty. The core of Schopenhauer's universe, far from beautiful, is contrastingly cold and frightening.

The contrast between Schopenhauer and Kant concerning reason's presence within this context, arises from their respective subject-oriented versus object-oriented approaches. In his aim to discover the absolute truth, Schopenhauer introspectively apprehends within himself a basic, blind, and driving force at the most fundamental level of his being. Kant's alternative concern is with the outward question of whether we can realize our moral obligations in daily life, and he orients himself towards the external world in his theory of beauty, observing systematic form in naturally beautiful objects, and wondering whether their design has an intelligent and potentially moral cause. These are important differences, but what we can gain through this association between Schopenhauer's Will and Kant's theory of beauty is some plausibility for Schopenhauer's notion of the aimless Will, since it seems incomprehensible at first.

To help render more understandable Schopenhauer's conception of the thing-in-itself as Will that strives or wills, but that strives for nothing in particular, we can further compare how Edmund Husserl (1859–1938) and Jean-Paul Sartre (1905–80) describe the nature of consciousness. Their view is that "intentionality" is the mark of consciousness: consciousness is always *consciousness of* some object or other, where the object can remain unspecified. This intentionality expresses "directedness," but due to its high level of abstraction, the direction consciousness takes remains unspecified. This is precisely because the theoretical aim is to characterize consciousness in general.[4] In sum, we can describe Schopenhauer's thing-in-itself not only as the *form* of all willing, or as a kind of purposiveness without a purpose, but as exhibiting the bare form of intentionality, or the bare form of consciousness.

iii life as embittering: schopenhauer and buddhism

Existential implications issue from Schopenhauer's metaphysics of the Will in conjunction with the PSR. Since the Will-in-itself is an absolute lack, each person – as a manifestation of this Will – experiences himself or herself as fundamentally empty, as always wanting something more, and as constantly driven to satisfy that lack. We experience ourselves as constantly reaching for some condition that, in principle, never arrives. We may attain what we want in this or that instance, but our essentially empty nature drives us to continue our search for fulfillment:

> All *willing* springs from need, therefore from deficiency, and therefore from suffering. Satisfaction brings the need to an end, but for every desire that is satisfied there are at least ten that are denied. Moreover, desiring lasts a long time, demands extend to infinity, satisfaction is short and is given out in small measure. Even the final satisfaction is itself only an illusion; every fulfilled wish makes room for yet another . . . Therefore as long as our consciousness is filled with our will, as long as we hand ourselves over to the crowd of desires with its constant hopes and fears, as long as we are the subject of willing, we will never have enduring happiness or peace . . . The subject of willing thus lies continually on the turning wheel of Ixion, is always scooping water in the sieve of the Danaids, and is the eternally thirsting Tantalus.[5]

All of those Schopenhauer mentions were punished for having killed people who were close either in social or blood relations. The former were condemned frustratingly to scoop water with a strainer for having killed the husbands who were forced upon them; Tantalus was condemned to eternal thirst for having murdered his son and having served him to the gods for dinner, deceivingly and cannibalistically. Ixion, the first human to shed the blood of his kin (specifically, his father-in-law), was bound forever to a winged, flaming wheel revolving in space and condemned to cry aloud "You should show gratitude to your benefactor." The closeness of kin involved suggests that these figures were hurting themselves in a broader sense, and in a more literary manner they allude to how the will "feasts upon itself." Schopenhauer also associates this self-feasting with guilt, and this underscores our earlier references to the violence-generating human cognitive condition, original sin, and the conception of humans as the descendants of Adam and Eve.[6] In all of these cases, the human condition is one of punishment:

> If one wants to know what people, morally considered, are worth as a whole and in general, one should consider their fate, as a whole and in general. This is want, misery, lamentation, torment and death. Eternal justice rules. If people, considered as a whole, were not contemptible, their fate would not be so pitiful. In this sense we can say that the world's courtroom is none other than the world itself. If one could put all of the world's misery on *one* side of the scale, and all of the world's guilt on the other, the needle would certainly point directly upwards.[7]

> The innermost core and spirit of Christianity is the same as that of Brahmanism and Buddhism: they all teach that as a consequence of its very existence, humanity carries a heavy guilt; it is only that Christianity fails to express this guilt directly and candidly, as do those older faiths.[8]

Although the PSR generates suffering by fragmenting the thing-in-itself as Will, the thing-in-itself is problematic in its own right, for it carries the seeds of suffering within itself. It is a lack, or a goal-orientation without any specific goal, and is the form of all instances of willing. Insofar as a lack entails suffering, the thing-in-itself as Will is none other than the very form of suffering.

The core of Schopenhauer's universe is consequently timeless, irrational, and cosmically lacking, and its form is a form of pain. This situates human beings in a maddening double-bind, for if we remain focused upon the daily world, we suffer from its violent and frustrating episodes; if we shift our attention to the Will-in-itself, we identify ourselves primordially with the very form of suffering that, when differentiated, fills the phenomenal world with misery. There seems to be no escape from either the form or the content of suffering, and this is consistent with Schopenhauer's statement that "all life is suffering."[9]

The statement that all life is suffering indicates a comparison to the first of the Four Noble Truths of Buddhism, and since he believes that Buddhism has pre-eminence over the other world's religions, it is useful to identify some of the fundamentally Buddhistic aspects of Schopenhauer's presentation of the world.[10] To coordinate the two, we can focus on the Four Noble Truths that as foundational tenets of the religion are at Buddhism's center. The First Noble Truth is often translated as either saying or implying that life is suffering, providing a statement of a prevailing spiritual illness. Buddhists also believe, as identified by the Second Noble Truth, that that suffering is caused by desire, paralleling Schopenhauer's estimation of our existential situation; the Third truth provides a decision upon whether or not the illness is fatal; and the Fourth, a prescription for better health. They are summarized as follows:

1 Life *as ordinarily lived* is frustrating and unsatisfactory.
2 There is a cause for this dissatisfaction, the most predominant of which is the presence of powerful strivings (that is, intense grasping for things; trying to "hold on" too much).
3 If these powerful strivings are reduced in their intensity, then daily life will be less frustrating and more peaceful.
4 There is a method for reducing one's powerful strivings, an important part of which involves realizing that every individual thing and condition is perishable, and that everything changes. Upon apprehending the world's constant fluctuation, grasping at things as if they were permanent becomes less meaningful and less attractive.

If we reflect upon the significance of the claim that "all life is suffering" in Schopenhauerianism and in Buddhism, some important differences also emerge between the two outlooks. Schopenhauer is convinced that life's pleasures are of relatively low value, maintaining that the two poles of daily human existence are boredom and pain: either we are briefly satisfied when we attain our goal and soon suffer from boredom, or we are engaged in attaining a goal, and suffer from the lack of having attained it. In the midst of this process, we die, tragically and comically. Since Schopenhauer believes that at bottom, no one desires death, we return ourselves to the frying pan of desire to avoid the ultimate shipwreck. Human life consequently embodies a triple bind of boredom, pain, and death that calls for some sort of escape from all three.

Traditional Buddhism's attitude towards the daily world compares to Schopenhauer's, but it is less bleak. We can see this by considering the First Noble Truth:

> This, monks, is the noble truth of painfulness [*dukkha*]: birth is painful, getting old is painful, death is painful. Sorrow, lamentation, pain, grief and despair are painful. Connection with the unloved, separation from the loved, that is also painful. Not to get what one wants, that is also painful. In a word, the five-fold aggregation based on grasping is painful.[11]

The Pali word "*dukkha*" typically means "painful," and it contrasts with "*sukha*," which means "sugar" or "sweet." This reveals the more metaphorical reflection that whatever is *dukkha*, can transform the flavor of a sweet mixture into something bitter or sour. Whatever is *dukkha* tends to spoil life in the way worms spoil fresh fruit. Life as a whole is not suffering, but life as ordinarily lived contains episodes that tend to produce embittered or soured feelings. As the First Noble Truth reminds us, this is typically when we lose our loved ones or when we are deeply disappointed, or, more generally, when we see the meanings we have established in the world – our families, social relationships, professional achievements, good deeds, etc. – begin to change in significance and disappear. These painful experiences can be like "maggots in the bread of life" as Nietzsche would say,[12] and Buddhism advises us strongly not to allow them to poison us spiritually. Becoming embittered as one gets older is as natural as the rotting of fruit, but Buddhism believes that there is a way to preserve a fresh and sound outlook on the world.

Buddhism's central prescription is also like that of Roman Stoicism: we should see things for what they are and avoid attitudes towards things that are inconsistent with their natures. The Stoic advises us to avoid trying to control things that are in fact out of our control. The Buddhist advises us to appreciate how everything in the daily world is a perishable item, and to realize that when we hold on to these items as if they were permanent, we engage with the world in an uninformed and unenlightened way that inevitably leads to suffering. Recognizing that the ordinary things that surround us are composite and perishable is the first step towards Buddhist enlightenment.

The Buddhist message is not, then, that all life is suffering. It is this: if one is not metaphysically aware, then life can become painfully bittersweet and easily spoiled. This is to say positively that by not holding on to perishable things as if they were forever enduring, we can considerably reduce suffering, retain a fresh outlook on life, and achieve a measure of happiness.

These reflections disclose the distinctively Buddhist philosophical attitude of adopting a doubtful stance towards anything that presents itself as permanent. When extended into the philosophical realm, it becomes a skeptical attitude towards eternal entities such as Platonic Ideas, unchangeable substances, and conditions that purportedly constitute the steadfast essence of reality. This marks a crucial difference between Buddhism and Upanishadic thought, for the latter acknowledges an unchangeable, eternal, and absolute substratum to the universe. The Buddhist world is more like constantly blowing wind, swirling smoke, burning fire, or flowing water, and nothing more.

The Upanishadic recognition of an unchangeable substratum did not satisfy Buddha, and it led him to reject ascetic yogic practices as a means to enlightenment. In his own efforts to become superlatively aware, he perceived that grasping for an unchangeable foundation on a transcendent dimension was only another attempt to hold on to something solid

schopenhauer's practical philosophy

and reliable, when grasping itself was the problem. To become enlightened, he realized that one must let go of everything.

As in Upanishadic thought, we see the same type of otherworldly grasping in Platonism, which originated through an interpretation of the daily world as one of constant becoming, and an associated effort to apprehend a non-spatial and non-temporal dimension to secure an unchanging truth. Buddhism, alternatively, acknowledges that nothing is unconditionally permanent, either in the daily world or in any other. This brings the experience of time to its forefront, since time is the destroyer of all perishable things and is an inescapable factor of human experience, both external and internal.

Schopenhauer's attraction to Buddhism is evident in the many passages in which he writes about it. For the most part, he is attracted to its conception of enlightenment (*Nirvana*) and to what he takes to be Buddhism's philosophical idealism. With respect to the latter, he celebrates Buddhism along with Brahmanism and Christianity, as expressing an attitude towards the daily world that regards it as dream-like, rather than as unconditionally and solidly present. To Schopenhauer, this is pleasingly consistent with the Kantian view that all human experience is conditioned by the PSR, and hence, is of a subjective and relative quality. Schopenhauer frequently contrasts Buddhism, Brahmanism, and Christianity – which he refers to enthusiastically as "pessimistic" religions – with Judaism, Islam, and Polytheism, which he interprets as more realistic and objectionably "optimistic" religions.[13] In these contexts, he does not highlight Buddhism exclusively, but discusses it affirmatively in conjunction with the other pessimistic religions.

More distinctive are Schopenhauer's discussions of Buddhist enlightenment, or *Nirvana*, for these reflect his extra-philosophical interest in revealing a state of consciousness that is independent of the PSR. For the present, we can note that Schopenhauer plausibly characterizes Buddhist enlightenment as not asserting any positive eternal truths, but as involving only a simple release from suffering. He also believes it coincides with his conception of the denial-of-the-Will:

> He [the Schopenhauerian subject of enlightenment] willingly gives up the existence with which we are acquainted: what instead comes to him in its place, is in our eyes *nothing*. This is because our existence, with respect to that other, is *nothing*. The Buddhist faith calls this *Nirvana*, i.e., utter cessation.[14]

> . . . the constant suffering and death of individuals is certain to life. To be freed from this is reserved for the *denial* of the will-to-life, through which the individual will tears itself away from the stem of the human species

and gives up its existence in it. Whatever it is that the individual will then becomes, we have no concepts; indeed, we have no data for such concepts. We can only describe it as that which is free to be the will-to-live, or not. For the latter case, Buddhism marks it with the word, *Nirvana*.[15]

Schopenhauer emphasizes the daily world's thoroughgoing suffering to a greater degree than does Buddhism, but their attitudes are similar: both believe that the daily world is typically unsatisfying; both agree that desire causes suffering; both prescribe that we can relieve suffering by desiring less. Nonetheless, in the manner of Brahmanism, Schopenhauer sometimes postulates a higher-dimensional reality that stands behind the worldly scenes. At other times, he does not take this transcendent step and conceives of enlightenment more simply and Buddhistically as a detached attitude that we can adopt within the daily world, that is, an attitude that does not require an extraordinary state of consciousness to relieve suffering. Schopenhauer has an Upanishadic metaphysics that equates the outer and inner aspects of reality, and he supplements this with a Buddhistic conception of enlightenment, often describing his end-state of enlightenment in a purely negative way. This combination of Brahamanism and Buddhism creates some tensions within his view that we will later explore.

The next several chapters describe Schopenhauer's various modes of salvation, attending initially to those that stand midway between the daily world of suffering and what he characterizes ultimately as *Nirvana*, or the extinction of the will-to-live. The leading idea is that since the PSR fragments the thing-in-itself as Will into conflicting parts that attack and feast upon each other, suffering will diminish if we can reduce the sense of multiplicity that the PSR generates. The PSR introduces multiplicity through space, time, and causality, so there will be less suffering within a more timeless and spaceless orientation towards the world, and less suffering if we resist interpreting the world scientifically in terms of cause and effect.

The compassionate aim to reduce suffering revolves around the principle that the more multiplicity one's experience contains, the more conflict and suffering there will be. Less multiplicity accordingly entails less conflict. Analysis generates suffering, whereas synthesis alleviates it; opposition generates tension, whereas reconciliation removes it; individuation leads to egoism and selfishness, whereas universalistic thinking leads to a more socially embracing sense of personality and moral awareness.

Schopenhauer's effort to eliminate oppositions between individuals – one especially evident in his conception of morality – is common to many thinkers of the time, including Kant and German idealists such as Fichte, Schelling, and Hegel. Among the latter, this is embodied in the dialectical logic of "position, opposition, and reconciliation," using the act of self-consciousness as their model. In a dialectical synthesis of opposites, differences between individuals are bridged and their opposition is dissolved in a more sophisticated amalgamation of what were opposing elements. We will explore this contrast between Schopenhauer and German Idealism in Chapter 12.

Schopenhauer, who was influenced more powerfully and conservatively by Kant's style of philosophizing, employs a more traditional Aristotelian logic whereby the reconciliation of opposites is achieved by disregarding the accidental differences between things to uncover a common essence. As a result, we usually see him aiming to apprehend universal ideas that are detached from the spatio-temporal individuals in which they inhere. He seeks this detachment because he regards the daily world as a nightmarish illusion that we generate through our cognitive activity.

Schopenhauer consequently identifies three different styles of reducing the sense of multiplicity in our daily experience, namely, aesthetic consciousness, moral consciousness, and ascetic consciousness. Each has a different object of attention and each provides a release from suffering to a different extent. Aesthetic consciousness attends to timeless Platonic Ideas. Moral consciousness highlights the timeless universalities related to people's characters and reveals the single act of Will that expresses itself as humanity as a whole. Ascetic consciousness centers upon the "denial-of-the-will" and leads to a difficult to describe universalistic mode of consciousness.[16] We will now consider each of these in turn.

notes

1 *WWR* (I), Book II, §27, P 147, HK 192–3, ZA 198.
2 *WWR* (II), Chapter XLVI, "On the Profound Emptiness and Suffering of Life," P 581, HK 392, ZA 680.
3 *CPR*, A21/B36. This style of abstractive thinking is at the basis of Schopenhauer's argument that the four roots of the PSR are distinct.
4 Along the same lines, even if we regard the will-in-itself as a positively productive power in general, rather than as a "lack" in the Schopenhauerian fashion, we arrive at a productive power that has no specification, and that achieves a specification only in some further context within which it can be given some determinate content. We encounter this view in Nietzsche, who speaks of the will-to-power as nothing more than a force of raw expansion and dynamism.
5 *WWR* (I), Book III, §38, P 196, HK 353–4, ZA 252.
6 *WWR* (II), Chapter XLVIII, "On the Doctrine of the Denial of the Will-to-Live," P 608, HK 426, ZA 712: "This original sin is itself in truth the affirmation of

the will-to-live, whereas the denial of the will-to-live that results from the rise of better knowledge, is salvation. What is moral is therefore located between these two."

7   *WWR* (I), §63, P 352, HK 454, ZA 438. Schopenhauer sets forth this judgment under the assumption of traditional Christian moral values. If one were to abandon these values, as Nietzsche does, then the conclusion that human beings have a low worth would not obviously follow.

8   *WWR* (II), Chapter XLVIII, "On the Doctrine of the Denial of the Will-to-Live," P 604, HK 421, ZA 707.

9   *WWR* (I), Book IV, §56, P 310, HK 401, ZA 389.

10 *WWR* (II), Chapter XVII, "On Man's Need for Metaphysics," P 169, HK 371, ZA 197.

11 That is, the desiring human mind itself, in its five components, is painful.

12 *Thus Spoke Zarathustra*, Book II, "On the Rabble."

13 For Schopenhauer, "realism" and "optimism" are disparaging terms. His own view lies more in the direction of idealism and pessimism.

14 *WWR* (II), Chapter XLI "On Death and its Relation to the Indestructibility of Our Inner Nature," P 508, HK 308, ZA 596.

15 *WWR* (II), Chapter XLIV "The Metaphysics of Sexual Love," P 560, HK 374, ZA 656.

16 Søren Kierkegaard (1813–55) also formulated his outlook in reference to the aesthetic, ethical, and religious standpoints, similarly locating the religious standpoint as the most enlightened. Kierkegaard's and Schopenhauer's respective articulations of the tripartite sequence sharply differ, however, since Kierkegaard regards each standpoint as conflicting with the others, whereas Schopenhauer regards them as aiming jointly towards the same universalistic end.

further reading

Dauer, Dorothy, *Schopenhauer as Transmitter of Buddhist Ideas* (Berne: Lang, 1969).

Janaway, Christopher (ed.), *The Cambridge Companion to Schopenhauer* (Cambridge: Cambridge University Press, 1999).

Sedlar, Jean W., *India in the Mind of Germany: Schelling, Schopenhauer and Their Times* (Washington, DC: University Press of America, 1982).

tranquility i: sublimity, genius, and aesthetic experience

i platonic ideas and aesthetic experience

To relieve the frustrations of constant desire, Schopenhauer advises us to change our ordinary attitude towards daily life. Since he believes that desire is the main cause of suffering, and that being an individual not only reinforces desire but also leads to conflict with other desire-filled individuals, he seeks ways of interpreting the world that are less individualistic and more universalistic. His view is that a more universalistic perspective will provide relief from the pushes, pulls, conflicts, and fleeting satisfactions that characterize daily life.

We can recall that in Schopenhauer's metaphysics of the Will, the thing-in-itself as Will *directly* objectifies itself through the principle of sufficient reason (PSR) (that is, through us) into a set of universalistic Platonic Ideas and *indirectly* objectifies itself (again, through us) into a set of individual spatio-temporal objects. As we aim towards greater universality and tranquility, the first step away from our ordinary interpretation of the spatio-temporal world accordingly brings us to the level of Platonic Ideas. For Schopenhauer, these are the prime objects of aesthetic experience, and he believes that their contemplation provides a measure of relief from the goal-oriented, selfish, and grasping nature of ordinary life.

This shift from the world of spatio-temporal objects towards the realm of Platonic Ideas takes place within our own construction of the world. As noted in our earlier discussions, Platonic Ideas cannot exist independently of human consciousness within Schopenhauer's view: our PSR has a general root and a set of four specific expressions, and when it operates, it generates two levels of objects that correspond respectively to its root and its fourfold expressions. At the PSR's root, the universal subject–object distinction invokes a level of universal objects, or Platonic Ideas, and the PSR's fourfold expressions produce the more highly individuated level of spatio-temporal objects. Since the PSR depends on our presence, there would be no PSR in our absence, and hence, no Platonic Ideas.

Although the PSR in its more specific fourfold application creates a violent state of worldly affairs, the less-individuating *root* of the PSR when considered in isolation, opens up a level of consciousness where differentiation and conflict, along with the significance of space and time, are noticeably reduced. Platonic Ideas are independent of the daily world within which suffering takes place, so the contemplation of these Ideas offers tranquility and relief.

As a general principle, Schopenhauer assumes that the quality of our consciousness mirrors the quality of the objects we contemplate. One is what one eats, so to speak. If we attend to finite objects, then our awareness assumes a distinctively finite quality; if we contemplate infinite objects, then infinity dominates our mind; if we reflect upon universal objects, then our thinking becomes more universalistic; if violent objects capture our attention, then we become more aggressive or defensive, and so on. Schopenhauer consequently holds that if we habitually contemplate Platonic Ideas, our outlook will become more universalistic, and hence, more liberated from daily desires and the suffering they cause.

It might seem strange that Schopenhauer associates aesthetic experience with the perception of Platonic Ideas, since Plato is so highly critical of artists and art. Plato's down-to-earth concern, though, is with developing a rational political leadership, rather than relieving suffering. By his lights, artists are out of touch with the eternal patterns of things, acting merely as mimics who present replicas of physical actions and objects. A two-dimensional picture of a fish, represents the timeless reality of "being a fish," far more superficially than does any actual, three-dimensional, full-blooded fish. A leader who learns about war only by watching movies and going to the theater does not compare to one who understands its grim reality by risking his or her life in actual combat. Since artistic representations provide less knowledge than do the actualities they represent, Plato believes that their artistic attractiveness is mainly a measure of our ignorance.

What Plato does not appreciate, and what Schopenhauer does, is that artists do not essentially copy or imitate things, either in a mechanical way, as does a camera, or in a merely pretending way, as occurs in children's play or mimicry. They interpret and often idealize their subjects, just as classical Greek sculptors idealized the human body in their perfectly proportioned and generically conceived statues. In traditional portraiture as well, artists do not merely copy a person's face, but aim to render the person's inner character visible by idealizing his or her physical form. Schopenhauer appreciates the amount of imaginative reinterpretation that artistic creation involves, stating that artistic activity is primarily about creating idealized images of things. He sees that a thing's artistic representation can (although it need not) present the thing's essence more clearly than would an ordinary, unpolished instance.

The word "aesthetic" derives from the Greek word "*aistheta*" [$\alpha\iota\sigma\theta\eta\tau\acute{\alpha}$], which means "sensory particulars" or "perceivable objects," and there is a general etymological connection between what is aesthetic and what is apprehended in sensory experience. For Schopenhauer, Platonic Ideas are not the products of literalistic and mechanical abstraction; they appear directly, immediately, imaginatively, and aesthetically within our perceptual experience:

> We do not allow abstract thought or rational concepts to take over our consciousness. Instead of this, we give the power of our mind over to perception, sinking fully into perception and letting our entire consciousness be filled with the pure contemplation of the actually present natural object, whether it be a landscape, a tree, a rock, a building or anything else. To use a pregnant German way of speaking, we *lose* ourselves completely in the object, i.e., we forget our individuality and our will, and remain constituted only as pure subject, as a clear mirror of the object. It is as if the object were there by itself, without anyone to perceive it, where one consequently cannot separate the perceiver from the perceived. Rather, both have become one, since the entire consciousness is completely filled and taken over by a single perceptual image . . . What is consequently known is no longer the single thing as such, but rather the *idea*, the eternal form, the immediate objectivity of the will at this level. In this perception the subject is conceived no longer as an individual, since the individual has lost itself in such a perception; rather it is a *pure*, will-less, painless subject of knowledge . . . Now in such contemplation the single thing, in a single stroke becomes the *idea* of its species, and the perceiving individual becomes a *pure subject of knowing*. The individual as such knows only individual things; the pure subject of knowing knows only ideas.[1,2]

Here, Schopenhauer describes a style of awareness wherein we disregard our individual will, and think of ourselves as only a "pure subject." As he characterizes it, we feel that we are "no longer an individual" as we become a "*pure* will-less, painless, *timeless subject of knowledge*." The possibility of coming close to experiencing such a will-less and timeless state of mind in actual life, is a leading feature of Schopenhauer's philosophy as a whole.

It is also fair to say that Schopenhauer describes this transcendent aesthetic state in exaggerated terms, for if we aesthetically contemplate a tree, for example, it is contradictory to maintain that the experience has *no* time-element, and implausible to claim that we become *entirely* unaware of the tree's individual perceptual details. While perceiving the tree's essence, we continue to look at the individual tree. Through an *idealizing act of imagination*, with the tree still there before us, we apprehend the timeless form of which the individual tree is an instance, shining through the detailed individual tree that wholly absorbs our attention.

The individual tree does not vanish from our perceptual field, but is perceived in light of its universal significance, just as when we look at another person and see beyond the person's individuality *per se* and attend more insightfully to the humanity that the person instantiates. As we perceive humanity shining through the person, the individual person does not vanish. Similarly, people do not vanish when we perceive this or that person as "the soldier," "the worker," "the calm person," "the courageous person," or "the dedicated person," holding the person's general qualities at the forefront of our attention.[3]

Since individuality does not dissolve completely in aesthetic perception, no one can become a pure, disembodied subject, be released from all pain, or have a timeless experience. It is more accurate to say that in aesthetic experience, our individuality, our pain, and our sense of time become submerged, diminished, and pushed into the background as we reflect upon the experience's more universalistic dimensions. We apprehend Platonic Ideas *through* temporal experience, and the experience's temporality does not vanish.

This existential consideration is consistent with Schopenhauer's account of the apprehension of the thing-in-itself as Will. Just as the thing-in-itself as Will cannot be perceived except through the thinnest veil of time, Platonic Ideas cannot be perceived except through the same thin veil. Schopenhauer's dramatic references to timeless, will-less, and purely knowing subjects are unrealistic, and his account of aesthetic experience needs to remain consistent with his foundational position that we cannot know the thing-in-itself in an absolute, time-free manner.

Noting how a thin, temporal veil always moderates our apprehension of Platonic Ideas, we are in a position to appreciate how Kant's theory of perception helps illuminate the nature of Schopenhauerian aesthetic experience. To recall, in Kant's theory we directly perceive an object that has intersubjectively invariant qualities (for example, extension, figure, and motion) along with subjectively-variable qualities (color, taste, texture, sound, or odor, for instance). We apprehend both sorts of quality in the object and distinguish colors from shapes, for instance, through an act of imagination.[4]

In the case of Schopenhauerian aesthetic perception, by analogy, we can imaginatively and idealizingly separate an object's unessential and transitory sensory details from the universal essence that shines through that individual object. This compares well to how Schopenhauer describes the experience of pure tones:

> Owing to the vibrations of its own material, there is no musical instrument that does not add an additional foreign component to the pure tone, which consists only of vibrations in the air . . . This introduces an accompanying sound through which each pure tone is distinguished as originating from, for example, either a violin or flute. The less this unessential mixture is present, the purer the tone will be.[5]

Schopenhauer often speaks as if we can experience Platonic Ideas in their purity, but aesthetic experience is more accurately modeled by the above example of a musical instrument (us, as we are in time) that intends to play a pure tone (apprehend a Platonic Idea, as it is timelessly). The presence of the musical instrument inevitably affects the quality of the played tone, although in an act of imagination and idealization, we can apprehend the tone's pure quality through the instrument's particular sound. This implies that aesthetic experience can relieve suffering to *some* extent, and perhaps to a major extent, but since it has a necessary temporal dimension, some minimal desire will remain within the experience. Owing to the presence of time, as thin as it may be, every example of apprehending universal qualities, aesthetic or otherwise, will involve desires of some sort.

Although when we conceive it in parallel with the apprehension of the thing-in-itself as Will the aesthetic experience of Platonic Ideas involves a necessary temporal component there is still plenty of room for it to relieve suffering. Consider a situation where one suffers as the result of a failed endeavor. Recognizing oneself as simply one among many in the universal community of those who have not succeeded can do much to relieve the disappointment. Here, one feels a consoling kinship with millions of other people who have suffered the same lot. Upon adopting this more universalistic standpoint, the unessential details of one's own failed effort recede into the background.

In sum, if we regard any given distressing situation as only an instance of a *type* of situation, and pay attention almost exclusively to the type itself in detachment from its particular objects and interests, suffering will diminish. Through this act of reinterpretation, the world transforms into a large theater, and one becomes an actor in a universal play, appreciating that others have played one's role, and that others will play the role again, in an endless recurrence. Schopenhauer believes that we can experience some substantial solace by adopting this less egoistic, more detached, universalistic, aesthetic and theatrical perspective, and he prescribes it to everyone as a way to reduce suffering.

ii artistic genius and the communication theory of art

Despite its therapeutic attractiveness, it remains difficult to perceive life's universalistic aspects in a continual manner. While drinking a glass of water, for example, few people perceive themselves as embodying the timeless thought of living beings that ingest liquids for their sustenance, identifying perhaps with some long-extinct dinosaurs who once gathered around a pond to drink. While speaking to their friends, few people perceive themselves as instantiating the timeless thought of living beings who communicate constructively with each other, identifying perhaps with aboriginal humans who gestured to each other in enthusiasm upon having discovered a new food source. When injuring themselves or upon becoming ill, few perceive themselves as instantiating the universal thought of beings that are injured, or of beings that become ill, identifying perhaps with some salmon in the stream, or a goat on a mountainside that suffered and died ten thousand years ago. Few people habitually look at themselves in the mirror and see the universal consciousness of humanity shining back at them. Owing to the practical pressures of daily life, it is natural to perceive ourselves as we are for the moment and to carry on within a narrow field of interests and reflections.

It takes a powerful imagination and willpower to apprehend constantly the universalistic aspect to everything one does. Some extraordinary people, however, experience this style of consciousness at a consistently high intensity. For Schopenhauer, they are "geniuses" who apprehend the world aesthetically in a relatively effortless manner. Unlike most of us, they attend to what is timeless within ordinary experience, and it is not an exaggeration to say that they live in an atmospherically different, non-ordinary world, where each individual action and object emits a universal glow, where personal desires are not important, and where the specifics of the situation count for very little.

Since the perspective of the genius is rare, and given Schopenhauer's assumption that suffering is important to alleviate, he assigns a special social role to the artistic geniuses within the world's population: they should serve the majority by portraying in the form of fine art visions of eternal truths.[6] By displaying the Platonic Ideas to those who would otherwise only vaguely apprehend them, artistic geniuses guide everyone towards a more distinctively universalistic, suffering-reduced perspective.

As a theory of artistic creation, Schopenhauer's exclusive interest in the apprehension and transmission of Platonic Ideas is open to criticism. Some fine artists simply do not conceive of themselves as transmitters of eternal truths. Also, during the creative process, not all artists have a complete vision of their work in its final form before working with actual physical materials; few merely transcribe a prior vision into a material medium, as W. A. Mozart was said to have done when he wrote his music. Furthermore, being able to apprehend universal essences does not in itself provide the technical talent required to express one's visionary experience well in a physical medium. All of this indicates that Schopenhauer's account of artistic creation applies only to certain artists and artworks, and not to all art.

We can also ask whether Schopenhauer offers a plausible theory of artistic appreciation. Questions immediately arise from the standpoint of the audience, for in relation to any work of art, we cannot be certain that the artist succeeded in portraying the Platonic Idea that he or she originally apprehended. It is also dubious that artworks serve mainly to communicate Platonic Ideas, as opposed to having other functions and values. Great works of art also admit of multiple, if not inexhaustible, interpretations, so that restricting each of their meanings to a single Platonic Idea conflicts with the richness of artistic masterpieces. As is the case for Schopenhauer's theory of artistic creation, such considerations reveal the limited scope of his account of artistic appreciation. This is perhaps the result of his having tailored it in conformity with an overriding interest in relieving suffering, rather than reflecting upon artistic creation and appreciation for its own sake.

Despite its limitations, Schopenhauer's characterization of aesthetic experience recognizes how it can involve a feeling of being transported to a higher state of consciousness, for the insights afforded by artistic masterpieces often provide some distance from our day-to-day difficulties and allow us to understand life with more wisdom. His theory of aesthetic experience might not be plausible as a general account of art, but it is appropriate for some important art.

Schopenhauer accounts for geniuses' extraordinary perceptual capacities – those of Picasso, Manet, or Michelangelo would be good examples – by asserting that they have a degree of intellect in excess of what ordinary perception requires, and that this intellectual excess detaches itself from the common interests of the will to operate on its own.[7] This detachment of intellect from will also generates a relatively painless state of mind:

> What one calls the activation of genius, the hour of holy inspiration, the spiritual moment, is nothing other than the intellect's becoming free. Temporarily relieved from its service to the will, it does not sink into idleness or weariness, but is active on its own for a brief time, by itself. Then it is of the greatest purity and becomes the clear mirror of the world, for since it is completely separated from its origin, namely, the will, the intellect is now – concentrated in *one* consciousness – the world as representation itself.[8]

All misery issues from willing, whereas on the other hand, knowing is in and for itself painless and cheerfully serene.[9]

The completely purified intellect entails painlessness, and to the extent that we *can* impersonally concentrate on purely intellectual matters, the less suffering we are likely to experience. As mentioned, however, the detachment from practical engagement can never be absolute. There are only degrees of disengagement, but the more one is detached, the better off Schopenhauer believes one will existentially be.

We might therefore expect geniuses to have tranquil dispositions. On a number of occasions, though, Schopenhauer indicates contrary features of the genius that temper the tranquility that this type of mentality can offer. For instance, he states that geniuses suffer *more* than ordinary people and that they are typically highly emotional, adding that "no plain, sober person can be a genius."[10]

These conflicting emotional qualities reveal how the genius's psychology is tension-ridden, and that profound tranquility and insight can combine with great suffering. The overall state of mind here is more sublime than it is consistently and peacefully beautiful, and it can reside anywhere along the spectrum between "tranquility tinged with terror" and "terror tinged with tranquility."

A comparable mixture of tranquility and suffering arises in the two further modes of transcendence Schopenhauer describes, namely, moral and ascetic consciousness. All three – which jointly constitute the essence of Schopenhauer's practical philosophy – admit of descriptions in terms of the aesthetics of the sublime.

iii the hierarchy of the visual and verbal arts

Schopenhauer's assorted reflections about the fine arts are grounded upon the hierarchy of the Platonic Ideas, where the objectifications range from inanimate nature to plants and animals to human beings. He refers to the ascending chain of Platonic essences to specify a sequence of artistic subject matters, and correlates various visual and verbal arts with different segments of this hierarchy, beginning with arts that refer mainly to the material forces of inanimate things, passing through those concerning plants and animals, and ending with arts that express human spirituality. He locates music in a realm of its own, since it does not obviously refer to the Will's immediate objectifications (viz., Platonic Ideas), but refers to a variety of the Will's immediate modes of subjectivity (viz., human emotions).

Schopenhauer's aesthetic theory – one centered in Book III of the first volume of *The World as Will and Representation* – is less systematically developed than what we find, for instance, in other German Idealist philosophers such as Hegel or Schelling. Schopenhauer uses the ascending sequence of Platonic Ideas as a guide for his discussions, but he sometimes offers analyses based on the nature of artistic media themselves, rather than upon artistic subject matters. Interwoven with these are statements of art-critical principles and evaluations of particular works of art. Within this context, as in others, Schopenhauer characterizes art in relation to relieving suffering. He consequently attends less to natural beauty, and more to the artistically-portrayed human condition.

His discussion begins with architecture, which expresses a basic conflict between the forces of gravity and rigidity, as these are embodied and clarified through the relationship between support and load. In company with architecture, Schopenhauer locates the aesthetic arrangement of water, as seen in fountains, cascades, waterfalls, and springs. At this base-level of Platonic Ideas that refer to inanimate objects and materials, he also includes paintings of architectural ruins and church interiors, drawing no important distinction between works of architecture and works of art that represent them.[11] Presumably, he would locate Zen rock gardens at this rudimentary level as well, owing to their inanimate materials.

Schopenhauer continues with discussions of art forms related to plant and animal life such as formal gardens, landscape painting, still-life painting, animal painting, and animal sculpture. This extends into those that reflect human activities, such as historical painting, historical sculpture, literature, and drama. The differences between the artistic media are mostly insignificant in this ladder-like conceptualization; the common subject matter captures Schopenhauer's attention and is what defines his theoretical arrangement of the arts.

At the pinnacle of the visual arts hierarchy, and in accord with Schopenhauer's wider philosophical interests, we encounter religious painting expressive of the innermost spirit of Christianity. The prevailing theme here is *resignation*, as found paradigmatically in Raphael's and Correggio's works. With this exemplary achievement in artistic expression, visual art fulfils its task and ends:

> Here is the high point of all art which, after it has followed the will in its adequate objectivity, viz., the ideas, through each and every level through which its nature is unfolded – from the lowest, where it is first affected by causes, then by stimuli, and finally, where it is affected by motives. Art now ends [*nunmehr endigt*] with the presentation of the will's free self-neutralization [*Selbstaufhebung*] arising through a great peacefulness that comes to it from the most perfect knowledge of its own nature.[12]

Although Schopenhauer's version is less historically structured, those familiar with Hegel's aesthetics will notice in the above excerpt, a similar, if undeveloped, "end of art" thesis. Hegel's own hierarchy of the arts focuses on artistic media and their respective capacities to convey the idea that self-consciousness is at the center of everything. In his view, the arts progress historically from the three-dimensional arts, to two-dimensional arts, to one-dimensional (that is, non-spatial) arts, attaining greater and greater semantic depth as they develop from architecture, to sculpture, to painting, to music, and to poetry. Hegel also claims that art, as the *sensuous* expression of metaphysical truth, reaches its finest expression or "end" in classical Greek sculpture, but, as it later becomes more spiritually introspective during the Christian era, it reaches a more adequate emotional and conceptual expression in the poetic arts.

With the progression of poetry through its epic, lyric, and dramatic forms, Hegel maintains that art reaches a final point at which other modes of expression, namely, religious and philosophical modes, more effectively take over the cultural task of expressing the centrality of self-consciousness. Schopenhauer's hierarchy is less systematized and less extensive than Hegel's, but they both describe fine art as a means to a spiritual end, and refer to art's end as the point where it succeeds in expressing its spiritual mission as best as it can.

iv tragedy and sublimity

Side-by-side with paintings that convey Christianity's atmosphere of resignation, the art of theatrical tragedy assumes an honored place in Schopenhauer's hierarchy of the arts. Unlike many of the other fine arts, tragedy portrays life's terrible side, and, in Schopenhauerian terms, it expresses the Will's self-attacking nature:

> . . . the unspeakable pain, the misery of humanity, the triumph of evil, the mocking domination of chance, the inescapable fall of the just and innocent are all here presented to us; and herein resides a meaningful indication of the quality of the world and existence . . . It is one and the same will that lives and appears in all of them, whose appearances struggle amongst themselves and tear each other limb from limb.[13]

Schopenhauer does not develop the view – as do Aristotle and Nietzsche – that tragic art idealizes or sublimates life's ills in a positive, life-affirming manner. To him, the theatrical portrayals of suffering simply represent people's genuine suffering and call forth the natural reactions of horror and repulsion. This fails to distinguish actual suffering from the artistic representations of suffering, but tragedy's artistic style nonetheless allows us to see more objectively, from an artistic distance, what life is viciously like. Its presentation of suffering compares to the Buddhist Wheel of Life, where Yama, the god of death, holds up a circular diagram of life's characteristic episodes, indicating how they constitute webs of suffering in which we are entrenched naturally, psychologically, and culturally. Yama holds up the wheel for us at an artistic distance, helping us to see life's typical contents more object-ively and with less involvement.

As this reference to the Wheel of Life makes obvious, Schopenhauer's characterization of tragedy has a Buddhistic resonance. It is also, how-ever, inspired by Kant's theory of the sublime – the section of Kant's aesthetics Schopenhauer believes is the most excellent.[14] When we experience overpowering phenomena such as waterfalls, mountains, or terrible storms whose forces have the potential to destroy us physically – if fear does not overwhelm us – Kant maintains that we are in a perfect position to appreciate an aspect of our being that physical destruction cannot touch, and that defies the will towards self-preservation that life-threatening situations provoke.

This higher sense of self is the awareness of our freedom, morality, and purely rational will, and, according to Schopenhauer, it reveals a time-less aspect of ourselves that is independent of any specific desires. Upon apprehending this seemingly invulnerable aspect, terrifying phenomena lose their threatening qualities and assume a more consoling dimension as they become symbols of a timeless existence beyond. A cadaver, a skull and crossbones, or a skeleton, do not represent the absolute end-point of physical death within the field of the sublime, but point instead to the prospect of eternal life.

As opposed to a peaceful theory of beauty, these reflections reveal a central role for the theory of the sublime within in Schopenhauer's view. We should add that Schopenhauer's own exposition gives a different impression, since he translates his theory of the aesthetic experience of Platonic Ideas into a theory of beauty and mentions only in passing that the sublime has the same goal as beauty (viz., to provide an awareness of the Platonic Ideas).[15] It is noteworthy, however, that the theoretical starting point for his account of aesthetic experience is the theory of Platonic Ideas, rather than the theory of beauty. The experience of Platonic Ideas is his main concern, and after describing what it is like to apprehend the Ideas, he equates the aesthetic experience with that of beauty.

It has been already mentioned above that the transition into the condition of pure perception arises most easily when the objects themselves are the most appropriate to that condition, i.e., when through their manifold and yet determinate and sharp figure, they easily become representative of their ideas, in which beauty in the objective sense, consists.[16]

Schopenhauer describes the experience of beauty as being will-free and related to a pure subject of knowing. We have already tempered his conception of a pure, will-free, timeless subject of knowing (recognizing that *every* experience is in time, no matter how extraordinary), and this is essential to keep in mind in what now follows, for the sublime more effectively captures this more realistic conception of a relatively will-free subject of knowing.

In the experience of sublimity, the fear that an object generates interferes with our attempt to contemplate it aesthetically, and the effort to reach that aesthetic awareness leads us to struggle against our desire for self-preservation. Schopenhauer claims that in the experience of the sublime some form of willing is always present, and this modifies the apprehension of the Platonic Ideas that would otherwise be known with less psychological tension in the experience of beauty. Since all experiences of the Platonic Ideas take place in time, however, they all have some dimension of will involved. It would therefore be more accurate to say that there is fundamentally a spectrum of the *sublime*, and that at its upper reaches, where the will is faint, we refer to the experiences as beautiful, owing to their predominant tranquility. The basic qualities of aesthetic experience that Schopenhauer intends to characterize remain the same under this reconceptualization and clarification; the difference is that beauty is now understandable more realistically as a species of sublimity, rather than vice versa.

This draws the concept of sublimity to the center of Schopenhauer's theory of aesthetic experience and the perception of Platonic Ideas. It also sets the scene for appreciating his references to the sublime in connection with moral and ascetic awareness. We will consider these in the next chapter. To accentuate and confirm this emphasis upon sublimity, we can note the following. He states, "our explanation of the sublime can indeed be extended into the ethical realm, namely to what one can describe as the sublime character"[17] and "the felt consciousness of what the Upanishads of the Vedas repeatedly express in such a variety of ways [is] . . . a rising above our own individuality, the feeling of the sublime."[18]

v music and metaphysical experience

For most of his life, Schopenhauer played the flute – that clear-sounding musical instrument whose presence covers the pure tone with the thinnest veil – and was intimately acquainted with music. Unlike the other arts – all of which he viewed as representational arts that express Platonic Ideas of a definite content – Schopenhauer was struck by music's wide-ranging formal and emotional qualities, and he accorded it a superior place within his aesthetics. Focusing on pure music without words, and recognizing musical values that are independent of historical or cultural references, he highlighted music's universalistic capacity to express emotion.

Schopenhauer's defining claim is that music expresses emotions in a detached and abstracted manner: when listening to sad music, for example, we do not experience this or that person's sadness in its emotionally painful condition; we experience it more contemplatively in abstraction from pain. One could say that we experience the emotion's *form* without its circumstantial matter and thereby experience it relatively painlessly. Such detachment from specific historical contexts lends a more timeless and remote quality to music, as if it were entering our consciousness from beyond the spatio-temporal world. At the same time, its expression of human emotion ties it closely to our subjective experience. This ascribes to music both otherworldly and profoundly intimate dimensions – ones that are enhanced by how we experience sound (as opposed to light, for instance) with a less noticeable spatial separation between ourselves and the sound's source. As is true for the experience of meditation, musical experience is both intimate and transcendent.

Schopenhauer accordingly places music on the subjective, as opposed to the objective, side of the universal subject–object distinction that characterizes aesthetic experience in general. In musical experience, we, as universal subjects, do not apprehend universal objects, but more reflectively apprehend universal qualities of our human subjectivity, namely, the emotions music expresses.

Schopenhauer's theoretical framework describes the Platonic Ideas as the immediate objectifications of the Will, and they stand as the universal objects of aesthetic apprehension. Music is not about universal objects, however, and in his effort to locate it systematically within his aesthetic theory, Schopenhauer asserts somewhat obscurely that music does not objectify the Will, but directly replicates it. One aspect of this close relationship between music and the Will (as we shall see in more detail) is that music symbolically contains at one fell swoop, the entire range of Platonic Ideas.

Aesthetic experience is grounded upon a universal subject–object polarity in which universal subjects (us, in a certain aspect) become aware of universal objects (Platonic Ideas). Schopenhauer's theory of music articulates the "universal subject" side of this equation, describing general qualities of human subjectivity that can be *directly* experienced as such through artistic expression. The structural correspondence between musical form (related to the subject-pole) and the hierarchy of Platonic Ideas (related to the object-pole) reflects within the aesthetic register the fundamental parallel between the world as will and the world as representation.

Schopenhauer claims in particular that musical form mirrors the ascending gradation of Platonic Ideas that ranges from inanimate to plant, animal, and specifically human forms. To mineral existence correspond the bass tones and also the fundamental tone; to plant existence, the tenor tones and the interval of the third; to animal existence, the alto tones and the interval of the fifth; to human existence, the soprano tones and the octave.[19] On other occasions, Schopenhauer states that the bass tones accord with mineral existence, that harmonies correspond to life in general, and that melody reflects human existence.[20]

These alignments are theoretically coarse and often criticized, but Schopenhauer believes that they reveal a philosophically important relationship between music and the rest of the arts. Whereas each art represents a specific sphere of existence corresponding to the level of Platonic Ideas it best matches, music represents the world as a whole in that it expresses in a single sweep the entire spectrum of Platonic Ideas. Every musical work is a microcosm. Every single note is also a microcosm, since the mere striking of a tone naturally generates a series of overtones that mirror the Platonic Ideas. Since music expresses human subjectivity, it also conveys the more determinate thought that the spectrum of Platonic Ideas and spatio-temporal world is an objectification not only of the Will but of human subjectivity as well, since the Will objectifies itself *through us* by means of the PSR.

Two further theoretical points are worth noting. The first is that Schopenhauer's theory of music is more formalistic, whereas his theory of the visual arts is more content-centered. Respective artistic media require different sorts of analysis, and Schopenhauer adjusts his discussions accordingly. In the realm of the visual arts, his theory focuses upon an object's perfection in relation to a defined ideal. This coheres with classical definitions of beauty as "the sensuous appearance of perfection." In the more subjective realm of music, where it is difficult to identify Platonic Ideas related to nature's physical patterns, he employs a more formalistic theory that allows him to discuss music as expressive of human emotion.

The second point is that Schopenhauer's theory of music fits systematically well with an observation made above, namely, that the thing-in-itself as Will can be seen as the abstract *form* of suffering. To recall, Schopenhauer characterizes suffering as lack, maintaining that the thing-in-itself as Will is an aim, or lack, without any specificity. As such it can be regarded as the general form of suffering. The thing-in-itself as Will does not itself suffer, but we can describe it as the abstract form of suffering, as well as the abstract form of consciousness (as the form of intentionality). With this in mind, Schopenhauer's reference to music as expressive of the form of emotions and his observation that music provides an experience of emotions in the absence of typical daily pain, make more systematic sense. His characterization of a Beethoven symphony is illustrative:

> If we take a look at purely instrumental music, a Beethoven symphony presents us with the greatest confusion whose basis, however, contains – through the most perfect ordering and arrangement – the most powerful struggle, which in the next moment is brought to the most beautiful resolution. It is *rerum concordia discors* [the concord of things through discord] . . . a true and perfect reflection of the nature of the world, which rolls on in the boundless tangle of innumerable forms and maintains itself through their constant destruction. But also being given voice from this symphony at the same time, are all human passions and emotions – joy, sadness, love, hate, horror, hope, etc. – in innumerable nuances, however at the same time only *in the abstract* and without any details. It is their mere form, without content, like a purely spiritual world, without material.[21]

> Music does not therefore express this or that particular and determinate joy, this or that sadness, pain, horror, cheer, merriment or peace of mind, but joy, sadness, pain, horror, cheer, merriment or peace of mind *themselves*, in a certain sense, *in abstracto*, according to what is essential to them, without any additional details, and therefore also without motives being attached to them . . . For music generally expresses the quintessence of life and its events, never these events themselves.[22]

Like the Will, music expresses the abstract form of suffering on the subjective side of things, except with more multiplicity and determinateness. People who can discern the essences of human emotions would consequently have the insight necessary for being excellent musicians. Schopenhauer tends to describe the artistic genius as someone with the ability to apprehend the objective Platonic Ideas, but artistic genius extends to musicians as well. Highly accomplished musical composers are arguably the most powerful examples of genius, owing to the proximity of music to the Will itself. The composer's focus is not upon the Platonic Ideas, however, but upon his or her own subjective constitution in its universal aspect – that is, insofar as one is a universal individual. Since music expresses the full spectrum of Platonic Ideas, one could say that the composer's mentality approximates the metaphysician's, except that the products of the composer's art provide a direct experience of the world's inner nature. It is consequently easy to see why Schopenhauer's theory of music was celebrated by philosophically-minded composers such as Richard Wagner and Arnold Schönberg, for it combines philosophical and musical greatness in a single person.

The connection between metaphysics and music within Schopenhauer's theory stimulates the speculation about the likely, if implicit, influence of the Upanishads on his conception of music. Upon surveying various philosophical theories of the world's foundations, it is unusual to encounter descriptions of the universe's foundation as a vibration or sound. Typically, we encounter substances, relationships, forms, or energies, that is to say, entities whose character stems from one of the five senses other than hearing, or if not from one of those four senses, then from pure thought.

In the Mandukya Upanishad (which Schopenhauer had in his own copy), the ultimate basis of the universe is presented as a sound, namely, the sound "AUM" which represents the last of four progressively enlightened states of mind attainable through the practice of yoga. These are: (1) ordinary waking state [A], (2) dream state [U], (3) deep dream state [M], and (4) the absolute state [AUM]. Here, apprehending the core of the universe is like listening to a fundamental sonic vibration. Chanting the vibration summons the universal essence to resound through one's being.

As one pronounces the sound "AUM," one's voice moves physically from the back of one's throat to the lips and passes through the entire range of the voice, thus representing the entirety of core vocal possibilities. This matches closely how, for Schopenhauer, the sounding of a single note resonates with a series of overtones that serve as metaphors for the spectrum of Platonic Ideas. The sound "AUM" and the single musical tone involve the same sort of metaphysical symbolism.

This link between Schopenhauer's theory of music-as-metaphysics and the Upanishadic mystical sound AUM reinforces how he recognized the potential power of meditational awareness to reveal the universe's ultimate nature. It also draws a link between Schopenhauer's view and Upanishadic thought, as opposed to Buddhism.

As we will discuss later, and as we have already touched upon briefly in Chapter 6, there is some ambiguity in Schopenhauer's views regarding the status of mystical states of awareness. Sometimes he acknowledges these states as a possible way to apprehend aspects of the thing-in-itself that remain inaccessible to either scientific or philosophic knowledge. Sometimes he acknowledges them as expressive only of a tranquil privation of desire. Either way, he associates the Upanishadic AUM with a level of consciousness where the subject–object distinction disappears and where a universalistic experience occurs.

We can interpret Schopenhauer on the details in whichever way, but he does state that the Upanishadic AUM represents the highest level of consciousness. In this regard, and in his simultaneous advocacy of Buddhism, it must be said that he overlooks some crucial distinctions between Upanishadic and Buddhistic thought, for he equates the Buddhistic conception of *Nirvana* with this Upanishadic highest state of consciousness.[23] We will discuss these distinctions between Buddhism and Upanishadic thought further in Chapter 10. In the present context, more generally relevant is how Schopenhauer perceives musicians, composers, and musical experience as close cousins to metaphysicians and philosophical thinking. Just as music expresses the nature of the world subjectively through the form of feeling, philosophy – whose materials are more conceptual – expresses the nature of the world objectively.

In *The World as Will and Representation*, Schopenhauer attempts to give us a philosophical presentation of the world, but his theory soon brings us to a non-philosophical, subjective, and feeling-oriented way to apprehend ultimate truths, namely, through music. He implicitly maintains that artistic (viz., musical) ways of expressing such verities are preferable to the more objectivistic, or scientific ways, since the various gradations of objectivity stem more basically from a single universal subjectivity at the core of things, and since music brings us closer to this core.

In view of the traditional aims of metaphysical reflection, Schopenhauer is essentially suggesting that to realize these aims we would do better as musicians and mystics, rather than as scientists or philosophers. The true philosophy points to and sublimates into artistic and religious expression, and does not crystallize into literalistic, precise, rigidified, and objectivistic scientific formulations. Schopenhauer's approach completely inverts the scientific attitude of classical positivism, where metaphorical and anthropomorphic religious expression gives way to abstract, literalistic, and speculative philosophy, and where philosophy yields to a no-nonsense, hard-headed, observation-based, mathematical, and scientific account of things. In this respect, his reflections on aesthetic experience reveal that he is an anti-positivist *par excellence*, and imply that art's handmaiden is natural science, rather than the other way around.

notes

1 *WWR* (I), Book III, §34, P 178–9, HK 231, ZA 232.
2 Focusing on the object itself need not lead to a universalistic consciousness, but might alternatively sink one into greater and greater detail in a Zen-like manner, or in a Kierkegaardian aestheticist manner. Universal consciousness does not follow from attending to the object itself in its "thisness" or immediate perceptual presence. Schopenhauer does not seem to have realized this, perhaps having been led too quickly by this metaphysical theory and existential interest in relieving suffering.

3 This universalizing mentality has an objectionable aspect, because it can lead to stereotypical characterizations of people (for example, racist, sexist, nationalist, etc.) and cause us to ignore the intrinsic qualities that issue from their individually unique features. One speaks not to "the Italian," "the Irishman," "the Spaniard," or "the German," in general, but rather to living, complicated individuals.

4 Kant's pure judgments of beauty involve attending only to an object's spatio-temporal qualities, for the sake of contemplating the object's design independently of the sensory qualities that vary from person to person (for example, the object's colors, tastes, odors, sound-qualities, and textures). Schopenhauer similarly refers to the aesthetic apprehension of an object as contemplating an object "without a purpose," directly echoing Kant's account of pure aesthetic perception as apprehending a "purposiveness without purpose" (*Zweckmässigkeit ohne Zweck*) in an object's form. (See *WWR* (II), Chapter XXXI, "On Genius, P 377, HK 139, ZA 446.)

5 *PP* (II), "Ideas Concerning the Intellect Generally and in all Respects," §49, P 64, ZA 74.

6 The activity of painting a dream for the sake of showing publicly what one had dreamt is closely related to what Schopenhauer describes. This loosely associates Schopenhauer's aesthetics with Surrealism.

7 "Genius consists in a fully abnormal, real excess of intellect, such as is not required for the service of any will." (*WWR* [II], Chapter XXXI, "On Genius," P 388, HK 153, ZA 459.)

8 *WWR* (II), "On Genius," Chapter XXXI, P 380, HK 143–4, ZA 450.

9 *WWR* (II), "On Genius," P 380, HK 144, ZA 451.

10 *WWR* (II), "On Genius," P 389, HK 156, ZA 461.

11 Schopenhauer's foundational equation of the "world as will" with the "world as representation," along with his idealistic view of the latter, might have unfortunately led him to downplay the differences between a thing, and the representation of that thing.

12 *WWR* (I), Book III, §48, P 233, HK 301, ZA 295.

13 *WWR* (I), Book III, §51, P 253, HK 326–7, ZA 318.

14 *WWR* (I), "Appendix: Criticism of the Kantian Philosophy," P 532, HK 155–6, ZA 647.

15 See *WWR* (I), Book III.

16 *WWR* (I), Book III, §39, P 200, HK 259–60, ZA 257–8.

17 *WWR* (I), Book III, §39, P 206, HK 267, ZA 264.

18 *WWR* (I), Book III, §39, P 205–6, HK 266, ZA 263–4.

19 *WWR* (II), Chapter XXXIX, "On the Metaphysics of Music," P 447, HK 231, ZA 526.

20 *WWR* (I), Book III, §52, P 258–9, HK 333-34, ZA 324–5.

21 *WWR* (II), Chapter XXXIX, "On the Metaphysics of Music," P 450, HK 235, ZA 529.

22 *WWR* (I), Book III, §52, P 261, HK 338, ZA 328–9. Richard Wagner repeats this position almost verbatim in his "Ein glücklicher Abend" (*Gazette Musicale*, nos. 56–8 [1841]).

23 *WWR* (I), Book IV, §71, P 412, HK 532, ZA 508.

further reading

Jacquette, Dale (ed.), *Schopenhauer, Philosophy and the Arts* (Cambridge: Cambridge University Press, 1996).

Knox, Israel, *The Aesthetic Theories of Kant, Hegel, and Schopenhauer* (New Jersey: Humanities Press, 1936).

tranquility ii: christlike virtue and moral awareness

i empathy as the foundation of moral awareness

Owing to his great respect for Kant, Schopenhauer sometimes refers to himself as a Kantian who merely develops Kant's insights. He accepts the doctrine of Kant's theory of knowledge that space and time are nothing without the human mind's presence, but rejects Kant's associated claim that twelve purely abstract, logically derived concepts further inform every perceptual experience. This stems from Schopenhauer's belief that rich, sensory apprehensions are the soil from which all abstract concepts issue, and that the latter cannot therefore be prior to experience. Schopenhauer does his best to preserve Kant's analysis of space and time, but he minimizes the significance of his twelve abstract, logical categories by reducing them to the one category of causality. He caps his argument by noting that animals perceive in terms of cause and effect relationships, which implies that causal thinking is not unique to humans.

Kant's moral theory also embodies a rationalistic, concept-centered style of philosophizing, and Schopenhauer similarly rejects its abstract, logical basis. As far as Kant can see, moral action is regulated fundamentally by a rational test that determines the permissibility of an action: if the rule (or "maxim") underlying any given action cannot be successfully enacted as a universal pattern of behavior, then we ought not to perform the action. Telling lies is the most-cited example. If, for instance, we extend the rule "one should lie whenever it is to one's advantage" to everyone's behavior, then the distinction between truth and lies will lose its meaning. Universalizing such a rule renders it impossible for anyone to trust anyone else, and this dissolves the very meaning of telling a lie. Dishonesty consequently "feasts on itself" and ought not to be enacted.

Kant's test for permissibility, viz., the above unconditional command or "categorical imperative" to behave consistently, measures an act's inherent rationality. The general concept of lawful regularity is at the center of the theory, and this concept has nothing intrinsically to do with contingencies or matters of fact about one's physical body, particular temperament, or particular feelings. This moral theory is appropriate for any finite rational being. Part of its attractiveness resides in its non-historical quality, which allows it to apply to people at any time or place.

Kant's moral theory is also appealing because it emphasizes, as does Jesus in his Sermon on the Mount, that the quality of our motivations makes all the difference in determining moral behavior. Of the Kantian moral essence is having self-respect for ourselves as essentially rational beings to the point where we embody the will to act consistently. Exactly *why* we do something is morally more important than *what* we specifically do, even though the latter might have beneficial consequences. Kant believes that there is something morally amiss about a world where motivations are skewed to the point where everyone acts in accord with their moral duty out of mere selfishness.

As philosophically trim, efficient, universally applicable, insightful, and consistent with traditional conceptions of human nature as Kant's moral theory may be, Schopenhauer doubts that it accurately describes how we in fact make moral decisions. He does not believe that morality has much to do with pure, detached rationality-as-consistency. To him, it is about having empathy, and he believes that empathy is not a feeling that we grow into through either abstract reflection or the development of rationality.

To appreciate Schopenhauer's moral theory, we can start with the non-moral, selfish standpoint as a background against which to set any moral outlook. Developing the latter involves stepping away from the selfish standpoint, and this requires a principle of unification that softens the confrontational, self-isolated, and egocentric barriers between people. Kant uses rationality for this purpose, and he believes that within moral contexts, we should view each action as an instance of a general sort of action, thus regarding our activity from the standpoint of a rational being in general. Within this perspective, social unification increases by adopting a universalistic standpoint based on reason.

An alternative way to overcome the selfish standpoint and to achieve social unification – one used by other thinkers of the time such as Fichte, Schelling, and Hegel – is to employ dialectical reason. Unlike Kant's style of abstractive reason, dialectical reason relies upon a synthesis of opposites. This synthesis is inspired by the paradoxical structure of self-consciousness, as when one says to oneself, "that is me" or "I am that." Here, the subject and the object are the same (S is O), but since subjects are by nature opposed to objects, they are not the same (S is not

O).[1] Dialectical reasoning similarly unifies opposites to form a new entity or sublimated condition that transforms the opposites while preserving them, as when copper and tin amalgamate to form brass, or as when friendship dissolves the barriers between bitter enemies.

Schopenhauer rejects dialectical reason, proposing instead a more strictly double-aspected approach that superficially drives a wedge between the objective "world as representation" and the subjective "world as will." It preserves a strong separation between the objective and subjective aspects of the world while acknowledging their underlying identity insofar as one aspect (viz., the objective) is the expression or manifestation of the other, more fundamental aspect (viz., the subjective). Since one aspect manifests the other, the two are substantially identical. However, since the manifestation appears in one specific form, as an ice cube manifests water, the specific manifestation appears superficially to be non-identical with that of which it is the manifestation.

To secure a sense of unification that coheres with this double-aspect theory, Schopenhauer begins with the apprehension of differentiated and apparently dissimilar individuals, and then develops this perspective to the point where it becomes plain that the individuals are manifestations of a single underlying being. Most importantly, he advances to this level of communal awareness, not through abstractive or dialectical reasoning, but through a certain kind of feeling.

Love and compassion are the popular candidates for the feeling of unification that grounds moral awareness, and Schopenhauer identifies with compassion. He refers to it as *Mitleid* (literally, "suffering-with"), which we can roughly translate into English as "pity," "compassion," "sympathy," or "empathy." The term "empathy" captures reasonably well what he has in mind. Empathy with another person entails that one imaginatively feel the other person's feelings *as one's own*, and Schopenhauer states that this type of experience is at the foundation of moral awareness:

> Only insofar as an action issues from empathy, does it have any moral worth. Moreover, every action issuing from any other sort of motive has none. As soon as this empathy is awakened, the joy and sorrow of others resides immediately in one's heart in exactly the same manner, if not exactly at the same intensity, as are usually only one's own. At that point, the distinction between oneself and another is no longer absolute.
>
> This occurrence is certainly astounding, and indeed, mysterious. It is in fact the greatest mystery of ethics, its primary phenomenon and boundary marker, beyond which only metaphysical speculation can dare step.[2]

Conversely, moral evil has to do with a lack of empathy and an alienated, isolated mentality. As history continues to confirm, when we fail to accord to others the respect we give to ourselves – whether this happens to involve religious, national, racial, institutional, educational, or familial definitions – arrogance, defensiveness, condescension, and awful inhumanities become possible.

ii intelligible, empirical, and acquired character

Schopenhauer's empathy-centered morality promotes feelings of social unity, and it draws our attention to more universalistic states of awareness. In his aesthetic theory, we have already seen him refer to such extraordinary states. On the objective side, he refers the apprehension of Platonic Ideas. On the subjective side, he describes how musical experience conveys an awareness of the universal forms of human feeling. With this in mind, let us continue with some additional reflections on Schopenhauer's theory of music, to gain further entrance into his moral theory.

Since music universally expresses human feeling, it provides direct access to the inner life of other people independently of historical details: we can experience forms of sadness, happiness, etc., through a composer's and/or musician's perspective, as these appear as universalized expressions of the composer's and/or musician's inner being. Although they are always tempered by the composer's or musician's personal character, the music conveys universal emotional meanings without the need for us to inform it with additional biographical details about the composer or musician.

Amongst the arts, the objective correlate to music is the set of visual and literary arts that portray Platonic Ideas. As subjective correlates to the Platonic Ideas themselves – and this is where we would philosophically locate what music allows us to apprehend more clearly – Schopenhauer refers to each person's timeless character. This is our "intelligible character," which, like music, resides on the *subjective* side of the universal subject–object distinction, just as the Platonic Ideas reside on the objective side. The term "intelligible character" stems from Kant's theory of freedom and Schopenhauer regards this idea as one of Kant's most profound philosophical contributions.

A main concern of Kant's philosophy is how to explain the possibility of human freedom if all natural events are mechanically explainable. He solves this by distinguishing between appearance and reality, and by situating nature as a whole – considered as a spatio-temporal expanse filled with physical objects and energies – exclusively within the realm of appearance. Mechanical explanation applies within this spatio-temporal dimension, but since it does not extend to the realm of things in themselves, we can locate human freedom within the latter realm. For each person we can thus indicate a source or ground for the person's individual freedom, and this would be their timeless character, the action of which is dispersed spatio-temporally as the physical movements of the person's body. Who each of us essentially is, resides in our respective intelligible characters beyond space and time, and these characters express themselves in our physical appearances and in our life's exact course of events.

Schopenhauer compares a person's intelligible character and its numerous manifestations in daily activity to how a single Platonic Idea has multiple instantiations in space and time. Just as the Platonic Idea of an oak is instantiated in every oak tree that has ever been and will be, a person's intelligible character is instantiated in all of the person's spatio-temporal actions as well as the person's physical form.[3] Any given person's worldly life is the manifestation of his or her otherworldly intelligible character. The person's freedom is expressed in the quality of his or her timeless intelligible character *per se*, not in specific choices the person makes in this or that context and which are (mistakenly) believed to be choices that might have been different.

Schopenhauer characterizes the thing-in-itself as a single timeless act that expresses itself directly through the human perspective as a set of timeless subjects and timeless objects. The timeless subjects are the billions of intelligible characters that constitute the respective essences of each person; the timeless objects are the numerous Platonic Ideas that include the definitions of all natural kinds as well as mathematical and geometrical entities. This realm of timeless intelligible characters and Platonic Ideas – this realm of universal subjects and universal objects – is the articulation of the universal subject–object distinction at the root of the principle of sufficient reason (PSR). Intelligible characters and Platonic Ideas, although both are timeless, are distinguished from the unitary thing-in-itself as Will, since there is a multiplicity of them.

Intelligible characters occupy an uneasy place within Schopenhauer's metaphysical arrangement, for they inconsistently stand midway between the world as will and the world as representation, and squarely in neither. Since there are billions of them, the phenomenal notion of individuation applies. This notion applies to intelligible characters just as it does to Platonic Ideas, of which there are also many. Since the intelligible characters are universal subjects rather than universal objects, however, we cannot refer to them as immediate "objectifications" of the Will. Schopenhauer refers to them as *acts* of the thing-in-itself as Will, as opposed to *objectifications* of it. Realizing the philosophical tensions involved, he admits the mystery of having to introduce individuation into the thing-in-itself as Will, as a way to account for the differences between people's intelligible characters:

It follows from this furthermore that *individuality* is not based only on the *principio individuationis* [i.e., space and time] and is consequently not merely and thoroughly *appearance*. It is rather rooted in the thing-in-itself, in the will of the individual, since this character itself is individual. How deep the roots go in this instance, however, is among the questions I do not try to answer.[4]

Each of us, therefore, is supposedly a single, timeless act of a certain personality-constituting quality. Each act manifests itself in space and time, and each of our lifetimes is the objectification of one of these acts, or intelligible characters. Our spatio-temporal existence expresses who we timelessly are, and the fourfold aspects of the PSR create the illusion that who we are changes over time and that we have the power to make individual decisions that alter the course of our lives. This is an illusion, since the spatio-temporal continuum is mechanistic and deterministic, and people's bodily movements are fully predictable.

When ascribing moral responsibility to a person, we consequently would not ascribe it to the person in reference to some particular choice, made at some particular time, in connection with some particular action. Instead, we would apprehend the person more eternalistically and ascribe the responsibility to his or her inner being, that is, to his or her timeless quality of character. Blame is assigned to who a person fundamentally is, just as we might characterize a type of animal or plant (for example, snake, deer, rabbit, fish, oak, maple, coffee) as having this or that sort of basic character. Just as it is senseless to expect a cat to change its natural disposition to hunt birds and fish and still remain a cat, it is senseless to expect a good or despicable person to change his or her character and still remain that person. Everyone's character is timelessly set in Schopenhauer's view, and all behavior is as predictable as the falling of a rock, if only the quality of the person's character were known, along with the specifics of the situation.

For the sake of theoretical clarity, Schopenhauer distinguishes various dimensions of a person's character. As we perceive ourselves and others, the observable, behavioral manifestation of one's own or another's timeless personal quality is the "empirical character." We are in experiential contact with our own empirical characters, and through them we can know, with various degrees of self-awareness, how we timelessly are. What we essentially are is not accessible in its purity, for we must always become aware of it through some experiences, that is, through our empirical character. The metaphysical situation compares to when we apprehend the thing-in-itself as Will, or when we apprehend a Platonic Idea: we always apprehend such beings through the thin veil of time.

Some people happen to be more knowledgeable about the sort of person they are, and, according to Schopenhauer, they consequently act more clearly in character. They exhibit their respective intelligible characters with greater depth, just as a fine work of art exhibits its Platonic Idea more clearly than do ordinary objects with the same theme. Schopenhauer refers to this refined expression of one's intelligible character as the expression of "acquired" character. Those who have acquired character apprehend their essential personality through their individual actions, as great musicians apprehend the universal structures of human emotion, or as artistic geniuses apprehend the timeless Platonic Ideas in the perception of individual things. In the case of acquired character, the perception of genius focuses upon oneself, and one's life consequently becomes a work of art:

> The *acquired character* is accordingly nothing other than the most perfect knowledge of our own individuality that is possible. It is the abstract, and consequently clearest knowledge of the immutable qualities of our own empirical character and of the measure and direction of our spiritual and bodily powers, and therefore from the entire strength and weakness of our own individuality. This puts us in the position, under the guidance of fixed concepts, to fulfill the unchangeable role of our own person thoughtfully and methodically, and to fill the gaps that are caused by caprice or weaknesses.[5]

When people speak generally of a person who "has character," Schopenhauer associates this with the display of acquired character, and it involves exhibiting empirically well what one timelessly is. This expression of one's character is a self-realization, a becoming-in-fact of what one ought to be. One is true to oneself, one knows exactly who one is, and through this awareness, there is a sense of self-perfection. We could also call this a sublime rendering of oneself, for we direct the mentality of the artistic genius upon ourselves, become our own genius, and discern what we are meant to be. Instead of contemplating Platonic Ideas as might a painter or sculptor, we contemplate the quality of our universal subjectivity as we become our own person. Having acquired character and self-knowledge also implies the expression of a single-mindedness, focus, and clear self-determination, since we become explicitly aware of the single, timeless act of Will that defines who we are and what we essentially want.

Having acquired character also acts as a catalyst for apprehending the intelligible characters of others. After having developed a universal consciousness with respect to one's own presence, it becomes possible to conduct social relationships with a greater focus on character-types. Our sympathies, attractions, repulsions, and appreciations are directed towards the sort of timeless intelligible character with whom we were dealing, rather than upon external accessories. A highly developed universalistic mentality of this type is not necessary for moral awareness, but it supports moral awareness through the decreased significance of transitory, spatio-temporal factors.

From a more critical standpoint, we can wonder how much damage Schopenhauer's postulation of intelligible characters does to the coherency of his leading metaphysical assertions. He intends to restrict individuation to the realm of representation and the PSR as much as he can, but since there are billions of intelligible characters, he cannot avoid having ascriptions of multiplicity drift closer to the thing-in-itself as Will. He cannot allow them to move too close, though, for the thing-in-itself would then no longer be purely one, and no longer be intrinsically immune from explanation.

Intelligible characters are hybrid states of subjective being that enliven each embodied person, and stand midway between the thing-in-itself and the realm of spatio-temporal consciousnesses. As subjective modes of being, they also differ from the Platonic Ideas. Intelligible characters are timeless, but they are timeless acts, not timeless objects. They nonetheless embody the root of the PSR, however, insofar as they constitute one pole of the universal subject–object distinction.

These reflections suggest that it is more consistent to conclude that individual human personalities are *not* non-phenomenal, mind-independent acts of the thing-in-itself, but rather, that they are as mind-dependent as are the Platonic Ideas. This implies that intelligible characters disappear when our consciousness dissolves. By regarding intelligible characters in this way, it becomes more plausible to say that at the deepest level, human individuality in both its spatio-temporal *and* timeless aspects is an illusory, phenomenal artifact of the PSR. Our being as timeless characters, that is to say, our fundamental self-conception, would thus require the presence of the PSR, just as does the being of the Platonic Ideas.

iii humanity's sublime anguish

For Schopenhauer, moral awareness is empathy-filled, and this underscores the idea that "virtue must issue from the intuitive knowledge that recognizes in someone else's individuality, the very same being as one's own."[6] It is noteworthy that moral awareness is at an even higher level of universality than the genius-like apprehension of one's own or another person's timeless personality, for beneath such character differences, there is the more profound unity that we are all manifestations of a single and general human reality, and ultimately, manifestations of the thing-in-itself as Will.

Within an empathy-filled, humane awareness, we overcome the differences between people and apprehend humanity as a single being with a subjective constitution of its own. Closely related to this, we can also more expansively apprehend all living things as the manifestation of the subjective constitution of "life itself." Most universally, at the level of metaphysical awareness, we can apprehend the entire, articulated world of representation as the manifestation of a singular, timeless, universal Will. Each of these levels is at a higher degree of universality than that which corresponds to the apprehension of intelligible characters.

The result of adopting any of the above universalistic standpoints – either that of humanity, of life in general, or of the world as Will itself – is the realization that other people are manifestations of the same being that constitutes one's own. We are like a set of independently appearing leaves and flowers on the surface of a pond, whose stems connect beneath the water to the same plant and single root. The same subjective energy flows through everyone. Even the differences between our intelligible characters do not ultimately matter, since moral awareness transcends our sense of timeless personality and sense of personal and individual responsibility.

This common metaphysical root entails that there is *literally* an identity between the aggressor and the victim, between the torturer and the tortured, and between the bad and the good. At the base of things and in reality, the torturer inflicts pain only upon a manifestation of his own metaphysical substance, the tortured person projects guilt or resentment only upon himself or herself, the bad person offends and attacks only himself, the good person helps and has empathy only for himself. The same inner nature bears both sides of the opposition. The people we help are essentially ourselves. The flesh we devour is our own, for in the world as representation, the Will feasts on itself. The achievements of others we can rejoice in as our own successes; the failures of others are nothing less than our own failures. This universalistic moral awareness submerges and transcends differences in sex, race, religion, and nationality.

Upon attaining such an empathy-filled consciousness, we realize that for any suffering being that existed, exists, or could exist, it is the same inner substance of us all that ultimately bears the suffering:

> According to the true essence of things, each person has all of the world's suffering as if it were his own; indeed he would regard all possible sufferings as actually existing for him, as long as he is the unwavering will-to-live, i.e., affirms life with all of his strength.[7]

The affirmation of life – saying "yes" to the world as representation – entails that we empathize with a virtually inconceivable amount of pain. The Christlike mentality implied here is obvious, for Jesus's having taken on the sins of the world reflects exactly the sort of universalistic empathy that Schopenhauer describes.

> Such a person who recognizes his own inner and true self in every being, must also regard the endless suffering of all living things as his own, and therefore must take upon himself the pain of the whole world. No suffering is foreign to him any longer. All of the miseries of others which he sees and is so rarely able to alleviate, all of the miseries that he knows of indirectly, and even those that he regards as merely possible, affect his mind exactly as do his own.[8]

We cannot reasonably describe this universal empathy as purely beautiful, tranquil, and detached. The consciousness involved is *sublime*. Its universalistic outlook provides only a measure of tranquility and joy, for this tranquility is counterbalanced by the perception of virtually innumerable and close-to-unimaginable instances of suffering whose accumulated pain would be in fact impossible to endure. Such, then, is the moral consciousness – it is a profound tranquility combined with an unbounded terror – that lifts oneself above the particular worries of individual existence, but which cannot provide a lasting salvation.

Indeed, it easy to imagine making a horrified retreat from life's affirmation, since saying "yes" to life involves empathizing with more pain than anyone could endure, even imaginatively. As episodes of war repeatedly show, humanity's inhumanity towards itself is more than painful: it is ghastly. Appreciating in any detail what it would be like to experience the pain of individuals who were burned at the stake is probably beyond most people's capacities. Appreciating in any detail what it would be like to experience the accumulated pain of an entire city, let alone that of a nation, or more broadly, of all of humanity, is simply beyond comprehension. *This*, however, is what is involved in becoming the consciousness of humanity, and to realize the universal being one is.

The tension-ridden aspect of Schopenhauer's moral theory is that while universalistic states of mind tend to distance us from much of the daily world's conflict, what it is like to experience universalistically "humanity itself" or "life itself" requires identifying with an unimaginable amount of pain. The inner nature of humanity and life is not only beautiful, tranquil, and joyous. It is also hideous, and empathic moral awareness reveals that permanent and peaceful salvation cannot be attained at this level of consciousness, as universalistic as it is. In fact, moral awareness reveals more poignantly a world from which resignation might be the most appropriate reaction, for despite the world's joys, the world's pains are heart-rending when considered with empathy and in detail. Moral awareness highlights the meaning of what it is like to face oneself, when one's very nature as a human being is a sublime tranquility mixed with terror.

Upon realizing that the torturer and the tortured are one, we arrive at a moral awareness that, at least ideally and in principle, leads us to empathize with all pain. This defines a Christlike-consciousness, but on top of this, and as mentioned in Chapter 7, it leads to a self-awareness that associates original sin with the world's violence. The suffering with which we try to empathize from a moral perspective, exists in the first place as a consequence of our own humanity: it arises from the activity of PSR upon a single, blind, timeless Will that manifests itself as the very being whose experience is informed by that principle.

The more profound difficulty arising in moral consciousness, then, is not the requirement to set aside one's individual interests for the sake of empathizing with as much of the world's suffering as one can endure; the difficulty is facing that we are responsible for this suffering to begin with. Our metaphysical being is identical to every suffering being and this grounds our empathy, but our projection of the PSR is responsible for the arena of violent individuals in the first instance.

Moral awareness thus produces a psychological burden in connection with the amount of pain we must assume, and this involves not simply the troubling feeling that metaphysically, when perceiving one individual who tortures another, one realizes that one is the torturer as well as the tortured. It involves a more reflective type of pain, for we torture ourselves upon realizing how we are the very creators of a morally repulsive spatio-temporal scene. We are the torturers and the tortured with respect to both our relationship with other people *and* with respect to our relationship to ourselves. The Will feasts upon itself on both non-reflective and reflective dimensions.

Schopenhauer concludes that moral awareness does not provide lasting salvation, and that it amounts to only another station on the way of despair that begins with ordinary day-to-day life and the endless pressures of desire. Beyond moral awareness, an even deeper realization is possible: affirming life in any way yields suffering:

> ... since he sees through the *principium individuationis*, everything lies equally near to him. He recognizes and apprehends the essence of the whole, and finds it constituted by a constant slipping away, an empty striving, an inner conflict and continual suffering. Wherever he looks, he sees suffering humanity, the suffering animal world and a world that passes away. All of this now lies just as close to him, as the ego does to an egoist. With such a knowledge of the world, **how could he now affirm this life** [emphasis added] through constant acts of the will and thereby bind himself, and press himself, even more tightly to it?[9]

> His will turns around; he no longer affirms, but denies his own essence that is mirrored in appearances. This phenomenon is revealed through the transition from virtue to *asceticism*. It is no longer sufficient to love others

as himself and to do as much for them as he would do for himself; rather, a repugnance arises in him towards the essence whose expression is his own very appearance – a repugnance towards the will-to-live, towards the core and essence of that world recognized as filled with misery. He consequently disowns this essence that appears in him and is already expressed through his body; his behavior reveals the fiction of his appearance, and appears in open contradiction to it.[10]

The above transition from morality to asceticism recalls the last line of the First Noble Truth of Buddhism, cited earlier: the nature of the mind is itself painful. This echoes Schopenhauer's awareness that the PSR is pain-generating in the direct sense of producing the nightmarish appearance of individual beings that insatiably desire, and in the more reflective sense of leading to the painful thought that our own nature is responsible for creating a suffering-filled appearance. As we will see in the next chapter, Schopenhauer's views have affinities with Buddhism that go even further than those already cited.

In the same Buddhistic vein, since the multiplicity of intelligible characters cannot be ascribed to the thing-in-itself as Will insofar as the latter is a single act, our individualities can only be regarded as PSR-dependent, as are the Platonic Ideas. When there is no PSR, there are no individual people. In a Buddhist sense, then, despite the timelessness of the intelligible characters, we cannot easily assert within Schopenhauer's view that they would exist independently of the PSR. They more obviously represent the essences of illusory egos. In this way, Schopenhauer's conception of personality can be interpreted Buddhistically, since it entails that there is no absolute permanence to our individual being, either timelessly or spatio-temporally considered.

The illusory nature of our timeless characters reinforces Schopenhauer's proposal that we empathize with other people to achieve a higher moral awareness, for this empathy is grounded in the idea that we are all of the same substance. This appears to be a non-controversial way to characterize moral awareness, but it does have a counterintuitive aspect. We are required to empathize with everyone, including the torturers and evil-doers, so we must imagine what is it like – including understanding what pleasures are attendant – to *be* a torturer and evil-doer. So at least at its beginning stages, moral consciousness cannot be a pure state of mind that is purged of all evil contents.

The very opposite is the result: Schopenhauer proposes that we should empathize with the full, complicated, tension-ridden, laughing, crying, suffering, ecstatic, depressed, enlivened, meditative, aggressive, passive – indeed multiply-complicated – amalgam of human emotions that constitute humanity itself. This is far from a naive, sheltered, and unsophisticated consciousness. Schopenhauer's moral consciousness is world-wise mode of awareness, understanding well what it is like to have a bloodthirsty mentality, but while being aware of this, apprehending with empathy the more extensive amalgam of mental states such as to experience sadness, if not nausea, upon apprehending the broader substance of who one is. This sort of awareness reflects upon the aggression one projects upon others, multiplies it by an unimaginably large factor, and becomes nauseated by the level of pain that extends from one's own substance. Owing to this sublime anguish, Schopenhauer believes that it is impossible to say "yes" to life.

notes

1 The structure of self-consciousness thus yields [(S is O) and (S is not O)], which is a contradiction. The German Idealists accepted the contradictory structure of self-consciousness, finding it more sensible to reject the law of non-contradiction (viz., [(S is O) and (S is not O)]) than question the fact that we are aware of ourselves, as paradoxical as that awareness may be.
2 *BM*, P 144, ZA 248.
3 Since the intelligible character is timeless, and since spatio-temporal circumstances vary, if one were born at a different time from that when one actually was born, a very different sort of life could be imagined in its details. In this respect, Schopenhauer remarks [*WWR* (I), §28, P 158, HK 207, ZA 211] that it makes no difference whether one plays for nuts or for crowns; what makes the difference is whether in general one plays honestly or dishonestly.
4 *PP* (II), Chapter VIII, "On Ethics," §116, P 227, ZA 248.
5 *WWR* (I), Book IV, §55, P 305, HK 393–4, ZA 382.
6 *WWR* (I), Book IV, §66, P 368, HK 475, ZA 456.
7 *WWR* (I), Book IV, §63, P 353, HK 456, ZA 440.
8 *WWR* (I), Book IV, §68, P 379, HK 489, ZA 469.
9 *WWR* (I), Book IV, §68, P 379, HK 489, ZA 469.
10 *WWR* (I), Book IV, §68, P 380, HK 49–91, ZA 470–1.

further reading

Atwell, John, *Schopenhauer: The Human Character* (Philadelphia: Temple University Press, 1990).
Atwell, John, *Schopenhauer on the Character of the World – The Metaphysics of the Will* (Berkeley: University of California Press, 1995).

tranquility iii: asceticism, mysticism, and buddhism

i the possibility of the denial-of-the-will

As the most effective way to overcome suffering and to achieve long-term tranquility, Schopenhauer advocates asceticism – an austere lifestyle that requires the minimization of earthly pleasures, cravings, and satisfactions. Often associated with monks and monasteries, this lifestyle focuses on self-sacrifice, stillness, renunciation, detachment from bodily desires, spiritual discipline, resignation, self-knowledge, self-purification, self-imposed poverty, and deep meditation. The phrase Schopenhauer uses to describe this attitude is the "denial of the will-to-live":

> Therefore it is here for the first time perhaps, that the inner essence of holiness, self-denial, extinguishing of one's own will, asceticism, is expressed abstractly and purified from all myth as *denial of the will-to-live*, which steps in after the complete knowledge of his own essence has become for him the quieter of all willing.[1]

Resignation from worldly affairs, Schopenhauer believes, is the enlightened moral reaction to realizing that owing to one's very presence, the world is filled with suffering, and that the practical and theoretical sides of our being involve pain. As intelligible characters and timeless acts of Will, each of us is essentially a single, unsatisfiable desire; as beings that apply the principle of sufficient reason (PSR) to individuate things in a quest for scientific comprehension, we introduce dividedness and hence, conflict.

This presents the dilemma mentioned earlier. If we remain in the grips of the daily world, we uphold a condition of insatiable desire and perpetual war. If we retreat to higher levels of universality, we arrive at less individuated mental states that afford a measure of tranquility in aesthetic and moral experience, but these lead ultimately to the form of suffering itself, viz., the thing-in-itself as Will, regarded as the universal and meaningless form of lack.

The intermediary stages between these extremes that we have considered so far – the aesthetic apprehension of Platonic Ideas and the moral awareness of either humanity itself, life itself, or the entire cosmos in its subjective being – offer some tranquility, but they also involve suffering. The artistic genius suffers as a sensitive and highly perceptive individual; the morally virtuous person suffers from empathizing with universal misery. Neither enjoys enduring tranquility. This motivates Schopenhauer to advance beyond these alternatives to a more potent "denial-of-the-Will" where the peace-of-mind is more profound.

Since we can apprehend the thing-in-itself as Will, and since Will constitutes everything, references to the "denial" of the Will, immediately raise the question of whether Schopenhauer contradicts himself. If we *are* Will through-and-through, it is impossible to deny or negate the Will absolutely, just as some say that matter can be neither created nor destroyed. At best, we might be able to modify specific forms and intensities of the Will's manifestations. On several occasions, Schopenhauer acknowledges this situation by stating that *per impossibile*, if any one of us were truly destroyed, the whole universe would be annihilated, since each of us is a manifestation of what is. To understand and evaluate his prescription that we deny the Will, it is important to explain how this attitude is even possible.

Schopenhauer's writings describe four ways to resolve the conflict between acknowledging an *all-permeating* thing-in-itself as Will and prescribing the denial-of-the-Will as a release from suffering. Moving from the least plausible to the most plausible, they are as follows:

1   We can distinguish between the "thing-in-itself as Will" and the more specific "will to live," and maintain that the denial-of-the-Will negates the "will to live," but not the substance of the metaphysical Will.
2   We can claim that the human mind divides sharply into two parts, namely, practical Will and theoretical knowledge, and that the denial-of-the-Will negates the active, practical Will, but not pure, contemplative knowledge.
3   We can claim that the thing-in-itself as Will does not exhaust the nature of the thing-in-itself, and that there are further dimensions to the thing-in-itself. This way, the denial-of-the-Will can negate the thing-in-itself as Will, but not negate the thing-in-itself as a whole.
4   We can claim that the absolute denial of the Will is impossible, and that the denial-of-the-Will occurs only as a matter of degree. Strong willing may transform into a weaker form of willing, or one sort of willing may transform into another sort, but we cannot annihilate the Will.

Let us consider the first option. By distinguishing between the will-to-live and the thing-in-itself as Will, we can equate the denial-of-the-Will with the denial of the will-to-live. This avoids asserting inconsistently that we can deny the Will absolutely, while it thoroughly constitutes us. Schopenhauer wavers on whether he believes that the thing-in-itself is thoroughly Will – and this offers another way to resolve the difficulty (see 3 above) – but we can set this first option aside because Schopenhauer clearly uses the terms "Will" and "will-to-live" interchangeably:

> The will, considered purely in itself, is without knowledge and is only a blind, unstoppable impulse that we see manifested in inorganic and vegetable nature along with their laws, and also in the vegetative part of our own life. Through such an emerging world of representation developed for its service, this will obtains the knowledge of its own willing and what it wills, namely, nothing other than this world and life, exactly as it exists. We have accordingly called the world that appears, the mirror or objectivity of the will, and because what the will wills is always life – exactly because life is nothing more than the presentation of that will within the field of representation – it is all the same and is only a superfluity if, instead of simply saying "the will," we say "the will-to-live."[2]

In its individuated manifestations, the Will always wills to be, and wills to affirm the world just as it is, with all of its inherent suffering. The Will, when manifested, is thoroughly life-affirming and can be called the "will-to-live." This returns us to the problem of how the denial-of-the-Will is possible, if our very substance is a life-affirming, life-desiring, and life-confirming energy. The denial-of-the-Will would seem to require a life-negating will towards nothingness that is inconsistent with our essential being. Such a self-negating Will makes sense, though, if we conceive of it as the will to dissolve merely our *individuality* within the field of PSR-generated illusion, since this would only involve a transformation of the Will's manifestations (option 4 above).

The "will towards nothingness" introduces the theme of suicide, and we should pause here to reflect upon the meaning of destroying our individual appearance. Even at this level, where self-destruction is possible, Schopenhauer maintains that suicidal tendencies do not typically express a denial of the Will, but rather an *affirmation* of it, as when, for example, a person kills himself or herself to avoid some present or anticipated pain. Here, the suicidal motivation rests upon a basic assumption that life would have been embraced, had pleasure been anticipated rather than pain. As the psychological opposite, Schopenhauer holds that the ascetic denial-of-the-Will involves shunning life's *pleasures*, since this more genuinely negates the lust for individuated life.

Continuing in our effort to articulate how the denial-of-the-Will is possible when the Will constitutes everything, we can consider

Schopenhauer's distinction between "willing" and "knowledge" (option 2 above). He claims frequently that we can detach ourselves from our desires to render them ineffective, and that at the extreme point of detachment we become a pure, will-less subject of knowledge that regards the world in an unconcerned and uninvolved manner:

> The will can be neutralized [aufgehoben] only through knowledge. There-fore the single way to salvation is this: that the will should appear without any obstruction, so that within this appearance it can come to know its own essence. Only as a result of this knowledge can the will neutralize and terminate itself along with the suffering that is inseparable from its appearance. But this is not possible through physical force, such as the destruction of a seed, or through the killing of a newborn, or suicide.[3]

The conception of a pure, will-less knower implicit in the above, has been criticized earlier as being unrealistic. A state of pure universality in abstraction from all individuality is impossible, since every experience occurs in time and must have some individualistic features. In any given experience, we can highlight the knowledge-component of experience as opposed to the willing-component, but we can never annihilate the latter.

Moreover, the sharp division between willing and knowing, or between practical and theoretical aspects of the human psyche, has a more typically Kantian than Schopenhauerian ring, for this division does not sit well with Schopenhauer's assertion that the world "as will" and the world "as representation" are at bottom identical. Given this identity, "knowing" must be the Will's manifestation and it cannot stand opposed absolutely to Will. Schopenhauer's references to a pure, will-less state of knowledge are consequently exaggerated, and it is more consistent to interpret his remarks with the assumption that some vestige of the Will is present in every experience.

This brings us to the third option, namely, that the denial-of-the-Will is possible, if the thing-in-itself has dimensions other than Will. This postulates a multidimensional thing-in-itself that includes Will as one dimension among potentially many others, some of which might be knowable only mystically, and some of which might not be knowable at all. The mystically-knowable dimensions would be unknowable within the parameters of empirical, merely phenomenal, knowledge and would be unknowable in philosophical terms. If there were any dimensions that are not knowable in any sense, as we have seen, Schopenhauer's position would transform into a canonical Kantian one.

This interpretation is familiar from Chapter 6, which presents Schopenhauer as claiming that the thing-in-itself is *philosophically* knowable as Will (where "philosophical knowledge" is a non-absolute intermediary between empirical knowledge and mystical knowledge), but that beyond this philosophical knowledge, the thing-in-itself could have dimensions that resist all forms of verbal articulation, and perhaps all access. This allows room for the denial-of-the-Will, since the thing-in-itself would have other dimensions that, after the Will's denial, would preserve the continuity between oneself and the rest of what is. Annihilating oneself as Will would not be annihilating oneself completely, if (questionably) the different dimensions of the thing-in-itself are not organically interrelated.

Aside from requiring us to assume that annihilating one dimension of the thing-in-itself would not entail the annihilation of all its dimensions, explaining how the denial-of-the-Will is possible by referring to multiple dimensions of the thing-in-itself generates two problems, the first of which demolishes Schopenhauer's philosophy. This, crucially, is if the thing-in-itself has innumerable dimensions, only one of which is "Will," then Schopenhauer cannot claim that the thing-in-itself is either only, or mainly, a mindless and amoral Will. If the thing-in-itself is not essentially Will, however, then there is no reason to expect that the world as representation will present a violent appearance. This is the problem. As we know, Schopenhauer accounts for the daily world's violence in reference to a single, blind Will that our PSR divides into individuals that stand against each other. Individuals selfishly and aggressively oppose each other owing to the metaphysical fact that their inner nature *is* blind Will, not because the nature of reality merely appears to *us* to be in itself Will, or because Will is only one of possibly an infinite number of the thing-in-itself's other dimensions.

Schopenhauer maintains that the PSR-generated world is a spatio-temporal expanse wherein each individual pits itself against every other. The PSR only has this violent effect, however, if the world in itself – the elemental being that the PSR prismatically divides – is a blind Will. If we are to preserve the features of Schopenhauer's philosophy for which he is most famous there is no choice but to interpret his claim that the thing-in-itself is Will in the most straightforward way, although we cannot absolutely equate the Will with the thing-in-itself (since we can only apprehend the thing-in-itself translucently through the thin veil of time). If the translucent apprehension of the thing-in-itself approaches transparency, however, and if whatever time occludes is insignificant – and this is the key point – then we can assert confidently that the thing-in-itself is aptly describable as Will. Otherwise, and more in line with the multidimensional view, it becomes difficult to explain why the world becomes so violent in the presence of the PSR. It also becomes difficult to explain why Schopenhauer equates the thing-in-itself with Will so often in his writings.

Second, the multidimensional interpretation undercuts the motivation to achieve tranquility through the denial-of-the-Will, for we deny the Will precisely because our projection of the PSR generates intolerable suffering. A multidimensional conception of the thing-in-itself provides less reason for denying the Will, since it introduces potentially uncountable and inscrutable dimensions that minimize the Will's metaphysical importance. Far more preferable is an interpretation that leaves intact Schopenhauer's view that the thing-in-itself is Will virtually through-and-through, and that implies that while one is alive, the will-to-live can never be completely negated or annihilated. This entails recognizing that there is a component of willing within the ascetic consciousness as well. Let us then reflect further upon this fourth option.

We can begin by identifying a basic type of experience that exemplifies the denial-of-the-Will. Examples are the experiences of overcoming an addiction, disruptive habit, obsessive need, or compulsive attraction. Upon quelling such powerful desires, feelings of freedom and tranquility issue from the realization that the driving hunger for things whose possession promises deep satisfaction is like the fruitless drive of a thirsty desert wanderer towards a shimmering mirage. Someone familiar with the desert would not allow such a mirage to stimulate his or her desire.

The resulting sense of composure and tranquility is a great relief, but this is not the experience of anything positive in its own right. We merely eliminate a nagging desire that was exerting itself with an oppressive weight. No longer a servant to such a desire, our consciousness becomes permeated with a feeling of "freedom from" or freedom as a kind of detachment.

Accompanying such a feeling of tranquility-as-detachment is an enlightening release from illusion, for one realizes that what had been previously controlling one's behavior as a desirable object, was the seductive bearer of false promises. There is a sense of release, of awakening from a dream, and of seeing things for what they are actually worth. As applied to desires and to the world in general, the result is to interpret the daily world as a large theater where the field of burning desire transforms into a fountain of illusory value:

> Nothing can frighten him anymore; nothing can move him. He has cut all of the thousand strings of willing that hold one bound to the world and which as desire, fear, envy and anger and pull us back and forth in constant pain. He now looks peacefully and smilingly upon the deceptive and illusory images of the world – ones that were once able to move and torment even his mind – that now stand before him so indifferently, as do chessmen after the end of the game, or as cast-off costumes appear in the morning, whose forms had been teasing and troubling on the Carnival night before. Life and its forms merely dangle before him like a fleeting appearance, as does a light morning-dream to one who is almost awake, through which reality is already shining and which can no longer mislead; and just like this morning dream, life and its forms finally disappear as well, without any violent transition.[4]

This underscores how the denial-of-the-Will involves neutralizing as many desires as possible, with the exception of the overriding, higher-level desire to neutralize every other desire. The situation reiterates microcosmically within the individual, the general image of the Will that feasts upon itself, where here, the desire that sets itself against all other desires is an empty desire that feasts upon other desires, and has a content and purpose only when there are other desires to oppose it.

The desire to eliminate all other desires is comparable to a destructive, nay-saying, skeptical consciousness that asserts "no" to any position it happens to encounter, as it aims to free itself of all positions and hold no position at all. In the case of the denial-of-the-Will, this negative attitude is directed by one aspect of the mind against another: a privileged aspect associated with reflection, disengagement, and non-clinging directs itself aggressively towards that aspect associated with individual desires, bodily drives, spatio-temporal consciousness, and practical attachment to the world. The ascetic consciousness engages in an internal war between the disinterested, reflective, and disengaged self and the practically-interested self. It is potentially self-destructive and inwardly-divided as it tries to cultivate self-awareness to the point where inner drives and emotions are no longer motivating, and where it can attain a virtually disembodied condition of tranquility-as-detachment.[5]

ii christian quietism, yogic ecstasy, and buddhist enlightenment

The ascetic typically expresses an attitude closer to Christian resignation than to Stoical detachment, for the ascetic is concerned with more than simply enduring emotional drives and demands without becoming ruffled. Schopenhauer consequently privileges the Christian, as opposed to classical Greek and Roman conceptions of tragedy, for instance, given the former's closer proximity to asceticism:

> Stoic equanimity is distinguished fundamentally from Christian resignation in that the former teaches only calm toleration and well-composed expectation of irreversibly necessary evil, whereas Christianity teaches renunciation, the giving-up of willing. The tragic heroes of the ancients accordingly display a steadfast subjugation under the unavoidable blows of fate; in contrast, the Christian tragedy displays the relinquishing of the whole will-to-live, joyful abandonment of the world in consciousness of its worthlessness and emptiness. I am completely of the opinion that modern tragedy stands at a higher level than that of the ancients. Shakespeare is far greater then Sophocles.[6]

Not long after Shakespeare's lifetime, the seventeenth-century Quietist movement also expressed a type of spirituality similar to the Schopenhauerian denial-of-the-Will. Its representatives include Miguel de Molinos (1640–97), François Fénélon (1651–1715), and Madame Jean Marie Guyon (1648–1717), and Schopenhauer positively lists these mystics in conjunction with Meister Eckhart (1260–1328), Johannes Tauler (1300–61), Antoinette Bourignon (1616–80), John Bunyan (1628–88), and Johann Georg Gichtel (1638–1710). He regards these individuals as jointly advocating the denial-of-the-Will and as describing states of consciousness that reflect the salvation he is aiming to articulate philosophically. Schopenhauer is sympathetic with mysticism, and the Quietists approximate the point towards which his view seems to lead. Quietistic mysticism, however, is not the only type of mysticism, and we can clarify Schopenhauer's discussion by distinguishing between a Upanishadic or Christian Quietistic version of mysticism, as opposed to a Buddhistic one.

For the Quietists, the reduction of desire is a way to minimize the feeling of finite individuality. The idea is that as long as one retains a strong sense of oneself as a finite individual, the entrance of God's infinite presence into one's consciousness also remains limited. Quietism thus advocates the denial-of-the-Will for the sake of allowing infinite and sacred content to enter freely into one's awareness. It compares well to any view that regards self-conscious willing and the awareness of oneself as an individual as standing in the way of attaining metaphysical knowledge.[7] We have already seen this type of subject–object parallelism in Schopenhauer's belief that the aesthetic experience of universalistic Platonic Ideas requires a corresponding universalistic consciousness on the part of the perceiver.

Quietistic mysticism is most compatible with the third of the above options where it is hypothesized that the thing-in-itself has many dimensions, only one of which is aptly described as Will. From the standpoint of philosophical theorizing, as noted, these additional dimensions are not knowable as empirical knowledge, nor are they knowable philosophically, although they could remain knowable mystically. Quietistic mysticism is also consistent with a panentheistic position that maintains that all is "in" God, where God is identified with the world we experience, but where God is also ascribed inscrutable dimensions far in excess of the world we experience. As we noted in Chapter 1, Schopenhauer's neighbor in Dresden during the composition of *The World as Will and Representation*, Karl Christian Friedrich Krause, may have been of some influence here, since he held views for which he coined the term "panentheism" and was interested in Upanishadic thought.

Whatever its historical source, we have seen how this mystical, Quietistic, and pantheistic interpretation of the thing-in-itself logically undercuts Schopenhauer's explanation of the world's violence, and it is best rejected in favor of preserving his more characteristic thesis that the thing-in-itself is Will, virtually through-and-through. This invites a *non-mystical* interpretation to the denial-of-the-Will, which acknowledges that we can significantly reduce the strength of desire, but denies the Quietistic supposition that the minimization of desire reveals any extraordinary mystical dimensions to the thing-in-itself. The tranquility that the denial-of-the-Will precipitates would in this case, not be a metaphysically-revelatory mode of awareness as we find asserted in Christian mysticism or Upanishadic yoga. It would simply be a release from the pressures of desire, as we typically encounter in Buddhism.

Schopenhauer's conception of the denial-of-the-Will is thus open to interpretation in two ways, either Buddhistically, where it provides only a sense of release from the pressures of desire, or in a more metaphysically revelatory, panentheistic, Christian Quietist, or Upanishadic manner. The latter imparts to ascetic tranquility, an apprehension of a higher metaphysical reality; the Buddhist interpretation values the experience of desireless tranquility without any metaphysical complications.

Schopenhauer refers supportively to Christian Quietism and Upanishadic enlightenment, so it is important to find a proper place for these modes of consciousness within his philosophy, if we assume that the thing-in-itself is simply Will, and is not multidimensional. Schopenhauer's framework indeed has an alternatively reasonable place for mystical experiences – one that lends them an important value, but which does not require us to assert that they reveal additional dimensions of the thing-in-itself. A place for mystical experiences is midway between the painful, ordinary state of mind and the ultimate, ascetic state, given that we are interpreting the ascetic state Buddhistically and non-metaphysically.

The Upanishadic and Christian Quietist modes of mysticism maintain that transcendent mystical experiences disclose an unchanging, absolute foundation of reality, sometimes referred to as God, the Absolute, or the Nameless. These sorts of timeless being fit easily within Schopenhauer's philosophy, for what has just been described as God or the Absolute is of the same order as timeless intelligible characters and Platonic Ideas (especially the Idea of the Good). These universalistic entities correspond to the poles of the universal subject–object distinction at the root of the PSR.

If we associate intelligible characters and Platonic Ideas with the apprehension of absolute permanence (as mirage-like as absolute permanence may be), then mystical experience of the Christian and Upanishadic sort shows itself to be related to the aesthetic and moral states of tranquility and transcendence that Schopenhauer describes. These are states of mind where the Platonic Ideas, music as the copy of the Will, and intelligible characters are the objects and subjects of universal awareness.

In these transcendent modes, we apprehend dimensions of timeless being, but if they are only manifestations of the root of the PSR, then reality as it is in itself is not being apprehended. They are projections of the human imagination, comparable to the peaceful and demonic gods that the meditational self projects in Tibetan Buddhism, for instance.[8] From the Buddhist standpoint that traditionally advocates a metaphysics of universal flux, moreover, such eternal beings are illusory, and Schopenhauer's claim that the Platonic Ideas are products of the imagination and of the PSR fits squarely into the Buddhist interpretation of such timeless, otherworldly beings. In sum, timeless intelligible characters, along with eternal and timeless states of mystical experience, are best located at the same level as the timeless Platonic Ideas, all of which are expressions of the PSR's universalistic root.

Schopenhauer does not distinguish clearly between Buddhistic, Christian, and Upanishadic modes of enlightenment, and this confuses his exposition. We often find them amalgamated in a single passage, leading us to believe that they are essentially the same. His grouping of aesthetic, moral, and ascetic styles of awareness as means to escape from the pressures of the Will also suggests that, while similarly oriented towards non-individualistic modes of awareness, their contents differ mainly in degree. There are some significant differences between the Buddhistic and the Upanishadic styles of enlightenment, however, and they reflect what supposedly led Buddha himself to reject yogic meditation. As the traditional account goes, upon extensive reflection Buddha rejected as illusory the eternal, timeless, and permanent state of mind to which the yogic practices he had followed aspired, for he found nothing permanent, either within or without, to grasp and metaphysically rest himself upon.

In Schopenhauer's works, Christianity, Upanishadic thought, and Buddhism have impressively positive roles in the associations he draws between their respective views and his own doctrines, and it is sometimes difficult to distinguish between these religious views within his exposition. One thing is clear, though: he was unsympathetic with Judaism and Islam because he believed that their core spirit is realistic. Schopenhauer maintained that, unlike Buddhism, Christianity, and Upanishadic thought, Judaism and Islam recognize our daily world as a real world, not as a dream or illusion of any sort. His accordingly set these two religions aside. Among his positive descriptions of the three above-mentioned religious views, Christian references predominate in Schopenhauer's works, but the spirit of his ultimately tranquil state of ascetic salvation often sounds like the Buddhistic sense of enlightenment, and rightly so if his most coherent position requires him to avoid admitting multiple and inscrutable dimensions to the thing-in-itself.

In sum, the strongest philosophical way to interpret Schopenhauer's doctrine of the denial-of-the-Will is to regard it as expressing a merely negative sense of tranquility and enlightenment: the denial-of-the-Will releases us from the pressures of willing, but the resulting tranquility does not reveal an alternative and positive reality on another dimension. Just as it is possible to claim, as did St Augustine, that evil is merely the privation of good and that only good positively exists, one can claim in reverse that Schopenhauerian tranquility involves only a reduction of the force of willing in some circumscribed sphere, and that metaphysically, only Will positively exists.

This sort of tranquility-as-detachment is exemplified by the Buddhist conception of enlightenment or *Nirvana*, and it is fitting that Schopenhauer refers to Buddhist enlightenment in the culminating last line of *The World as Will and Representation*. At this point in his manuscript he has characterized the ascetic state of consciousness as one which, from the standpoint of the world as representation, looks like "nothing," while yet from its own standpoint regards the world as representation as "nothing." Each outlook regards the other as either incomprehensible or as valueless, and there is a mismatch and mutual failure of communication between the two perspectives.

Schopenhauer's conception of ascetic tranquility is particularly Buddhistic in the coincidence between Buddhism's elementary dictum not to hold on to anything as if it were absolutely permanent and Schopenhauer's claims that his philosophy ends with a negation and, most importantly, that all happiness has a negative character. According to all forms of Buddhism, all composite things are devoid of absolute permanence and are consequently metaphysically the wrong sorts of objects towards which we should grasp. This doctrine conflicts with the Upanishads and yogic practice, where we seek and acknowledge a timeless, permanent self.

It remains that Schopenhauer often speaks Upanishadically and in accord with both a yogic consciousness and a subject of experience that is pure, timeless, and painless. As noted, this is at odds with what is arguably his more fundamental and non-negotiable position, following Kant, that all experiences are in time. Given this, all forms of mysticism that refer to timeless states of mind are impossible in Schopenhauerian terms, and are understood better on the model of apprehending Platonic Ideas through the form of time. It is consequently more reasonable to advance the more qualified, tranquility-as-detachment view – a view that is more Buddhistic in spirit and more plausible as an overall interpretation of Schopenhauer's conception of ascetic enlightenment.

iii asceticism and spiritual purification

Independently of whether Schopenhauer's emphasis on attaining tranquility is interpreted in an Upanishadically-revelatory or Buddhistically-empty sense, it is important to emphasize that according to Schopenhauer's own rendition, even the ascetic consciousness involves a tranquility that is less permanent and pure than we might at first suspect. As is true for both aesthetic awareness and moral awareness, he recognizes a noticeable amount of discord and struggle in the ascetic's mind as well:

> We should not suppose, however, that after the denial of the will has entered upon the scene through the knowledge that acts as its tranquilizer, that it never falters, and that one can rely upon it as one would rely upon an inherited quality. Rather, it must always be freshly achieved through a constant struggle . . . Therefore we also see those who have once attained the denial of the will try to stay upon this road through self-enforced renunciations of every sort, through a penitential and hard lifestyle, and by directing themselves towards what is unpleasant to them – all in order to subdue the will, which continually rises up again and again.[9]

In view of our earlier discussions of the aesthetic and moral consciousness, we can appreciate how Schopenhauer is here outlining a process of spiritual purification that involves struggle and pain. In this respect, his philosophy is in the religious tradition of St John of the Cross (1542–91) who referred to a series of ascending stages of spiritual development, all of which involve struggle, denial of the will, and disorienting uncertainty. Hegel's *Phenomenology of Spirit* (1807) describes a comparable "way of despair," except that Hegel's path to salvation employs dialectical reason as opposed to the denial-of-the-Will. Chapter 12 will explore this connection to Hegel. In relation to Schopenhauer, it is not long before we start to wonder whether each of his ideal types – the genius, the moral soul, and the ascetic – suffer to an extent that matches those who remain unenlightened. The only difference seems to be the periodic experience of tremendously elevated states of tranquil, insight-filled consciousness.

Once again, we encounter here the sublimity that the aesthete and the morally virtuous person share. They attain a measure of tranquility, but only as flesh-and-blood individuals who cannot avoid feeling the Will-to-live pulsing through them in their effort to transcend this

Will. Schopenhauer's various modes of salvation are thus more sublime than beautiful, owing to the inescapable facts that our experience is in time, and that as spatio-temporal beings, we will inevitably suffer. The difference between the ordinary person and the person who achieves salvation depends upon how each respectively uses or manages his or her suffering, for Schopenhauer acknowledges that salvation is not without its price:

> Whoever imagines through such observations how necessary deprivation and suffering often are to our salvation will recognize that we should envy others not so much for their happiness but for their unhappiness.[10]

If pain and death are inevitable, no matter how enlightened we become, Schopenhauer's view harbors some paradoxes. He claims that we should appreciate our sufferings rather than our pleasures, since our sufferings, and not our pleasures, lead eventually to the denial-of-the-Will. He adds that we should deny the Will from a motivation to shun the *pleasures* of the world rather than from a motivation to shun its pains, sharply opposing the denial-of-the-Will to suicide. At the same time, the reason why we are led to deny the Will and to resignation is because the world is so filled with suffering, such that when we empathize with it as much as we can, we become repulsed. Suffering is both attractive and repulsive, and confusingly so.

We should not, therefore, try to avoid suffering in search of pleasure, even though the presence of universal suffering is repugnant enough to stimulate us to detach ourselves from the world altogether. Indeed, it is not so much the physical pain and physical suffering *per se*, but life's essential fruitlessness and meaninglessness, that motivates Schopenhauer's sense of resignation, as it combines with the guilty awareness that we – as cognitive projectors of the PSR – are responsible for the world's violence, frustration, and suffering. As we observe from a moral standpoint, resignation arises from feeling repulsed by our creation of an immoral world. It is also to say more locally that the more miserably we behave towards each other, the more meaningless life becomes.

There is sufficient evidence that Schopenhauer believed that mystical experience provides a relief from suffering. We have noted how he tried to explain this by asserting that the thing-in-itself could have other aspects aside from Will, and that these aspects are what mystics might be blissfully experiencing. Independently of accepting or rejecting this speculation, it remains that in both editions of *The World as Will and Representation* (viz., of 1818 and 1844), Schopenhauer expresses the view that time is necessarily involved in the apprehension of the thing-in-itself as Will, and he positively advocates mystical states. He did not become more mystical as the years went on, for we encounter the following remark in the first edition:

> Were there to be, however, some absolute insistence for some sort of positive knowledge about that which philosophy can provide only a negative expression as the denial of the will, there would consequently remain for us nothing left but to refer to that condition which all those who have attained a perfect denial of the will have experienced, and which is indicated by the names ecstasy, rapture, enlightenment, union with God, etc. This condition, however, should not actually be called knowledge, because it no longer has the form of subject and object; moreover, it is accessible only through one's own experience that is not further communicable.[11]

The difficulty in interpreting Schopenhauer's philosophy resides in the distinction between philosophical expression and mystical expression implicit in the above excerpt. Schopenhauer develops a philosophical characterization of the world and within these constraints he acknowledges the limits of philosophy, which, for him, are circumscribed by the presence of the subject–object distinction. Beyond the limits of philosophical expression he admits that there might be other realms of being, and it is here that he locates mystical experience, maintaining that the thing-in-itself might have other dimensions aside from its being Will. Schopenhauer is on plausible ground in his positive acknowledgement of mystical experience; with respect to maintaining the systematicity of his outlook, his philosophical error is to interpret such experiences as indicating that the thing-in-itself might have countless other dimensions aside from its presentation to us as Will.

In sum, and to reiterate, Schopenhauer's philosophy remains the most organically integrated if we interpret him as stating that there is a single reality called "Will" and nothing significantly beyond this. We can apprehend this reality translucently and almost transparently, and we can apprehend it well enough to know that the universe lacks a rational or meaningful core. Universalistic states of mind – aesthetic, moral, and apparently transcendent states of a Upanishadic and traditional mystical sort – offer some salvation, but their very universality and presence arises from our own projection of the root of the PSR.

Aside from these universalistic states, a more disengaged and more practical state of mind is possible, namely, one where desires are gradually stilled and where we appreciate the tranquility of not being pushed to and fro by the pressures of desire. Metaphysically, there is no higher reality to be revealed beyond the fact that the thing-in-itself is Will, and, experientially, there is at best only a higher state of consciousness – akin to a Buddhistic state of enlightenment – through which the reality of the world as Will is not allowed to cause undue suffering to the point of generating an embittered attitude.

From a moral and social standpoint, we might ask whether the Schopenhauerian outlook at which we have now arrived is either pessimistic or defeatist. On the positive side, the denial of otherworldly states of consciousness as having a metaphysical validity is useful for generating a more practically-oriented, down-to-earth outlook. From this angle, Schopenhauer's view assumes a more Buddhistic, and even existentialist, flavor. Ultimately, the end-state is one where this world is acknowledged as the place where one exists as an individual, but where, within this spatio-temporal existence, one is clearly appreciative of the psychological benefits that having less desires can bring.

One can only imagine the positive social impact if a majority of people – quite independently of the theory's metaphysical truth – adopted a Schopenhauerian attitude that aims explicitly towards the reduction of craving, greed, selfishness, and violence. Unfortunately, Schopenhauer is portrayed often as an escapist and pessimist, but his view can be of tremendous practical and spiritual value, if we attend to the simple project of minimizing one's desires. It requires no gods, no meaningful core to the universe, and no personal afterlife to advocate the importance of self-tranquillization, compassion, and the reduction of suffering as much as the world's imperfections will allow. His final key is always to want less.

notes

1   *WWR* (I), Book IV, §68, P 383, HK 494–5, ZA 474.
2   *WWR* (I), Book IV, §54, P 275, HK 354, ZA 347.
3   *WWR* (I), Book IV, §69, P 400, HK 517–18, ZA 495.
4   *WWR* (I), Book IV, §68, P 390, HK 504–5, ZA 483.
5   As we shall see in Chapter 12, this is the dialectic of the "unhappy consciousness" that Hegel describes in his *Phenomenology of Spirit*, except that in Hegel's account there is a further development into the standpoint of reason.
6   *WWR* (II), Chapter XXXVII, "On the Aesthetics of Poetry," P 434, HK 213–14, ZA 511–12.
7   Taoism, for example, would fit into this category insofar as it advocates that one not seek fame, not make plans, and simply dwell in the infinite in a state where one is aware of all that is. In such a state of mind, the Tao can more easily flow through one's being.
8   For instance, see *The Tibetan Book of the Dead*, trans. Robert A. F. Thurman (London: The Aquarian Press, 1994), pp. 133ff.
9   *WWR* (I), Book IV, §68, P 391–2, HK 505–6, ZA 484.
10 *PP* (II), Chapter XIV, "Additional Remarks on the Doctrine of the Affirmation and Denial of the Will-to-Live," §170, P 320, ZA 348.
11 *WWR* (I), Book IV, §71, P 410, HK 530, ZA 506.

further reading

Goldman, Daniel, *The Meditative Mind: The Varieties of Meditative Experience* (Los Angeles: Jeremy P. Tarcher, Inc. 1988).

Luft, Eric von der (ed.), *Schopenhauer: New Essays in Honor of his 200th Birthday* (Lewiston, NY: Edwin Mellen Press, 1988).

Neeley, G. Steven, *Schopenhauer: A Consistent Reading* (Lewiston, NY: Edwin Mellen Press, 2003).

schopenhauer in perspective

schopenhauer, nietzsche, and eternal life

i the question of life's value

We are now in a position to consider Schopenhauer's philosophy through three different lenses. In this chapter, we will compare and contrast Schopenhauer's and Nietzsche's outlooks, noticing how the "cadaverous perfume" of Schopenhauer's philosophy permeates some central Nietzschean doctrines more than Nietzsche himself seems to have realized. In the next chapter, we will compare Schopenhauer and Hegel. At almost every turn, Schopenhauer bitterly criticizes Hegel, and rarely are these two German Idealists viewed in harmony. Schopenhauer's penitentiary themes and their relationship to alienated labor will bring the two theorists together. Finally, we will discuss Schopenhauer's impact on Ludwig Wittgenstein's earlier and later philosophies as a way to locate a significant strand of Schopenhauer's twentieth-century philosophical influence.

Many agree that a sound understanding of Nietzsche's philosophy requires a familiarity with *The World as Will and Representation*, but there is a wide range of opinion about the degree to which Schopenhauer and Nietzsche stand in close philosophical proximity. Nietzsche suggests in his final autobiographical work, *Ecce Homo* (1888), that he departed from the Schopenhauer's pessimism after the 1870s, and it has been common to assume that Schopenhauer's influence on Nietzsche is as Nietzsche describes: Schopenhauer inspires the sorts of existential problems Nietzsche addresses, but Nietzsche's mature solutions are substantially anti-Schopenhauerian.

As we shall soon see, a leading Schopenhauerian theme persists, nonetheless, across Nietzsche's writings. We can refer to this as "eternalism" – a positive philosophical orientation towards eternal realities, where these consolingly absorb, expand, and transcend our daily, finite selves. Both Schopenhauer and Nietzsche offer eternalistic solutions to the problem of how death tends to undermine life's meaning, and it is a testament to Schopenhauer's influence that in most of its eternalistic guises, Nietzsche's philosophy remains very Schopenhauerian.

To discern this eternalistic dimension, it helps to recall the many-aspected concept of life that dominated nineteenth-century intellectual thought in general. Life involves growth, expansion, self-maintenance, health and decline, reproduction, instinct, development, goal-orientedness, the realization of naturally given potential, nourishment, modification of forms, competition, violence, internal balance, and organic unity, among a number of salient qualities. As philosophers emphasize certain of these aspects and downplay others when formulating their life-inspired philosophies, the resulting outlooks exhibit different attitudes and vary in their respective contents and prescriptions.

The Hegelian philosophy, for instance, conceives of human history's development as a culminating contribution to the universe's organic unity, and it describes a series of conflicts and increasingly integrated resolutions to reach this harmonious end. The Schopenhauerian philosophy regards history as driven blindly by instinct, violence, and individual selfishness, without any goal, moral or otherwise. The Nietzschean philosophy similarly emphasizes instinct, violence, and, most importantly, the quest for power and health within a vision of history that again, is without any overriding moral goal.[1]

The question of life's meaning governs Schopenhauer's and Nietzsche's philosophies, and this question can appear generally as What is the value of existence? What is the value of life? Is human life worth living? Is it better not to have been born? Is suicide the most reasonable action to take? Why bother to be good? or Why absolutely value anything? As is evident, these formulations focus on existence as a whole, or on earthly life in general, or sometimes more specifically upon people, either as a group or individually.

Schopenhauer and Nietzsche agree that raw existence has no intrinsic value, but they hold different views about the value of suffering and about whether daily life can *acquire* a positive value. Schopenhauer scornfully believes that daily life is hardly worth the suffering it involves and he aims to retire from it; Nietzsche enthusiastically believes that life can be worth suffering for, and he formulates ways to live each day positively, healthily, and wilfully.

Although one philosopher says "no" to life and the other "yes," they employ the same general model to resolve the question of life's meaning. This involves eternalistic content that leads us either to a retirement from daily suffering (in Schopenhauer's case) or to a glorifying reinterpretation of suffering (in Nietzsche's case) for the sake of action. Schopenhauer locates the eternalistic content of his solution in a dimension beyond the daily world, but Nietzsche locates it in the daily world itself, aiming to enhance life's value.

ii funereal imagery and nietzsche's theory of tragedy

For Nietzsche, the assertion that life is not worth living expresses a form of nihilism, and he opposes it. As nihilistic spokespersons whose views he proves to be unhealthy, he introduces two fictional characters, the classical Greek god Silenus, who appears in *The Birth of Tragedy* (1872), and a soothsayer who appears in *Thus Spoke Zarathustra* (1883–5). Silenus announces the disappointing truth that the best thing for people is that they should never have been born – that they should be nothing – and that the next best thing for them is to die soon. In *Zarathustra*, a soothsayer preaches that every individual thing perishes, that everything that can happen has already happened, and that the world is boringly always the same. The sermon's effect renders its hearers weary, drains their life-energy, and diminishes their motivation.

Nietzsche aims to dissolve such dreary, life-negating feelings and he advances anti-nihilistic doctrines that present a more enthusiastic outlook. In *The Birth of Tragedy*, this takes the form of his theory of classical Greek tragedy; in *Zarathustra* it takes the form of the doctrine of eternal recurrence. The logical opposite of Silenus's nihilistic doctrine is that the best thing for people is to live eternally, and that the second best thing is to live as long as one can. With this in mind, Nietzsche sets forth an aesthetics of classical Greek tragedy in which a joyous and thrilling immersion in the trans-individual, eternalistic energies of life in general diminishes the threat that death poses to one's personal meaning.

As we know, Schopenhauer believes that the two highest art forms are tragedy and music, and some immediate evidence of his influence on Nietzsche is in the title of the latter's 1872 work, *The Birth of Tragedy Out of the Spirit of Music*, where the two art forms thematically conjoin. To account for the great healing powers of classical Greek tragedy – ones he associates with the dynamic nature of art itself – Nietzsche incorporates Schopenhauer's two most powerful art forms, hoping to apply his own theory of Greek tragedy therapeutically to redeem his debilitated and nihilistic nineteenth-century European culture.

The nihilism that Nietzsche perceives within the classical Greek culture is the same one he feels within his own. He consequently infers that the Greek's solution to the problem, viz., the development of tragedy as an art form, can resuscitate his own culture, and, by implication, dissolve the depressing Schopenhauerian attitudes he is witnessing around him. Somewhat paradoxically, Schopenhauer's eternalistic aesthetic theory supplies Nietzsche with the tools to overcome Schopenhauerian pessimism.

In Nietzsche's interpretation, Greek tragedy artistically and religiously resolves the problem of meaninglessness that issues from anticipating our personal death. On the face of things, people are born, they struggle, they suffer, they reproduce, they sometimes triumph (but more typically they do not), and they die; new people step into their place and do the same, with the purpose of the long, automatic, and re-iterative process remaining unclear. Since time will bring about one's own death and probably humanity's extinction as well, it is natural is to ask What is the point of our strong instinct to introduce new people into the world, if they are destined to suffer and die? or Why are we here at all, if extinction is inevitable? On a more meditative note, we can ask with Ecclesiastes, why we should struggle for wisdom if death befalls both the wise and the foolish, and if, someday, we will all be forgotten.

Schopenhauer responds to these concerns by advocating states of mind that minimize our sense of individuality: we can contemplate eternal Ideas, contemplate humanity in general, or detach ourselves from as many individual-related desires as possible. Realizing, for instance, that a rose is no less beautiful if it endures only briefly, he advocates attending to the eternalistic quality of rose's beauty, as opposed to lamenting about the individual rose's wilting and death. He prescribes more universalistic states of consciousness and an effort to transcend time, assuming that the more effectively we can contemplate universal realities, the less troubling and eerie the prospect of our absolute extinction will be.

Nietzsche judges that Schopenhauer's well-intended prescriptions sacrifice life's daily value, and, to preserve this value, he develops a more life-affirming view in *The Birth of Tragedy*. Focusing on the metaphysical consolation that classical Greek tragedy seemed to provide for its ancient audience, Nietzsche characterizes tragedy in terms of the interplay between two opposing forces – an Apollonian individuating force and a Dionysian universalizing force – that he discerns at the root of Greek tragedy and Greek culture in general. Experiencing this consolation, he believes, will awaken a more welcoming and enthusiastic attitude towards life.

On the one hand, Greek tragedies portray horrifying scenes of patricide, incest, bad luck, mutilation, and heart-rending woe, as they show some of the most upsetting kinds of events that fate can throw at an innocent person. Such scenes depict, in effect, the frustrating and terrifying nature of the daily world of individuals in social interaction; in Schopenhauerian terms, they theatrically depict the will "feasting on itself." On the other hand, the environmental setting of these Greek tragedies is the springtime festival of Dionysus, where the springtime season is of the essence. This setting supportively frames the scenes of death and destruction within more powerful surroundings that express life's return, new growth, resurging feral energies, youth, beginnings, love, sexuality, elation, intoxication, and cyclical balance.

A key to Schopenhauer's influence on Nietzsche and to understanding Nietzsche's philosophy as a whole lies in reflecting upon how, for some, Greek tragedy developed out of funeral ceremonies for a dead hero. If we consider this funereal context, it is intriguing how the basic *structure* of the Greek tragic experience according to Nietzsche – and this structure highlights an image of overwhelming life that surrounds, frames, and supports an image of death – compares to a lavish floral display that encircles a corpse at a funeral ceremony. As an image, the burning of incense is of a similar character, for the constant aroma of incense's perfume as it diffuses through the environment, provides a stable frame within which to observe the process of decay in the incense's burning. Central to all of this is the upbeat springtime season that surrounds and tempers the horrific tragic images. Each of these examples expresses a tranquility (the springtime, the flowers, the perfume) tinged with terror (the tragedy on stage, the corpse, and, more distantly, the process of decay) that resonates with the aesthetics of the sublime – an aesthetics that we have seen in earlier chapters as forming a defining undercurrent within Schopenhauer's philosophy.

The death scenes on the tragic stage during a springtime performance produce a sublime metaphysical consolation: by transcending and eventually absorbing everyone, the universal power of life mitigates the death of each individual. Insofar as we identify our essential selves not with our individual bodies but with the life energies that flow through all living things, we become one with a virtually undying force that minimizes the significance of our finite individuality and impermanence. It is particularly Nietzschean that this vital life force does not transcend space and time in a Schopenhauerian, life-negating manner. As a form of naturalistic energy, it remains earth-bound, and like an ocean in contrast to a raindrop, it constitutes, and yet far outweighs, the specific forces that pulse through any particular living body. To the extent that we can identify with these life energies that surge through all living things now, in the past, and in the future, our individual deaths will matter less than they do when seen from a more mundane, matter-of-fact perspective.

In its logical structure, the above solution to the problem of nihilism matches Schopenhauer's, for it similarly advocates that we identify with a sublime and universal force that transcends individual existence. Nietzsche's style of universality differs in that we affirm the universal will-to-live, rather than timeless Platonic Ideas. His solution nonetheless expresses an everlasting, eternalistic, and universalistic quality, for, instead of finding salvation in a timeless world that opposes the daily world, he regards the daily world from a perspective that encompasses a time frame that extends far beyond our individual lifetimes, encouraging us imaginatively to subsume and dissolve our individuality into the wider processes of life itself.

In this limited sense, we can experience a feeling of being eternal. Within the experience of tragic theater this involves identifying with the springtime, the music, the singing, and the supportive and observing choral voices. Given the rapture Nietzsche describes in connection with Greek tragedy's metaphysical consolation, we can say that classical Greek tragedy generates the feeling that despite the terrifying violence and eventual death that daily life generally involves, life itself, and as a whole, is something to love. Tragic art, Nietzsche believes, can inspire us to fall in love with life itself and to feel at home in the world.

Within this theory of tragedy, we can discern Schopenhauer's characterization of moral consciousness. When we identify with life itself in Nietzsche's view, we identify with each living individual in a collective sense, feeling ourselves participating in the wider community of living things. Here, we identify empathetically with our natural surroundings, imaginatively feeling the winds blowing through the leaves on the trees, now felt to be our own leaves, the water pulsing through the life of the sea, now felt to be our own life, the bitter fighting between the species, and the suffering, joys, contentments of each living thing, all now felt as our own. We find ourselves in a sublime condition akin to what Schopenhauer's moral theory directs us to experience.

In the Schopenhauerian moral consciousness with which we are familiar, we identify empathetically and compassionately with all people, with the torturer and the tortured, the good and the bad alike, in a way that leads us to a powerful and screaming mix of devastating emotions. Nietzsche describes the feeling of becoming one with life itself in the same way, observing how life's overwhelming power can so easily break a person apart. Just as Schopenhauer finds the immersion in the consciousness of humanity to be close to unbearable, Nietzsche finds the immersion in life itself to be psychologically overwhelming.[2]

Schopenhauer and Nietzsche differ noticeably, however, in their respective evaluations of the universalistic contents of this amalgamated style of consciousness. Schopenhauer describes the bittersweet and intense mix of human emotions as sublime, but as morally repulsive; Nietzsche experiences it as more uniformly wild, dangerously thrilling, and yet comforting in its death-defying content.

iii schopenhauer's moral awareness and eternal recurrence

As an upgrade to his theory of Greek tragedy, Nietzsche later formulates his doctrine of eternal recurrence as a further – and yet remarkably similar – solution to the problem of nihilism. Although Schopenhauer foreshadows it, the doctrine of eternal recurrence first appears in

Nietzsche's writings in 1882 at a time when his friendship with Richard Wagner – a friendship that inspired *The Birth of Tragedy* – had already dissolved. By this time, Nietzsche had passed briefly through an anti-Wagner, science-friendly phase in the late 1870s in *Human, All-too-Human* (1878), and had begun to write the works for which he became a world-historical philosophical figure. Nietzsche himself stated that the doctrine of eternal recurrence is one of his leading philosophical ideas, so it is revealing to note here how it is saturated with eternalistic Schopenhauerian content.

Nietzsche initially presents the doctrine of eternal recurrence through a "spirit" that appears during one's "loneliest of lonelies." The spirit appears when one is depressed, when the most painful experiences and memories are in view, and when one is in isolation from all comforting social support. The question we hear is simple, but pointed: How would you feel, if you had to live your life over and over again, with no prospect of changing any details?

Nietzsche believes that supremely healthy people will enthusiastically welcome an endless reiteration of their lives, despite the pains their lives contain. He also believes that significantly unhealthy people will gnash their teeth in agony upon hearing the spirit's proposition, anticipating the eternal reiteration of their sufferings as a most terrible prospect. The spirit delivers the healthy people to heaven; the unhealthy, to hell. Nietzsche views the Last Judgment, so to speak, as ultimately decided by a person's health.

In its finer details, the doctrine of eternal recurrence admits of many interpretations, and within our present context, it is most revealing to reflect upon the reiterated contents of our lives from the internal, experiential, or subjective standpoint. This contrasts with observing our lives replay as if we were watching a theatrical performance played by others. Important for Nietzsche is the evaluative contemplation of accumulated pains, sufferings, disappointments, struggles, pleasures, joys, and satisfactions in an experiential way, so that we can determine whether life is worth living from the perspective of *what it feels like* to be alive.

Typically, the hypothesis of eternal recurrence stands as a test of health that each person can apply, where each person's experience is considered unique, and where each arrives at his or own particular response to the spirit's question. Within such a formulation – and this is how Nietzsche originally presents the doctrine in *The Gay Science* – the answer to the spirit's question depends on the individual's attitude to the specific contents of his or her own life. An appropriate response would be, "relative to what happened to me and relative to my attitude towards those experiences, it would be joyful to learn that my life will be infinitely reiterated." Anyone who could affirm this would have a healthy attitude towards life, so it would seem.

This personal formulation does not resolve the problem of nihilism in a sufficiently generalized way, however, for we are not yet addressing the philosophical question of whether life *in general* is worth living, independently of the variable proportions of favorable versus adverse circumstances that any given person might experience. In *Zarathustra*, however, Nietzsche seems to appreciate the limitation of the personal formulation, for he expresses the doctrine in a way that replaces its relativistic, individual-relative application with a more demanding consideration.[3] Since the problem of nihilism concerns health in light of how *life in general* happens to be, not health in reference to whether fate has been kind or unkind to this or that person, he adds a dimension to the doctrine that emphasizes the interconnectedness of things, asserting that no one is isolated from the rest of the world. When one says "yes" to the reiteration of one's *own* past, whatever its contents might have been, one must affirm the reiteration of the people with whom one had been in contact, and by extension, to the entire history of civilization. Saying "yes" to a single pleasure entails affirming – and, in effect, taking responsibility for – *all* of the suffering that has ever been, since the world is of a single piece. Whatever the contents of one's life might have been, either pleasurable or painful, Nietzsche sets the same heavy price upon saying "yes" to life.

A more careful contemplation of the spirit's proposition consequently leads us to reflect upon whether daily life is worth living in view of empathizing with every person's worst moments, best moments, and merely uneventful moments. This more accurately amounts to asking whether life in general is worth living. Enjoying the sunlight and the cool breeze upon one's face in a joyful affirmation of life at this moment, entails acknowledging the torturers, earthquakes, disease, and sorrow over the centuries that has brought one to this very moment, not to mention the suffering and sorrow that is likely to continue into the imaginable future. Moreover, upon reflecting upon humanity's worst episodes, one considers them empathetically as one's own, as one identifies with life in general.

When appreciated in this way, Nietzsche's doctrine of eternal recurrence, like his theory of tragedy, generates an empathetic consciousness akin to Schopenhauer's moral consciousness, for these views require us to identify with everyone past, present, and future, and to understand what it feels like to be both the torturer and the tortured. Through such a thought-experiment, we imagine ourselves to embody the accumulated consciousness of humanity itself, condensed within ourselves. Upon further empathizing with not only humanity but with life in general, we become one with the animals and plants. The suffering of a bull, chicken, pig, or lamb in the slaughterhouse becomes as psychologically close to us as if we were the bull, chicken, pig, or lamb ourselves. The pleasure in eating the meat of the bull, chicken, pig, or lamb, becomes a complicated pleasure infused with the knowledge that, in a more universal sense, we are eating our own flesh. The doctrine of eternal recurrence requires us to engage in this sort of universal empathy, and it is what Schopenhauer describes as characteristic of moral awareness.

If we reflect upon some of the symbolic and literary aspects of Nietzsche's doctrine of eternal recurrence, some further commonalities emerge between eternal recurrence, the consoling experience of classical tragedy as he understands it, and Schopenhauerian eternalism. As mentioned above – and this is a vital point – the core image of Nietzsche's theory of tragedy is that of a death-image, decay-image, or suffering-image surrounded by, tempered by, and dominated by a soothing and overpowering image, typically linked with life, health, laughter, or consolation. This core image has a surprisingly extensive set of examples. The funerary image of a casket or corpse surrounded by fragrant flowers, a perfumed and embalmed corpse where the perfume and fragrant preservatives (for example, myrrh) prevail, a burning stick of fragrant incense, or a violent tragedy on stage supported by springtime and choral surroundings, are exemplary.

Further images resonating within Nietzsche's writings include the downward march of the 205 Cathars from their mountaintop refuge at Montsegur in 1244, singing, as they walked into bonfires set for their execution. There is also the medieval dance of death in which the festivity of the farandole dance overcomes the fear of the approaching grave. We can also recall the many instances where laughter serves for Nietzsche as a healthy reaction to meaninglessness and futility. These all counteract death's nihilistic force with more powerful energies of singing, dancing, laughing, rejoicing, being cheerful, buoyant, celebratory, and hopeful. They bring to mind how the new springtime growth is hopeful in its promise of life that overpowers the previous winter's stage of death.

Just as the springtime image of life frames the individual tragic episodes in Greek tragedy, Nietzsche's character Zarathustra inters in the trunk of a tree the corpse of a daring tightrope walker who had fallen to his death. In much the same way, the doctrine of eternal recurrence frames the sufferings and pains of all living things in an overall feeling of love for life in general. Somewhat unexpectedly, Christian imagery contains similar images. For instance, there is the wooden cross – an instrument of torture and death – depicted as intertwined with fragrant and beautiful roses.[4] Finally, we can add the image of the risen Christ, glowing in a white halo, while bearing and displaying on his hands the wounds of his crucifixion.

These examples consolingly situate an individual's death within a more positive frame of life, beauty, or love everlasting, and in this respect, Nietzsche's doctrine of eternal recurrence is as eternalistic as his earlier theory of tragedy, and as Schopenhauer's theory of moral consciousness. Indeed, if we consider Nietzsche's views at this level of abstraction and amalgamate the various images mentioned above into a single theme, we can see that a substantial portion of Nietzsche's philosophy – at least that within his early period and from 1880–5 as portrayed so far – resonates with the basic funereal image of a corpse lavishly surrounded with flowers. The examples range from the theory of tragedy to Zarathustra's laying of the tightrope walker into the tree trunk.

Such reflections suggest how a foundational *Christian* imagery underlies Nietzsche's thinking as so far described, for his outlook expresses a conception of an eternal life that overcomes each individual death. This connection helps explain why Schopenhauer's theory of moral consciousness, which itself aims to capture Christian views, bears a close affinity to Nietzsche's theories of tragedy and doctrine of eternal recurrence.[5] From a structural standpoint, moreover, the similar logic of eternal recurrence and Christian moral consciousness is visible in the comparable psychological difficulty Nietzsche himself faces with respect to the idea of affirming life and eternal recurrence. The spirit's message in *The Gay Science* eventually leads Nietzsche (as Zarathustra) to summon the strength to say "yes" to the eternal recurrence of mediocre and weak people. He is nauseated by the thought of their continual presence, not to mention the awareness of his own limitations, and he struggles to overcome his desire to purge himself and the world of mediocrity and weakness. This is Zarathustra's spiritual struggle in *Thus Spoke Zarathustra*.

The Christian faces the same type of challenge, except that in place of the mediocre, weak, uncreative, and unhealthy people who need to be celebrated joyously within an all-affirming Nietzschean outlook, the Christian is presented with offensive and vicious people whom he or she is compassionately obliged to forgive and accept all-lovingly. Nietzsche's difficulty in summoning the strength to love mediocre, weak, uncreative, and unhealthy people matches the Christian's difficulty is mustering the strength to love those who are murderers, thieves, and outrageous aggressors. In both cases, the ideal is to love everyone equally in an attempt to fill one's vision with an all-permeating affirmation of the world, either in light of a particular moral vision, or in light of the love of life. Nietzsche accepts enthusiastically that life itself contradicts traditional moral values, but he has more difficulty accepting how life itself rarely produces perfect specimens, and that the demands of health require us to love it unconditionally nonetheless.

In sum, these assorted affinities between Christian imagery and Nietzsche's solution to the problem of nihilism reveal a strong Schopenhauerian undercurrent to Nietzsche's solution. This is expressed in the logic of Schopenhauer's eternalistic model for resolving the problem, and it appears in Nietzsche's thought partially on account of Schopenhauer's originally having influenced him so profoundly when he was in his early twenties. Both share the problem of estimating life's value, both share the same violent vision of the world, and both share the same style of eternalistic solution. It is no wonder, then, that although Nietzsche sought to free himself from Schopenhauer, the Christian style of Schopenhauer's solution – here symbolized funereally by a corpse, highly perfumed, or surrounded with a lavish and fragrant floral arrangement – remains strong in Nietzsche's writings.

iv the eternalistic illusion of supreme health

Nietzsche's final years, 1887–8, present us with a change in philosophical tone and orientation – one suggestive of a departure from Schopenhauerian, or more generally universalistic, themes. Nietzsche retains his characteristic interest in life to the very end, but he emphasizes its health-related aspects in less broadly philosophical ways, opting instead for more localized, psychological, historical, and physiological analyses. These recall his earlier work, *Human, All-too-Human*, although Nietzsche was at that time less friendly to art than he was during the early 1870s and 1880s.[6]

In his final writings, Nietzsche approaches the question of health in detailed and local analyses of specific phenomena, which he classifies as being more or less healthy or unhealthy, case by case. He addresses Schopenhauer's views by discussing the meaning of "ascetic ideals" – ideals of which he believes Schopenhauer is a prime advocate and representative, and which he believes cohere with an unhealthy cultural perspective that has done widespread social damage during his own time and earlier. We find this discussion in *On the Genealogy of Morals* (1887).

Within the category of ascetic ideals, Nietzsche includes religious ideals. Schopenhauer's philosophy consequently emerges as a contemporary example of a philosophical perspective set forth in exactly the same spirit as the world's main religions, locating Schopenhauer himself within the company of religious leaders – the ascetic priests – that includes figures such as Buddha and Jesus. Nietzsche admits that the postulation of ascetic ideals constitutes a possible solution to nihilism, and he appreciates how such values can provide a meaning for existence, if only in a negative way that recommends detachment, denial-of-the-will, and hopes for transcendence.

When viewing Schopenhauer's asceticism through the perspective of life, Nietzsche concludes that it is unhealthy. We should note that he does not consider whether Schopenhauer's ascetic prescriptions are scientifically grounded or philosophically true, but examines whether they are *healthy*, in full awareness that health often, and perhaps even typically, requires deception, lies, and a subordination of truth to the interests of health. He medicinally evaluates Schopenhauer's definitive prescription of asceticism as we might reflect upon the health-value of a plate of food, climate, daily regimen, or style of clothing.

On the face of things, we encounter here an explicitly anti-Schopenhauerian tone in Nietzsche's rejection of asceticism, which suggests that by the end of his active intellectual life Nietzsche had distanced himself significantly from the Schopenhauerian, eternalistic style of solution to the problem of nihilism that we meet in his theory of tragedy and doctrine of eternal recurrence. As we will see in a moment, this departure from Schopenhauer is only apparent, since eternalistic content continues to reside in the subjective quality of a supremely healthy attitude.

Nietzsche philosophizes from the perspective of life as opposed to other perspectives, and this leads him to reject transcendent and permanent ideals. Any focus upon states of consciousness that are not spatio-temporally determined, he tends to devaluate, disparaging all predominantly speculative and universalistic philosophical styles. At this point in his writings, he works primarily with the concepts of health and power, and applies them in specific contexts in ways that resist wider philosophical speculation. He discusses nutrition, environment, the dispositions of individual people, personal tastes, and historical contingencies, usually offering only local and circumscribed conclusions to the effect that this or that constellation of values, social phenomenon, or theoretical structure is healthy or unhealthy.

Within this case-by-case framework, it is difficult to draw lasting conclusions, and Nietzsche sometimes appears to be at a loss for specifying any specific philosophical doctrines that compare in their universality to his theories of Greek tragedy and eternal recurrence. He instead advocates cheerfulness, a will to deception, and the creation of new values, but in the absence of any detailed vision of how what these values should be defined, aside from asserting generically that they ought to be healthy and powerful. This is not an objectionable point at which to arrive philosophically, but it indicates that when one's perspective becomes more and more down-to-earth and existentially-centered, there is increasingly less to rely upon, except for sets of variable and contingent facts.

The implicit solution to the problem of nihilism at which we arrive, then, is not an explicitly philosophical solution but a practical one. Nietzsche aims to foster health, and he manages this through biological, psychological, and environmental analyses and prescriptions. This motivation to be healthy is understandable as motivated in part by the following philosophical consideration: in a supremely healthy condition, the problem of nihilism simply no longer arises, for the perspective and feelings of health undermine depression, debilitation, and the weakening of energies that attend nihilism.

Nietzsche admits that for those who suffer from nihilistic feelings, a philosophy such as Schopenhauer's can be therapeutically useful as a means to recuperate, and he compares it to how one often needs to retreat, hibernate, and rest in order to revitalize oneself when ill or weak. For those who are already healthy and strong, he sees no need to adopt a Schopenhauerian attitude. The very presence of the problem of nihilism indicates that one is unhealthy, and, accordingly, the problem dissolves once one re-establishes one's health.

Rather than solving the problem of nihilism in a theoretical fashion, Nietzsche finally dissolves it by formulating ways to transform one's perspective on life itself from an unhealthy perspective to a healthy perspective. Within this later Nietzschean framework, the problem of nihilism compares to being unable to taste one's food well due to a stuffy nose, and it is a problem dissolved by becoming healthy again and free of one's spiritual head cold. Nietzsche approaches nihilism as a doctor would, and he literally treats it as a disease.

We can inquire of this Nietzschean therapeutic approach, of course, whether the dissolution of a philosophical problem can satisfactorily take the place of a positive solution to it, and whether switching one's perspective to dissolve a philosophical problem introduces the danger of self-deception. Nietzsche consistently responds by regarding self-deception as unproblematic, as long as the mode of deception generates or sustains a great health. Health is more important than truth because, as living beings, the perspective of life defines the very possibility of our experience, and health is a necessary condition for a flourishing life.

Among the most thought-provoking aspects of Nietzsche's later response to the problem of nihilism – and the point where we can begin to see how this response embodies the same basic, Christian–Schopenhauerian structure as before – is how the generation of illusion in one's perspective is itself a feature of supreme health. When one is extremely healthy, death does not much matter, for it typically remains imaginatively far away and practically unlikely in light of one's strong and wholesome condition. When one is supremely healthy, one feels as if one will live forever.

It is common knowledge that when serious illness interrupts one's health, it can generate a feeling of waking up from a dream, as one perceives that death could be very near. This dissolution of meaning attending the closeness of death shows, by means of contrast, how *an illusory sense of eternity* issues from the condition of being in supreme health.

The great health that Nietzsche advocates in the culmination of his philosophy has the psychological effect of generating the illusion of eternal life, and, in this sense, it embodies a Schopenhauerian dimension in its eternalistic quality and resonates with the doctrine of eternal recurrence. For Schopenhauer, as we have seen in earlier chapters, the otherworldly Platonistic Ideas are illusions that, when contemplated, provide an eternalistic feeling as well, so Schopenhauer's and Nietzsche's eternalistic solutions to the problem of nihilism are closer than they at first appear to be.

The above considerations suggest that Nietzsche ultimately remains Schopenhauerian and eternalistically oriented throughout most of his philosophy. A main difference between the two philosophers resides in their alternative ways to express a redeeming eternalistic content. Schopenhauer's eternalism is fundamentally otherworldly insofar as it leads us to focus on a timeless and spaceless dimension as a relief from the pressures of daily life. Nietzsche's eternalism is more worldly, for it is expressed either as an identification with life itself, as an identification with the continual flow of physical events evaluated positively in reference to love, beauty, or laughter, or as a personal feeling of supreme health that overshadows with an eternalistic halo any feelings of personal demise or degeneration.

v nietzsche's madness and eternalistic consciousness

Although Nietzsche's descriptions of the world tend to accentuate the depressing, frustrating, and violent aspects of life somewhat less than Schopenhauer's, it is open to speculation that Nietzsche might have himself become too immersed in the imaginative requirements of Schopenhauer's moral theory and his own theory of eternal recurrence. The contents of what he wrote immediately after his mental collapse are consistent with this speculation, for his letters appear to have been written by someone who had adopted in fact, rather than merely imaginatively, the consciousness that he or she is essentially "everyone."

In a letter to Jacob Burckhardt dated January 6, 1889, Nietzsche refers to a recent criminal case and states that he, Nietzsche himself, "is" the criminal, that he also "is" the criminal's father, that he had already literally witnessed his own funeral when he had seen the funeral of others, and, amazingly, that he is indeed "every name in history." Such statements have an insane ring, but they accurately describe the consciousness of someone who has immersed himself into the heartbeat of life to such an extent that there could be felt a first-person, empathetic identification with every person who had ever lived. More than once

Nietzsche stated that such an immersion into the energies of life itself would drive a person mad.

No one will ever know whether Nietzsche's madness constituted a state of salvation for him, but it is worth reflecting briefly that the contents of his writings immediately after his mental collapse echo the state of eternalistic consciousness that appears across his writings as a mode of salvation and solution to nihilism. They are also consistent with Schopenhauer's observation that genius and madness are closely linked. The irony is that Nietzsche's state of consciousness did not emerge from a supreme state of health, but from what appears to have been a debilitating illness, and this suggests that we cannot stretch the eternalistic feeling that supreme health provides to the universalistic point where we literally lose the power to discriminate between ourselves and other individuals. It is both eerie and remarkable that Schopenhauer's characterization of moral consciousness – a sublime state of mind that can be used to characterize the mentality of a person such as Jesus, who is described traditionally as having assumed to himself all of the world's sins – has even the slightest resemblance to Nietzsche's remarks during the initial days of his mental collapse.

notes

1 Nietzsche sometimes departs from this when referring to the superhuman (that is, most healthy) type of person as the goal towards which less healthier people should strive, but he does not have a theory of necessary historical development. In a July 30, 1881 postcard to Franz Overbeck, for instance, Nietzsche wrote how his own views agreed with Spinoza's, emphasizing how he and Spinoza both denied that there is freedom of the will, teleology, and a moral world order.

2 See *The Birth of Tragedy* (1872), §21. In Chapter 20 of *Middlemarch* (1871–2), George Eliot (Mary Anne Evans) coincidentally expresses the same idea.

3 This reflection is expressed in *Thus Spoke Zarathustra*, but it is also present in Nietzsche's writings in 1878, before the 1882 formulation of the doctrine of eternal recurrence, for example, *Human, All-too-Human* "From the Souls of Artists and Writers," §208.

4 Martin Luther's personal seal, "Luther's Rose," has closely related imagery, as does the "Rose Cross" of the Rosicrucians.

5 In Nietzsche's own 1886 self-criticism of *The Birth of Tragedy*, he observes in §7 that there is a Christian quality to the "metaphysical consolation" he associated with Greek tragedy. Nietzsche maintains that he overcame this dimension of Christianity in his later work, but the argument of the present chapter is that although Nietzsche might have overcome Christianity's otherworldliness, he retained Christianity's eternalism.

6 Nietzsche's most Schopenhauer-independent phase is arguably centered around the short time (late 1876–7) when he was living with his friend Paul

Rée and writing *Human, All-too-Human*. The problem of nihilism is difficult to locate as a predominating theme in *Human, All-too-Human*, and Nietzsche's own attitude towards the value of life in that work displays an even, non-preoccupied neutrality.

further reading

Fox, Michael (ed.), *Schopenhauer: His Philosophical Achievement* (New Jersey: Barnes & Noble Books, 1980).

Nietzsche, Friedrich, "Schopenhauer as Educator" in *Untimely Meditations*, trans. R. J. Hollingdale (Cambridge: Cambridge University Press, 1983).

Simmel, Georg, *Schopenhauer and Nietzsche*, trans. Helmut Loiskandle, Deena Weinstein, and Michael Weinstein (Urbana and Chicago: University of Illinois Press, 1991).

schopenhauer, hegel, and alienated labor

i the world's essence: rational or irrational?

T he majority of Schopenhauer's irreverent characterizations of Hegel appear after the latter's death in 1831, and it is easy to suspect that Hegel meant more to Schopenhauer than Schopenhauer meant to Hegel. As we shall see below, it is likely that by the time Schopenhauer was applying for his teaching position in Berlin in 1820, Hegel had long believed that he had transcended Schopenhauer's style of intuition-grounded metaphysics. He wrote his *Phenomenology of Spirit* (1807) over a decade before Schopenhauer published *The World as Will and Representation* (1818), and in 1820 he is likely to have regarded Schopenhauer as a young and talented philosophical amateur with much to learn.

Schopenhauer's references to Hegel – for example, "charlatan," "scribbler," "windbag," "tedious," "dull," "common" – perhaps reveal less of Schopenhauer's resentment of Hegel's philosophical abilities than they express the pain of feeling neglected by the academic philosophical establishment. Throughout his years of estrangement from the university community, Schopenhauer retained his aristocratic pride, his self-confidence, and his energy for belittling the most established and respected professors of his time, consistently conveying the impression that his philosophy remained superior to those of his slightly older and more renowned contemporaries such as Fichte, Schelling, and Hegel. In 1820, when Schopenhauer was 32 years old and was aspiring to make a scholarly mark in Berlin, Fichte had already been dead for six years, having succumbed to typhus in his early fifties. Hegel was himself then 50, teaching in Fichte's former university chair. Schelling had already been enjoying academic honors since the age of 25 and was then 45, with fate holding in trust for him to receive 21 years later in Berlin, a university position in Hegel's chair.

Schopenhauer's estimate of his own philosophy is accurate enough: *The World as Will and Representation* offers a philosophy that differs radically from Hegel's in crucial respects. Whereas Schopenhauer maintains in a no-nonsense and individualistic fashion that life is a continual war of all against all, Hegel asserts with a forceful social spirit that we are essentially all for one and one for all.[1] Schopenhauer advocates intuitionism, mysticism, ahistoricism, anti-teleology, irrationalism, a traditional Aristotelian logic, and a miserable view of human nature that dooms us to continual frustration, suffering, and war. Hegel advocates the possibility of an explicit comprehension of the cosmos, historical awareness, teleology, rationalism, dialectical logic, and the view that we are the crown of creation, set confidently on the path to realize higher and higher levels of self-consciousness, social harmony, and mutual respect.

Moreover, in the form of the principle of sufficient reason (PSR), Schopenhauer regards rationality as a source of pain, frustration, illusion, and original sin. In the form of dialectical logic, Hegel regards rationality as the key to the cosmos and as the ultimate and divine reconciliatory principle. Within Schopenhauer's view, reason generates metaphysical falsity and the world of appearance; within Hegel's, it generates truth and reality.

Schopenhauer's dim view of Hegel's metaphysics is also widely known. From abstract concepts such as "being," "nothing," and "becoming," along with an extensive sequence of unfolding abstractions that constitute the rest of his *Logic*, Hegel dialectically derives space and time, along with the rest of the great chain of being in his *Philosophy of Nature* and *Philosophy of Spirit*. In the course of this unfolding, he describes how concrete human society emerges as the self-articulation of what starts logically, conceptually, and metaphysically, as purely abstract being. As we have seen, Schopenhauer objects to this grand procession of thought, since he believes that Hegel's metaphysics elaborately expresses none other than the ontological argument for God's existence. Convinced that Kant had definitively refuted this argument, he considers Hegel's system to be wrongheaded from the very start.

Accepting Kant's view that space and time are subjective forms that stem from the human psyche, Schopenhauer believes that it gives too much credence to appearances if one asserts that the elementary core of things gradually brings itself to fruition in historical, spatio-temporal development. To aggravate matters, Hegel's difficult technical verbiage, complicated expositions, and vague philosophical references to his predecessors sometimes confuse even the most sympathetic Hegelians, and Schopenhauer has little patience with it. For his own part, Schopenhauer is certain that his philosophy has solved the most profound problems of human existence, and when reflecting upon Hegel's fame, he cannot but feel that a charlatan in conjunction with a gullible population has prevented his public recognition as a leading philosopher of the time.

It is tempting to conclude from all of this that Schopenhauer's and Hegel's philosophies are miles apart. Such an estimation, though, would overlook their fundamental accord in rejecting Kant's claim that metaphysical knowledge is forever beyond human reach. Against Kant, both argue that, since the same being that constitutes the rest of the universe constitutes us as well, when we know ourselves we simultaneously know the world's essence. Schopenhauer and Hegel drift apart because their introspections reveal different foundations at the core of human being: Schopenhauer discerns an ever-striving, blind, unintelligent, and meaningless Will; Hegel discerns the dialectical, rational, and reconciliatory structure of self-consciousness.

Despite this difference, the underlying formal structures of their views are alike. Both assert that the non-material essence of the world objectifies into an array of self-opposing forms; both assert that this objectification begins with inanimate matter, ascends gradually through plants and animals, and arrives at the human being. Both assert that the human being represents the most developed stage of this objectification. Both formulate their philosophy in terms of a single principle (viz., Will or self-consciousness) in reference to which we understand everything else.

Each accordingly employs a logical style (dialectical logic in the case of Hegel; manifestational logic in the case of Schopenhauer) that aims to unify opposites and reveal that an all-permeating oneness, rather than a duality or diversity, is the universe's underlying quality. Both articulate their philosophies according to the model of an integrated and healthy organism in which the parts of their respective views depend upon each other in a mutually supportive fashion, where the beginning presupposes the end, and vice versa. In sum, although each starts with a different philosophical grasp of the world's essence, they elaborate their philosophies along structurally similar lines.

ii labor, imprisonment, and christianity

The correspondences between Schopenhauer's and Hegel's philosophies do not end with their structural likenesses. Further affinities stem from their common assumption that the true philosophy coheres with Christianity's central beliefs. Hegel, impressed by the notion of divine incarnation, develops the religious idea that human beings are made in God's image and that God is a morally good, rational being. He expresses this in a distinctively philosophical way, proposing that self-consciousness is divine, and that the universe is the physical realization of self-consciousness. Schopenhauer, impressed by the Christian message that compassion is both a moral and divine quality, develops a compassion-based moral theory whose leading feature is a universalistic, Christ-like transformation of consciousness that follows from adopting an empathetic attitude. Acknowledging the presence of this empathetic awareness in Buddhism and Hinduism, he furthermore regards his philosophy as uniquely cosmopolitan and not as exclusively Christian.

An equally resonant agreement between Schopenhauer and Hegel concerns their shared perception that labor, suffering, work, and self sacrifice inhere in the human condition, and that these are necessary for personal development, salvation, enlightenment, and the apprehension of truth. The image of Jesus carrying the cross to his physical death and spiritual ascension inspires both philosophers, and they develop philosophies that express in abstract terms Jesus's torturous passion and heavenly end. Hegel's version is historical; Schopenhauer's, ahistorical. Hegel's tone is more theistic; Schopenhauer translates the Christian moral message into an atheistic format that is compatible with other religions.

Hegel envisions human history as a slaughter bench that recalls Jesus's crucifixion and salvation, whereas Schopenhauer perceives history as an endless self-flagellation of the Will that feasts on itself, subject to periodic relief through universalistic modes of awareness. Both presentations contain an unimaginable amount of violence, blood, and pain, and although they interpret the meaning of this violence differently, they imagine equally attractive endpoints and consolations: for Hegel, the world-historical endpoint is a future society of mutually respecting, Jesus-like people. For Schopenhauer, an ascetic and tranquilizing denial-of-the-Will preserves a standing capacity to produce peace of mind for anyone, at least in principle.

Schopenhauer's characterizations of the Will as a blind, constantly striving, irrational, and unconscious force are well known, but it is rarely noticed that these characterizations also join Schopenhauer to the tradition of labor-related, Hegelian, and Marxist social theorizing. This tradition aims to overcome alienation within social relationships and the workplace, and it projects a genuine hope for a more harmonious society. Schopenhauer tends to dwell upon individual transcendence, eternalistic states of consciousness, and the denial-of-the-Will, but his philosophy also offers a constructive response to the conditions of alienated labor, undesired servitude, and frustrated human relationships.

To discern this labor-related aspect of Schopenhauer's philosophy, we can consider some of his characterizations of the human condition:

> From the start, the intellect is a hired hand assigned to a miserable task at which its overly demanding master, the will, keeps it busy from morning until night. If there is an occasion during an hour of leisure, however, when this hard-driven, drudging servant produces a piece of work of his own free

will, from his own initiative and without any secondary motives, merely for his own satisfaction and delight, then this is a genuine work of art, and indeed, if taken to great heights, a work of genius.[2]

. . . the intellect has originated merely to serve the will. But it is exactly in that respect that we have it in common with the animals. The intellect is the slave of need, carries the stamp of our miserableness, and we appear in it so fittingly like *glebae adscripti* [soil-bound serfs].[3]

The intellect, as a mere slave and bondsman of the will, is not αυτο µατος [*automatos*] like the will, or active from its own power and own impulse. Hence it is easily pushed aside by the will, and through the latter's wave, brought to silence. While for its own part, it can hardly bring the will to a short pause with the most extreme effort, in order to be able to speak.[4]

. . . then the peace that was always sought on the first path of willing, but that always escaped us, appears all at once on its own, and all is completely well for us. It is the painless condition that Epicurus prized as the highest good and as the condition of the gods. For we are rid of the contemptible pressure of the will at that moment; we celebrate the Sabbath of the penitential work of the will. The wheel of Ixion stands still.[5]

Schopenhauer regards daily life as comparable to that of a slave, serf, or prisoner. Similar to animals as well, our physical desire provides few moments of relaxation, for our will-to-live pushes and pulls us, like a marionette, to eat, want, grasp, and move forward to some next goal. Animals are slaves to the Will and have no freedom; people tend to be dominated by their animality, and to that extent slave-like conditions prevail. Such is Schopenhauer's vision of daily life, as he notes further how a feeling of bondage arises from realizing that we are not essentially animals, as we sense that the worldly desires that drive us physically are alien to our true, timeless personality.

Schopenhauer's taskmaster is not a factory owner, landlord, or tyrant. It is the thing-in-itself as Will in its human manifestation. The oppressor is the very kernel of the world as it appears with its myriad, shifting divisions crystallized by us through the lens of the PSR. As manifestations of the Will, we condemn ourselves to slavery and cast ourselves out of the Garden of Eden, simply by following our natural drives in the quest for scientific knowledge. We enjoy the fruits of worldly knowledge, but we do so within a dungeon of work, suffering, and bondage to human desire. Schopenhauer consequently regards the world as representation – the daily world – as a vast penitentiary. His escape manual is *The World as Will and Representation*, which describes the layout of this prison and reveals how we can liberate ourselves through the universalistic doors that lie hidden in the prison's spatio-temporal walls.[6]

In the world as representation, reason is typically the slave of the passions, but Schopenhauer adds that the exercise of reflective disengagement can minimize the driving force of our natural tendencies. Insofar as we are intelligible characters, however, we are essentially independent of space and time, and of our physical bodies and drives. By reflectively raising ourselves to a level of consciousness that is detached from the individualized, spatio-temporal Will, we can position ourselves to become authentic creators and behave more truly in accord with our timeless being. In this way, the freedom from the Will comes to the foreground of consciousness through artistic creation, and non-alienated labor peacefully and contemplatively becomes a reality.

Artistic activity is one of the few liberating activities within Schopenhauer's philosophy that involves a strong engagement with the spatio-temporal world. Such activity matches what Hegel and Marx identify as free human labor, as opposed to frustrating master–servant relationships that carry with them demeaning exploitation and incomplete forms of human recognition. Within Schopenhauer's outlook, the emergence of acquired character is a special type of artistic creation, and both are positive responses to the problem of alienated labor.

If we interpret Schopenhauer's prescription of the denial-of-the-Will as a call to disengage ourselves from a merciless taskmaster, his philosophy becomes a theory of liberation that resonates with Stoicism – a contemplative viewpoint that ascends to spiritual freedom within the context of material imprisonment. His philosophy also reflects the situation of early Christians, who were subjected to Roman oppression and who followed Jesus's assertion that the true world is not of the earthly type but is located in a realm beyond.

As is now becoming obvious, Schopenhauer represents a familiar position that describes us as enslaved to our animal drives, where disinterested activity partially releases us from this servitude, and where a purely contemplative state of consciousness provides an ultimate disengagement and liberation. It is fundamentally intolerable for Schopenhauer that we remain suffering as the slave of the Will. It improves the situation if we are creative artists, and if we dwell in a mostly desire-free, detached state of consciousness, it is close to ideal.

Labor, struggle, and suffering also permeate the atmosphere of Hegel's philosophy. In his *Phenomenology of Spirit*, he argues that we can reach absolute knowledge only by working through a hierarchy of ever-more comprehensive outlooks, beginning with rudimentary, sensation-oriented perspectives and progressing to increasingly complicated, culturally sophisticated ones. He describes the process as a series of stations along the way of the soul, recalling Jesus' carrying of the cross to his execution, where each stage marks a kind of death. The development of each perspective, no matter what it happens to be, requires that we forsake its seemingly unshakable assumptions, for only in this way can we experience a metanoia or metamorphosis into a more comprehensive and more truthful outlook. To become a mature tree, we cannot remain a seed, and every seed must shed its life as a seed before it can unfold its stems, leaves, buds, blossoms, and fruits.

In Hegel's mature philosophy, the world's developmental process follows the above type of pattern: through internal conflicts that require war, death, and suffering each period of human history develops its rational potential laboriously and painfully towards a more enlightened social system. Just as an individual must suffer to enjoy the standpoint of surveying human history from a wider and unconditional perspective, human beings as a whole must suffer to enjoy the future condition of a perfectly harmonious society and ultimate self-understanding. Both Schopenhauer's and Hegel's philosophies of labor present the same kind of end: we, either individually or as a social collectivity, endure a long and painful path to a state of consciousness where tensions are resolved or sublimated, where knowledge prevails, and where a feeling of unity dominates within a relatively timeless awareness.

Schopenhauer emphasizes the feeling of unity in a personal, private, and non-spatio-temporal manner that accentuates the experience of universal content almost exclusively; Hegel emphasizes the feeling of an ideally social unity amidst a complicated diversity of historical details in a more public, down-to-earth fashion. Schopenhauer's heaven is a meditative, if open-eyed, detachment from the spatio-temporal world; Hegel's heaven is the sphere of enthusiastic, mutually respecting social involvement, matching a more liberal and reformed interpretation of Christian ideals.

iii *the world as will and representation* and "self-consciousness" in hegel's *phenomenology*

We can informatively contrast Schopenhauer's and Hegel's conceptions of salvation against the background of Hegel's analysis of self-consciousness, for this analysis sheds a different light on Schopenhauer and probably reflects how Hegel was interpreting Schopenhauer's philosophy when he met him in 1820. Hegel's 1807 discussion valuably includes the Schopenhauerian style of outlook as a passing phase, implicitly criticizing the finality Schopenhauer ascribed to his own view.

It is unfortunate that we rarely read or discuss Schopenhauer's *The World as Will and Representation* in conjunction with the famous "Self-Consciousness" section of Hegel's *Phenomenology*, since this section encapsulates Schopenhauer's view so well. Hegel begins with the perspective of a self-confident, self-centered, combative, and antisocial consciousness, foreshadowing how Schopenhauer conceives of the egoistic, will-driven, craving-consumed individual. "Desire" is the prevailing state of mind, in which we aim to destroy or control whatever presents itself to us as an alien being. When filled with a consuming desire such as raw hunger, for instance, the thought is only of self-preservation and individual freedom, as we aim aggressively to eliminate all threats to the realization of our desire.

Hegel agrees with Schopenhauer that it is impossible to satisfy oneself completely in a condition of self-centered desire, since this mentality's controlling and destroying attitude undermines itself. To begin, it is impossible to control or destroy everything that enters threateningly or attractively into view, but, beyond this, insofar as we succeed in destroying or controlling these things, our dependence on them increases, rather than decreases. Trying to secure our freedom by means of aggression only tightens the bondage to the things from which we aim to be free. An attractive dwelling or social status, for example, may first stand as a something that "someone else" has, but after we acquire the desired item, bondage to it follows, since its loss would diminish our sense of security.

If we attend not to physical objects but to other people who threaten our freedom and the realization of our desires, repeating the strategies of destruction and possession yield the same self-defeating results. By trying to kill others, we eliminate the very people we require to recognize our victory. By choosing instead to control them, as if they were our property, we receive a respectful sort of recognition as their superiors, but this superior position provides a meager satisfaction, since the recognition comes from inferiors for whom we have little respect. Equally frustrating is the inferior position, for although inferiors receive recognition from superiors whom they respect (or at least fear), the superiors' recognition is condescending and disrespectful.

It is consequently futile either to allow ourselves to be subjugated, or to act as a superior, aggressive, commanding type for the sake of feeling free, since the inevitably attendant, asymmetrical social relations create a prison of their own. This insight sums up the first half of Hegel's analysis of self-consciousness, and it likewise applies within Schopenhauer's world of representation, where the will-to-live selfishly dominates. The second half of Hegel's analysis reacts to this frustrating situation by describing some styles of disengagement from the world, since the hopelessness of violently securing our freedom by destroying or owning other things and people has now become clear. These styles of disengagement correspond to Schopenhauer's prescriptions for minimizing suffering.

Hegel identifies the attitude of stoical detachment as the initial style of withdrawal from the daily world of destroyers, aggressors, consumers, possessors, predators, and exploiters. Schopenhauer also advocates this kind of withdrawal, but Hegel gives it an interpretive twist of his own, observing that the stoical consciousness – since it now has little to think about in its detached state of mind – suffers from a feeling of emptiness. This is a new type of frustration, leading the Stoic to return attention to the spatio-temporal world to experience a more knowledge-filled awareness. Hegel gives no weight to the meditative possibility of contentedly submerging oneself Buddhistically in a field of pure emptiness.

The Stoic consequently attends once more to the spatio-temporal world for the sake of a more complicated, less boring experience. This, however, requires a new attitude: preserving the reluctance to engage positively in the frustrating daily world, the Stoic engages with it, but does so in a thoroughly hostile way, reintroducing the aggressive strategies typical of raw desire in a sublimated form. Whatever sensory detail, proposition, or theory happens to present itself, the Stoic does not try to destroy it, but instead effaces it by asserting "no" in every instance. This nullifying attitude accordingly transforms the Stoic into a Skeptic.

The skeptical consciousness does not differ substantially from the desiring consciousness whose project is to destroy alien objects. The Skeptic is not an outright destroyer, but projects a comparable level of aggression on a more conceptual level by denying and refuting entities such as beliefs, propositions, and theories. The Skeptic expresses desire in a modified form, but this does not prevent him or her from exhibiting the same sorts of problems that accompany raw desire.

Schopenhauer's prescription of the denial-of-the-Will corresponds to this skeptical attitude. For any desire that presents itself, Schopenhauer advises us to say "no" to the desire in an effort to free ourselves from its domination. No desire is exempt. Hegel's Skeptic refutes theories, assertions, and propositions, whereas Schopenhauer's Ascetic renounces desires, motivations, stimuli, and impulses, but both embody the same negative attitude in their engagement with the world.

Hegel observes that this nullifying attitude backfires, since the activity of denying whatever proposition happens to present itself entails the assimilation of contradictory views. What the Skeptic acknowledges today, it denies tomorrow, and it consequently becomes confused and destabilized over time. As a path to inner peace, skepticism works poorly.

The Skeptic eventually attains a relatively stable self-conception by coalescing its chaotic condition into two opposing aspects: it conceives of itself as a desire-driven body and a pure, reflective mind. It seeks stability and truth by identifying solely with the pure, reflective mind, and by denying that the desire-driven body is essential to who he or she is. This transforms the skeptical consciousness into a religious consciousness, in which one aspect is held up to be true, essential, unchanging, and divine, and in which the other is cast down as false, unessential, changing, merely animalistic, and fleshly. This religious consciousness – now polarized into superior and inferior aspects of its own – aims to exist exclusively as its superior, divine aspect. This mental purification is also the *prima facie* aim of Schopenhauerian asceticism.

Hegel's description of this inwardly divided religious consciousness – the "Unhappy Consciousness" as he calls it – closely reflects Schopenhauer's characterization of the human situation and accompanying quest for salvation. Following the Kantian distinction between intellect and will, Schopenhauer similarly divides consciousness into two opposing aspects, namely, the pure, painless, Will-less, universal subject of experience and the Will-infected, suffering, individual subject of experience. The former, in its ascetic effort to deny the Will, strives to turn the tables on the desire-driven Will.

We thus have a single consciousness within which a life-and-death struggle takes place, fought between the universal subject and the individual subject. Each personality tries to dominate and to annihilate the other's presence. The desire-driven, individual subject tries to lower the universal subject into the condition of an instinct-driven animal, while the universal subject of experience tries to renounce as many worldly desires as possible, aiming to achieve pure transcendence and peace. In the course of the battle, sometimes the individual subject prevails and sometimes the universal subject prevails, as flesh and spirit fight bitterly with one another and alternatively dominate.

Within this internal life-and-death struggle, the ascetic, universalistic consciousness is as hard on the individual, desire-driven consciousness, as the desire-driven consciousness is on the ascetic. Both are relentlessly oppressive, each aims to annihilate the other, both use force, and both aspire equally to be master of consciousness as a whole. Schopenhauer believes – and this *prima facie* marks the culmination of his philosophy – that the ascetic consciousness can win this war, and that it can realize a condition of relatively permanent tranquility. He also believes that few are spiritually strong enough to prevail, and that most are doomed to do the biddings of insatiable desire.

Hegel's analysis does not end at this point, and he describes how the religious consciousness continues to transform. A benefit of his analysis resides in the more refined interpretation of Schopenhauer's asceticism that it makes possible. According to Hegel, after the inner war between the flesh and spirit continues with neither aspect experiencing total victory, there is a dawning realization. It is that this life-and-death conflict between two aspects of one's consciousness – the divine aspect and the worldly aspect – *itself* constitutes an intimate and repulsive instance of one's inherently violent nature. This reflection causes the ascetic to identify with *neither* its divine aspect *nor* its worldly aspect and to locate its more enlightened point of tranquility in the non-substantial interface between the two. The ascetic consequently ceases to identify with either aspect of its conflicted consciousness and, like the skeptic, it says "no" to both halves of itself. It identifies with a sheer point of nothingness by more reflectively detaching itself from its own violent quest for independence. This reveals a more advanced stage of self-consciousness in which even the general desire not to desire anything is set aside, and it more closely matches the Buddhist conception of nirvana as the extinction of desire.

Hegel's analysis of the Unhappy Consciousness continues even beyond this Buddhistically suspended consciousness that, resting in a highly reflective condition, identifies with neither spirit nor flesh. For Hegel, this point of suspension serves only to reintroduce the problem of Stoicism, for he believes that the suspended self-consciousness cannot but experience a terrible emptiness and feeling of being absolutely lost. This triggers a descent into nihilistic despair as both flesh and spirit lose their value, as there is no longer anything with which to identify, except for a dimensionless transitional point or a "nothing."

This doubly-interpretable, nihilisitic/nirvanic point of suspension marks the genuine crossroads between Schopenhauer and Hegel, for Hegel's analysis continues on the assumption that a positive engagement with the spatio-temporal world is inevitable, whereas Schopenhauer maintains that the suspension of consciousness from painful engagement with the world is a tranquil end in itself. Hegel conceives of this Schopenhauerian state of mind as nihilistic and despairing, but this is because he is convinced that a sense of personal meaning is possible only through positive, rationally motivated activity in the daily world. Schopenhauer, alternatively, discovers a value in rest itself and in taking worldly meanings lightly, including the meanings associated with the hard, self-disciplined life of the ascetic.

In the end, we can interpret Schopenhauer's philosophy as concluding not with a victorious mystical ecstasy that sets one's fleshly being to nought, but with a more practical, universal indifference to the daily world, accompanied by a deep peace of mind. The contentment associated with having acquired such a peace of mind overcomes any sense of boredom that might otherwise arise, for boredom itself arises only when one is immersed in a field of desire that is not satisfied by one's present position. This state of peace would perhaps define a more enduring rest, since the desire for mystical ecstasy only throws one back into the frustrating and unwinnable war against the desire-filled human body.

notes

1   The phrase is a modification of the slogan – "one for all, and all for one" – of the three musketeers in Alexandre Dumas's novel of the same name (*Les Trois Mousquetaires*, 1844).

2 *PP* (II), Chapter III, "Ideas Concerning the Intellect Generally and in all Respects," §50, P 68–9, ZA 79.

3 *PP* (II), Chapter III, "Ideas Concerning the Intellect Generally and in all Respects," §50, P 70, ZA 80.

4 *WWR* (II), Chapter XIX, "On the Primacy of the Will in Self-Consciousness," P 212, HK 426, ZA 247.

5 *WWR* (I), Book III, §38, P 196, HK 254, ZA 253.

6 Michel Foucault (1926–84), similarly concerned with the theme of liberation, used the image of the penitentiary as a model for social institutions in general. See his book *Discipline and Punish – The Birth of the Prison* (1975).

further reading

Fox, Michael (ed.), *Schopenhauer: His Philosophical Achievement* (New Jersey: Barnes & Noble Books, 1980).

Lauer, Quentin, *A Reading of Hegel's "Phenomenology of Spirit"* (New York: Fordham University Press, 1976).

McGill, V. J., *Schopenhauer: Pessimist and Pagan* (New York: Haskell House Publishers, 1971).

Marx, Karl, "The Economic and Philosophical Manuscripts of 1844," in *The Marx–Engels Reader*, ed. Robert C. Tucker (New York and London: W. W. Norton & Company, 1978).

Soll, Ivan, *An Introduction of Hegel's Metaphysics* (Chicago and London: The University of Chicago Press, 1969).

Solomon, Robert C., *In the Spirit of Hegel* (Oxford: Oxford University Press, 1983).

schopenhauer, wittgenstein, and the unspeakable

i the quest for absolute value

Although outside of academic circles his name is often only vaguely recognized, Ludwig Wittgenstein (1889–1951) was one of the most influential and enigmatic philosophers in the twentieth-century Anglo-American tradition. Among his works, his *Tractatus Logico-Philosophicus* (1921) and his posthumously published *Philosophical Investigations* (1953) have influenced scores of leading writers in the philosophies of language, art, morals, logic, mathematics, and science.

Categorizing Wittgenstein as an Anglo-American philosopher only partially reveals his significance, since his thought also reflects the *fin-de-siècle* Viennese culture within which he grew up. Wittgenstein's father, Karl, was one of the wealthiest industrialists in the Habsburg Empire, and his socially powerful family was filled with talented, aesthetically minded individuals. As Wittgenstein matured within this privileged environment, he developed an interest in mechanical engineering (working on airplane propeller designs), and as he reached maturity it transformed into a more reflective desire to understand the philosophical foundations of logic and mathematics.

To advance his education, he corresponded with one of the foremost mathematician-logicians of the time, Gottlob Frege (1848–1925), who recommended that Wittgenstein study in England with the relatively younger Bertrand Russell (1872–1970), another leader in the field whose work in mathematical logic had been refining and developing Frege's insights. Wittgenstein consequently moved to Cambridge in 1911 with a background steeped in music and art and stamped with the philosophy of one of the most popular writers among the Viennese intellectuals at the turn of the century – namely, Arthur Schopenhauer.

While at the University of Cambridge, Wittgenstein studied mathematical logic and the philosophy of language, and, from a quick glance at the technicality and rigor of his work, it would be surprising to learn that Schopenhauer had any significant influence on him. That presence is evident, though, in Wittgenstein's first book, the *Tractatus Logico-Philosophicus* – a work that is solidly grounded in his logical studies with Russell, but which explores the Kantian question about where the limits of human comprehension reside. Wittgenstein develops the position that formal logic establishes the basic contours of what we can factually express, and that formal logic's limits define the limits of the scientific world.

Wittgenstein read Schopenhauer's *The World as Will and Representation* as a teenager and probably again in his late twenties, as an Austrian soldier during World War One. This is clear from a few passages in his 1916 wartime notebooks that respond directly to Schopenhauer's text. These concern the meaning of life and are upshots of Wittgenstein's environment at the time, for he was asking himself how he would react under combat conditions, and was testing himself by bravely volunteering for dangerous assignments. He filled his wartime notebooks with technical logical reflections, but there is a scattering of entries that address the nature of good, evil, and life's meaning. At the time, he was also carrying a copy of Leo Tolstoy's *Gospels in Brief* for moral support.

Some of these notebook entries reappear in the concluding passages of the *Tractatus*, published shortly after the war, but, since they are cryptic and few, it has been common to interpret them as serving superficially to render the logical conclusions merely more dramatic. Owing to the placement and limited number of these meaning-of-life-oriented remarks, Schopenhauer's influence on Wittgenstein initially presents itself as having been of only minor significance. He seems to have briefly stimulated Wittgenstein's reflections about life's meaning during a stressful time, and some of the remarks – most of which are presumed to be unessential for understanding the *Tractatus*'s lines of argument – appeared innocuously in this latter work.

This impression is reinforced by the fact that, to date, Schopenhauer's name does not appear substantially, if at all, in many books on Wittgenstein. Most studies tend to portray his philosophical interests as either predominantly logical, mathematical, linguistic, pragmatic, or essentially secular in nature. Adding to this impression is Wittgenstein's own reluctance to speculate about traditional metaphysical questions, not to mention his later view that such questions lack linguistic meaning.

There is an interpretive issue, then, about whether Schopenhauer influenced Wittgenstein beyond his having been among the first philosophers he read as a youth and whom he recalled briefly during the war in soul-searching times. It is indeed easy to suppose that after World War One, Wittgenstein left behind the influence of Germanic philosophy with the *Tractatus*'s publication and slowly gravitated into a different style of philosophizing – the one for which he became famous – that focuses on ordinary linguistic practices. With an extraordinarily pragmatic mind-set that is absent in Schopenhauer, Wittgenstein's later work concentrates on how we use words in the course of daily life, and on how everyday linguistic practices and their underlying grammar are the final court of appeal for describing, interpreting, and evaluating philosophical problems. With respect to determining the degree of Schopenhauer's influence on Wittgenstein, it is thus important to consider the extent to which Wittgenstein's later philosophy retains the spirit of his earlier thought.

On the surface of things, the *Tractatus* exclusively concerns formal logic and linguistic meaning, and, at the time of its writing, Wittgenstein believed that formal logic establishes the basic structure of all possible facts. As noted above, he defines the world as the set of all facts, adding that since formal logic circumscribes the limits of what we can say literalistically, it consequently circumscribes the limits of the world.

This thematically aligns Wittgenstein's *Tractatus* with Kant's *Critique of Pure Reason*, for both examine and define the limits of human capacities in reference to logical structures. Wittgenstein uses logic to define the preconditions for articulated thought and literalistic linguistic meaning; Kant uses it more specifically to define the preconditions for human experience. Both agree that logic plays an essential role in establishing such limits, and both assert that beyond the limits of logic, strictly speaking, we can say nothing definitive. In the face of the unknown, the unknowable, and the non-provable they officially adopt an attitude of silence.

Wittgenstein concludes the *Tractatus* with the often-quoted remark, "whereof one cannot speak, thereof one must be silent," provoking his readers to wonder immediately how to interpret this silence, either as thin and empty, or as deep and profound. If all thought is linguistically constituted, then the silence would be non-indicative and meaningless. If not all thought is linguistically constituted, however, then the silence could carry a wordless significance that could only be pointed to, shown, or hinted at.

In the *Tractatus*, Wittgenstein has in mind the second, affirmative form of silence, for he distinguishes facts from values, positively acknowledges values, and associates values with silence. For him, the world is only a set of facts that are valueless in themselves. Value, he maintains, resides outside of the world (*Tractatus*, 6.41) and by "value," he intends *absolute* or *necessary* value, or, as he describes it, value that is actually *worth* something, as opposed to being merely accidental and transitory. Wittgenstein locates ethical value and aesthetic value here, in an otherworldly, foundational, and transcendent realm.

We need not examine the coherency of this position to estimate Schopenhauer's influence. More revealing is the coincidence between Wittgenstein's realm of facts (that is to say, what he calls "the world") and the "phenomenal world" of both Kant and Schopenhauer. The latter philosophers describe this world as one wherein the way we apprehend things does not present how those things are in themselves. This is also a world where there are no absolute values, for these reside elsewhere, outside of space and time. Equally importantly, the Kantian and Schopenhauerian phenomenal world is a thoroughly describable scientific world, purely factual, and governed by logical modes of thought.

Given these correspondences, Wittgenstein built the *Tractatus* upon some of the basic distinctions and questions that underlie Kant's and Schopenhauer's theories. As do Kant and Schopenhauer, he also divides everything into two spheres – variously definable as the spheres of "fact vs. value," or "science vs. morality," or "the sayable vs. the unsayable" – maintaining that without the otherworldly sphere of values, daily life would have no meaning. The difference is that in the place of Kant's logically-derived categories of the understanding and of Schopenhauer's principle of sufficient reason (PSR), Wittgenstein substitutes a more advanced form of mathematical logic to the same, if not more wide-ranging, philosophical end, since he aims to define the limits of linguistic meaning in general, rather than the narrower sphere of possible human experience.

When considering Schopenhauer's influence on Wittgenstein, it consequently helps to ask whether Wittgenstein's views in the *Tractatus* and in his later philosophy also have a Kantian resonance. We will see that his views stand exactly between the two. After the *Tractatus*, it is difficult to find Wittgenstein articulating any of the arguments that distinguish Schopenhauer from Kant, but he does express what Schopenhauer and Kant have in common.

As we know, Schopenhauer argues that the ultimate nature of things is describable as Will, whereas Kant holds that the absolute truth is unknowable. Kant speculates that it could reasonably contain God, freedom, and immortality, but he admits this as only rational speculation. In an early notebook entry from October 1916, Wittgenstein refers in a Schopenhauerian way to the "world-will," but by the time we reach the *Tractatus* and his later works it is difficult to find him subscribing to any view that positively describes the ultimate nature of reality. Noticeably remaining is a Kantian tone of reservation in the face of the unknown.

We therefore need to look equally towards Kant as towards Schopenhauer in forming an appreciation of the overall impact

Schopenhauer had on Wittgenstein. The evidence suggests that Wittgenstein initially read Schopenhauer, discerned an illuminating Kantian thread that he retained in the long run, and only temporarily subscribed to the Schopenhauerian metaphysics of the Will. As his philosophy developed, and as the Kantian thread became more salient, he became increasingly non-expressive in his later works about whether there is anything beyond the daily world to which we can meaningfully refer. Central to this attitude is the claim that all knowledge in the factual, scientific sense, is restricted to the daily world, that is, the world of space and time.

Wittgenstein's linguistic orientation is squarely in tune with, and significantly definitive of, the spirit of twentieth-century Anglo-American philosophy. With this linguistic attentiveness of Wittgenstein's in mind, we can read one of Kant's most influential passages in a different light, speculating how it might have inspired Wittgenstein when he read it himself at the end of World War One. In this vein, we can interpret Kant as referring to the bounds of *linguistic* meaning of the term "space," when he states famously that outside of the human standpoint, space stands for nothing:

> We can therefore speak [*reden*] about space, of extended things, etc., only from the human standpoint. If we depart from the subjective conditions under which we can alone have outer intuition, which is namely our capacity to be affected by objects, the representation of space has no meaning at all [*bedeutet gar nichts*].[1]

Since Kant refers here to what we can speak about, and since he directs our attention to the linguistic meaning of the word, "space," this passage might have led Wittgenstein to develop a Kantian approach to philosophical problems, using mathematical logic in the place of Aristotelian logic, space, and time. If we furthermore acknowledge a distinction between linguistic meaning and mystically apprehended meaning, then a position for Wittgenstein opens midway between Kant and Schopenhauer. This agrees with Kant in that we can publicly say nothing knowingly about the absolute truth, while it agrees with Schopenhauer in that we can nonetheless know this truth, albeit mystically and privately.

ii what the *philosophical investigations* cannot say

The influence of Schopenhauer's metaphysics of the Will on the early Wittgenstein is evident from the latter's First World War notebooks. In the *Tractatus* as well, a Schopenhauerian spirit remains in the

Kantianism we can discern. The question to ask next is whether Schopenhauer's positive influence persists in Wittgenstein's later works. These refute the *Tractatus* insofar as they deny the fundamentality of formal logic and substitute ordinary language in its place. This gap between the *Tractatus* and the later works suggests that Schopenhauer did not significantly influence the later Wittgenstein.

One would consequently assume that the paradigm work of this period, the *Philosophical Investigations* (published posthumously in 1953, but written by Wittgenstein during the mid-1940s), simply embodies a different, anti-metaphysical spirit. To appreciate how this is not obviously the case, and how there is a thematic continuity of Schopenhauerian import between the earlier and later Wittgenstein, we can consider some remarks Wittgenstein made in his Lecture on Ethics of 1929, which continue his reflections on the nature of absolute value.

In this lecture, Wittgenstein defines ethics as the inquiry into the right way to live. This is a way that reflects what is absolutely valuable, essentially important, and makes life worth living. His practical concern is with living in tune with absolute value, rather than living in accord merely with relative or conditional values, all of which he believes are reducible to factual descriptions. In the *Tractatus*, Wittgenstein defines the world as the set of facts, and it follows both there and in this Lecture, that absolute values – and the meaning of life – reside outside of science, facts, and, most importantly, linguistic expressibility. In the daily world, we do not encounter what ultimately counts, and if we try to speak definitively about absolute value, we speak nonsensically. This, once again, leaves us with an ambiguous silence, either as indicative of an inexpressible realm of absolute value, or as a non-entity that makes no sense even to indicate. The former, following Schopenhauer, we can refer to as a relative nothingness that does not preclude a mystical apprehension of absolute value. The latter would be an absolute nothingness that renders unconditional value meaningless, and that leaves the daily world, ordinary language and customs, as the only world that there is.

This ambiguity about whether there is anything significant beyond words inheres in Wittgenstein's later philosophy as well. We find it in his claim – similar to that of the *Tractatus* – that we cannot speak meaningfully about anything that surpasses the bounds of our ordinary language. Many of Wittgenstein's remarks suggest that he recognizes nothing positive beyond these linguistic bounds, and they invite the judgment that he is either a relativist, or, worse yet, a nihilist who regards philosophical problems as nothing more than grammatical jokes:

> The problems arising through a misinterpretation of our forms of languages have the character of *depth*. They are deep disquietudes; their roots are deep in us as the forms of our language and their significance is as great as the

importance of our language. – Let us ask ourselves: why do we feel a grammatical joke to be deep? (And that is what the depth of philosophy is.)[2]

This excerpt compares nicely to how Kant believes that our reason
leads us, quite inevitably, to speculate about what lies beyond the
bounds of possible human experience, and how these speculations yield
no knowledge. Kant refers to them as reason-generated illusions: we
expansively project truths beyond human experience, but our human
finitude denies their proof. Kant admits that these rational speculations
(about God's existence, for instance) are meaningful, and he allows for
faith in their truth. Wittgenstein, however, goes a step further and
denies the meaningfulness of linguistic formulations that express traditional philosophical problems. The deadly effect is to send centuries-old
philosophical problems into oblivion, for once we realize that these
problems issue from the inner workings of our language itself, like the
rumble in a car engine, their objective significance disappears, just as a
joke reduces to insignificance, what we once believed to be serious.

Dissolving the linguistic significance of traditional philosophical
problems does not imply, however, that the questions are ignorantly
motivated. It remains that an unspeakable, non-linguistic awareness can
answer to these problems, and that whatever philosophy strives to
express through precisely worded arguments can only be addressed by
someone in his or her own wordless privacy and solitude. This amounts
to mysticism, or the idea that absolute truth reveals itself through a
kind of subjectivity, for which there are no consistent expressions.
Wittgenstein's *Philosophical Investigations* remains open to this kind
of reading, for he is exceedingly careful to restrict his discussions to
what can meaningfully be said, and his attack on philosophy to linguistic formulations *per se*.

We can also discern in *Philosophical Investigations* the interest in
absolute versus relative values that Wittgenstein expresses in his
Lecture on Ethics. He maintains in his 1929 lecture that there are values
that we *can* talk about meaningfully, and that these are only relative
values. In his later philosophy of the 1940s these relative values find
their expression within a specific form of life and its associated set of linguistic practices, since everything that can be said remains relative to
the constraints of one's language. Again, this does not imply that there
are no absolute values, but rather that if there are any, they can only be
mystically, personally, and wordlessly apprehended.

Consistently enough, Wittgenstein does not discuss such a wordless
state of mind, and everything that he does talk about avoids it. Another
way to express this peculiar situation more colloquially is to say that all
linguistic (that is, public) formulations of philosophical problems are
necessarily misleading, and that whatever substance they have remains

exclusively, as the saying goes, between the person and God. Philosophical concerns are not public issues, and we can say nothing about them, even to ourselves, on pain of immediate distortion.

In contrast to this mystical interpretation, Wittgenstein sometimes speaks as if the linguistic dissolution of traditional philosophical problems draws an end to the matter, purely and simply, without indicating any private, language-independent relationship with the cosmos as an alternative. He refers to these philosophical problems as linguistic situations where we do not know our way around, do not know what to say, and are tormented because we feel so semantically lost (*PI*, §133). He also refers to the dissolution of such problems as psychologically relieving and as a therapeutic path to achieving some peace of mind. This sense of relief counts against the mystical interpretation, for if the difficulty resides in merely making the mistake of using public language to express an essentially personal, existential concern, we would expect that upon dissolving the linguistically formulated philosophical problem, the existential concern, and probably a significant amount of free-floating anxiety, would rise to the psychological surface more explicitly.

This yields a more worldly reading of the later Wittgenstein. Here, we can compare the irresolvable puzzlement that philosophical problems are notorious for producing to Schopenhauer's characterization of the perpetually unsatisfied Will, in reference to which one achieves tranquility by means of extinguishing the Will. The picture is non-mystical, and with its implicit identity between linguistic possibility and what is thinkable, it is inescapably embedded in what can only be described as relative conditions and values, much like Buddhism.

We thus encounter in Wittgenstein the same ambiguity about the significance of transcendent states of mind and of "the unspeakable" that we find in Schopenhauer. In both thinkers, the emerging silence allows for two interpretations, either a mystically transcendent interpretation, or a worldly, relativistic, and contingency-based one. In our examination of Schopenhauer, the more worldly interpretation proves to be more consistent, lest the acknowledgment of countless mystical dimensions undermine his metaphysics of the Will. In connection with Wittgenstein, the more transcendent interpretation is more attractive as a token of Schopenhauer's influence, lest Wittgenstein's linguistic philosophy reduce to a pragmatism that extinguishes all private religious spirit. To support this preference, we can recall a criticism that Hegel directed at Kant, note how it applies constructively to Wittgenstein, and add a supporting remark from Wittgenstein about his own positive attitude towards religiosity.[3]

Kant and the early Wittgenstein define the limits of human capabilities in reference to the limits of logic, and, arguably, the later Wittgenstein continues the same project in his *Philosophical*

Investigations, substituting ordinary language for formal logic. In this later work, he states that language, concepts, and sentences are "instruments" (*PI*, §421 and §569). As expressive of a "form of life," he regards our language as an instrument that we use to interact with each other, and his *Philosophical Investigations* examines closely how language works. This is worth noting because Kant similarly regards *reason* as an instrument – one that we use to grasp the truth – whose effectiveness needs to be brought to trial. Kant, like Wittgenstein, concludes that logical structures, or ordinary language in the later Wittgenstein's case, render it impossible for us publicly to know absolute truth or values. In the absence of public knowledge, Kant continues to speculate about these ultimate values; Wittgenstein more consistently remains silent about them.

Hegel's critique of Kant challenges the latter's assumption that our rationality is a single-edged "instrument" that we can use effectively to secure empirical knowledge, but which is simultaneously useless to establish a positive relationship between us and metaphysical truth. The argument, as we have seen in previous chapters, is simple: we cannot assert consistently that any structure – and this can apply to reason, logic, ordinary language, cultural values, and the like – can stand absolutely between us and metaphysical truth, because we are not separate from this truth, but are constituted by it. Whatever governs the cosmos flows through us as well, so examining ourselves can reveal the answers to traditional philosophical problems.

If this post-Kantian insight is sound, it indicates generally that our human finitude does not preclude the awareness of absolute truth and values. Such an awareness can take the form of a publicly-accessible and communicable truth, as Hegel espoused, or it can take the form of a private and inexpressible mysticism, as Schopenhauer sometimes set forth. If we apply this post-Kantian argument to Wittgenstein's discussion of the limits of language, meaning, and forms of life, it reveals that he need not be interpreted as a relativist or nihilist, but that his restriction of meaningful discourse to what our particular form of life publicly dictates, compares to Schopenhauer's and Kant's restriction of factual, objectively valid knowledge to daily life or to mere phenomena. Beyond this, Schopenhauer further admits mystical knowledge (although he hesitated to call it "knowledge" *per se*) and locates it in the realm of the unspeakable. To this extent, the mystical interpretation of Wittgenstein bears a closer resemblance to Schopenhauer than it does to Kant, who was no mystic, and who, although he recognized a realm of absolute value as a matter of principle, precluded our apprehension of it in every way.

Wittgenstein can consequently be seen as residing in an intermediary position between Kant and Schopenhauer, if we take seriously

Wittgenstein's remark in the late 1940s that he regarded every problem from a religious point of view.[4] He contrasts with Schopenhauer and compares to Kant in that he resists public linguistic expressions of absolute truth. He contrasts with Kant and compares to Schopenhauer if we admit that this linguistic philosophy is not all-encompassing and allows some space for what can only be described as a wordless, non-conceptual, purely intuitive apprehension of the ultimate nature of things, lest our lives otherwise become existentially meaningless and without an iota of private religiosity.

In accord with this interpretation, the thematic consistency between Wittgenstein's early and later writings, along with its connection to the philosophical problems addressed by both Kant and Schopenhauer, combine to set Wittgenstein's writings within a wider historical context as extended reflections on the quest for absolute value. Ultimately, we can see that the distinction between the private and the public is at the core of Wittgenstein's philosophy, that he is religiously and profoundly silent about absolute values, and that he goes to great lengths to allow no one to speak meaningfully about them.

Owing in part to the different times in which they lived, the contrast in perspectives between Schopenhauer and Wittgenstein remains pronounced. Wittgenstein remains utterly private to himself, focusing his writings and philosophizing exclusively within the public, observable, practical realm, and eliminating the significance of private sensations in his account of public linguistic meaning. Schopenhauer, writing a century earlier, always returns to the inner standpoint, and he subordinates to this first-person standpoint at virtually every turn, the significance of the daily world of linguistic practices and their associated forms of life. We can appreciate these complementary temperaments in the following excerpts. The first is from Wittgenstein; the second, from Schopenhauer:

> Always get rid of the idea of the private object [e.g., the experience of redness or of pain in connection with the meanings of words such as "red" or "pain"] in this way: assume that it constantly changes, but that you do not notice the change because your memory constantly deceives you.[5]

> An optimist tells me to open my eyes and to see how beautiful the world is with its mountains, plants, fresh air, animals, and so forth. – Naturally these things are beautiful to *behold*, but to *be* them is something quite different.[6]

notes

1 *CPR*, A26/B42.
2 *Philosophical Investigations*, §111.

3 This argument is found in the Introduction of Hegel's *Phenomenology of Spirit*.
4 Norman Malcolm. *Ludwig Wittgenstein – A Memoir* (Oxford: Clarendon Press, 2001), p. 83.
5 *Philosophical Investigations*, Part II, §xi.
6 Schopenhauer, MS III, p. 188.

further reading

Janik, Allan and Stephen Toulmin, *Wittgenstein's Vienna* (New York: Simon and Schuster, 1973).

McGuinness, Brian, *Young Ludwig: Wittgenstein's Life, 1889–1921* (Oxford: Oxford University Press, 2005).

Monk, Ray, *Ludwig Wittgenstein: The Duty of Genius* (New York: Penguin Books, 1991).

Weiner, David Avraham, *Genius and Talent: Schopenhauer's Influence on Wittgenstein's Early Philosophy* (London and Toronto: Associated University Presses, 1992).

conclusion: idealism and the will to peace

i the plausibility of schopenhauer's idealism

For many readers, Schopenhauer's philosophical idealism diminishes his philosophy's plausibility, for common sense and scientific knowledge suggest that long before human beings emerged, the physical universe existed mind-independently with its suns, moons, chemical elements, atomic particles, space, and time. We have seen Schopenhauer argue to the contrary that space and time depend on the presence of conscious awareness – "no object without a subject," he maintains – setting forth a philosophical idealism, following Kant, the appreciation of which requires an imaginative power far beyond the norm. Kant's philosophy has been historically influential, but his doctrine of the mind-dependence of space and time is its most frequently contested feature. Immediate disbelief is therefore more likely than not, upon reading the following:

> Just as the present is, so also is the past from which that present arises, namely, dependent upon the knowing subject and it is nothing without it.[1]

Establishing a more direct road to Schopenhauer's idealism would help render his metaphysics more attractive. One way to do this – and Schopenhauer suggests this method himself – is to imagine what the inanimate physical world is like "in itself" or from within its own perspective, so to speak. If we think of a time when the physical universe contained only inanimate matter, and imaginatively remove ourselves *entirely* from the scene, the result is chilling.

From the internal standpoint of a lifeless universe, that is, from the standpoint of having removed from within it all living standpoints, including imaginative presences, it becomes difficult to distinguish a lifeless universe from there being nothing at all. There is certainly no experiential difference, because a lifeless universe's condition is in fact impossible to imagine from the first-person standpoint, for it has none. Trying to project a first-person standpoint into a physical universe that contains only inanimate objects and no perceivers, amounts to imagining what it is like to be dead. Perhaps one can approximate the uncanny sense of emptiness by thinking about where one "was" when dinosaurs were ruling the Earth.

To accentuate this reflection, let us suppose that life had *never* come into being, and that from the dawn of existence, only inanimate matter had been present. One might ask in this instance, "present to whom?" Things would be, but no one would ever know it, including the things themselves. From an imagined standpoint interior to that universe, there would be no difference between a forever-lifeless physical universe and nothing at all. Such a physical universe forever devoid of conscious beings – without people, animals, spirits, gods, etc. – would be senseless in all respects. To admit that no experience would exist in such a world, amounts to casting doubt on that world's very presence, for if we try to imagine what it is like to "be" that world, it is striking that there is nothing to imagine.

It is nonetheless natural to suppose that the foundation of things is a mind-independent, inanimate being, for otherwise it becomes difficult to explain how, for instance, the configuration of leaves on a tree remains the same when we turn our attention away from it. Day after day, the arbitrary configurations of objects – on one's table, in the rooms of one's dwelling, etc. – appear identical to how one left them the day, and sometimes the year, before. The world's *stability* in its minute contingent qualities is what ordinarily leads to postulating an inanimate mind-independent being. The strange thing is that this inanimate being seems to exist only for us, since in itself, it does not know that it exists.

ii the explanatory weakness of a blind and senseless will

Schopenhauer explains the world's stable and predictable appearance by appealing to the principle of sufficient reason (PSR) – the principle that precipitates, through us, the Will's objectification into the hierarchy of Platonic Ideas. This explains some of the stability within our experience, but a reference to the thing-in-itself as Will is required to account for the exact details of the daily world. The formal structures of the mind explain neither why the colors of the trees, beaches, and deserts have the qualities they do, nor why, in their infinite details, they remain relatively constant and predictable from day to day. Only the thing-in-itself can complete the account for this, and from the standpoint of formulating adequate explanations, it helps if the thing-in-itself were infused with intelligence. The intellectually frustrating aspect of Schopenhauer's metaphysics is that he defines the Will as blind, senseless, and unitary. Unlike God – a being that upholds the world within other non-materialistic philosophies – Schopenhauer's thing-in-itself as Will has no intrinsic intelligence and, unlike the physical world, it has no articulation within itself.

Schopenhauer assigns all rationality, rule-governedness, and spatio-temporal individuation to the PSR. Since the PSR prescribes only general modes of stability, however, the world's contingent features remain without an explanation. This is not to say that the materialistic alternative does not have the same problem. If we suppose that our presence can be traced back to a foundational set of subatomic particles, the question of why these particular sorts of subatomic particles should exist as opposed to others also remains unexplained. Aware of this, Schopenhauer states that we can never get to the inner nature of things from without.[2] Whether he offers a significantly more satisfactory view, though, is questionable.

From the standpoint of formulating explanations – a standpoint that Schopenhauer associates exclusively with the PSR – Schopenhauer's metaphysics of the Will leaves us in a condition of philosophical frustration. We can apprehend that the thing-in-itself is Will, but it is out of bounds to ask why this Will would objectify itself into a being, namely, the human being, that always "asks why." Neither are there reasons why, or how, the thing-in-itself becomes objectified into the specific world we experience, with its particular sets of colors, sounds, tastes, odors, and textures. These questions remain outside the scope of the PSR and, therefore, outside the scope of possible explanation.

Since Schopenhauer's metaphysics refers us to a principle of the universe that is unintelligent, blind, unitary, and meaningless, we can ask a challenging question: if the thought of an inanimate physical universe existing mind-independently on its own brings us so close to thinking about nothing at all, what are we to say about the Will? In-itself, it has no self-consciousness, does not know that it "is," and compares to a person in a deep and dreamless sleep who might never wake up. Within Schopenhauer's view, there is no necessity that the Will must objectify itself in an act of self-awareness. There seems to be little difference between the thing-in-itself as Will, and a mind-independent, inanimate physical universe, if we consider them from the inside, from the standpoint of what it is like to *be* such beings. From the inside, both are indistinguishable from the standpoint of death (that is, no standpoint) and are from that standpoint, non-entities. When the universe contains no experience, it makes no difference whether the ultimate substance is material or non-material. Schopenhauer's Will may have a small metaphysical edge over inanimate matter, since it is not a mind-independent being, but once we remove the reflective human element from among its manifestations, we arrive at not much more than a dreamless, non-explanatory sleep.

From a more practical angle, though, we can construe Schopenhauer's philosophy constructively in existential terms as an attempt to formulate an acceptable life-strategy in the midst of a worst-case spiritual scenario. This is a world where there is no God, no eternal meaning, where the present life meaninglessly pushes and pulls one to and fro like a marionette, and where the future holds nothing more than a reabsorption and absolute extinction into the comatose nothingness from which we have mysteriously emerged. If it is possible to live contentedly in a universe so bleak, then it is possible to live happily under any more fortunate outlook.

This practical standpoint allows us to appreciate Schopenhauer's advanced place in the development of post-Kantian philosophy, for although he believed that Fichte and Hegel were worth skipping over, his view marks a distinctive step in a path from Kant that includes these influential post-Kantian German Idealists. We can reiterate this path briefly and schematically to illustrate Schopenhauer's central role.

As we know, Kant maintains that human beings are forever precluded from knowing the absolute truth, but he also speculates that the universe has a rational core, and that freedom, immortality, and God are possible endpoints in which we can consistently invest our rationally grounded faith. Fichte and Hegel transform Kant's speculations into knowable metaphysical realities, holding that the universe is grounded on either an intrinsically rational act (for Fichte) or rational state of being (for Hegel), and that this is necessarily unfolding into a harmonious and moral society. Kierkegaard – a person who is usually not included in this philosophical sequence – deifies the divine act that grounds the universe, but in recognition of this act's absolute freedom, removes the rational aspect. The god that he finds within himself resonates with the nominalistic God of the fourteenth century – a fearsome and unintelligible God who chooses to do whatever he wants, whenever he wants, for whatever reason.

In light of these various conceptions of the universe's grounding act, Schopenhauer stands as someone who, like Kierkegaard, eliminates rationality from the universe's core, but more consistently refers to this core as blind, meaningless, and as virtually demonic. This precipitates his famous pessimism, for despite his advocacy of asceticism, he does much to dissolve otherworldly hopes. This also reveals Schopenhauer as one of the forefathers of mid-twentieth-century French existentialism, since he refers to the thing-in-itself as non-rational, and since one can equally refer to it as absurd, as do Jean-Paul Sartre and Albert Camus.

More revealing than characterizing the universe's core as either non-rational or absurd, is to refer to it as being unconscious, foreshadowing Sigmund Freud's psychoanalytic theory of the human mind that would be developed in later decades. Schopenhauer removes the often-supposed mind-independent objectivity of the physical world and sets aside the conception of a mind-independent reality altogether. For him, there is only a single subjective energy that he calls "Will" and in itself this Will is unconscious. The model that thereby presents itself to Schopenhauer, as we have noted earlier, is the Upanishadic one from the Mandukya Upanishad that refers to ultimate reality as residing in the fourth state, beyond the waking, dream, and deep dream states. The thing-in-itself as Will, as it objectifies itself, engages in a process that compares to dreaming.

Given his violent conception of the world as representation, the production of the world as representation is more precisely like the production of a nightmare. Schopenhauer's frequent remarks that life is like a dream, point to the more literal meaning that human reality, that is, world history, is the Will's nightmare. For the purposes of salvation from this nightmare, we must escape not only the contents of the nightmare; we must escape also from the unconscious source of the nightmare, namely, the thing-in-itself as Will, which is our very substance. Hence arises Schopenhauer's central doctrine of the denial-of-the-Will and its accompanying attitude of thoroughgoing psychological indifference.

iii the prospect of peace

We can conclude by reflecting once again upon the sort of person Schopenhauer appears to have been, and asking how closely the present interpretation of his philosophy is consistent with that characterization. Schopenhauer was a person of developed aesthetic and moral sensibilities, cosmopolitan sophistication, and religious sensitivity who harbored a dim view of common humanity and who, despite his adequate material surroundings, endured a fair share of frustration and disappointment in his personal affairs and long-term hopes.

Although his overriding interest was in philosophy – and specifically in the philosophies of Kant and Plato – Schopenhauer was friendly to most of the world's main religions and to the natural sciences, as he aimed to achieve a level of philosophical enlightenment that could do justice to religion, philosophy, and science alike. From his attraction to the arts and to aesthetic experience in general, he cultivated a sense of disinterested attention as he celebrated the psychological activities of mental distancing and disengagement as a way to relieve suffering, and as a way to achieve a measure of salvation, tranquility, and meaningful living within a meaningless universe.

To remain consistent with this picture, this study has grounded its interpretation of Schopenhauer by acknowledging first and foremost his Kantian belief that human beings cannot but apprehend reality in a human way. This aspect of humanity – contrary, however, to Kant's conclusions and consistent with Schopenhauer's – has been interpreted as akin to the color of lenses through which we look, or as the faint cloudiness of a piece of translucent glass, either of which introduces a minor imprecision or distortion in our perception of some object. We see it reasonably well through our colored lens or translucent glass, but we do not see it in its absolute purity. This is like hearing a sound as played by a musical instrument: we can discern the pure tone, but only as it is affected by the quality of the instrument through which it sounds, whether this happens to be a flute, trumpet, or violin.

Schopenhauer refers to the distorting human quality within this mode of apprehension as the principle of sufficient reason, which is, for him, a two-layered principle that projects the subject–object distinction in both universalistic and individualistic forms. Individual subjects and objects, and universal subjects and objects, are the productions of our own psyche, leaving in itself at the core of reality nothing more than a blind Will that we can apprehend directly in its bare unity and simplicity. Here, even our timeless, intelligible characters reveal themselves to be artifacts of our general human presence, as shadow-like or as dream-like as the Platonic Ideas. Apprehending the ultimate truth of who we are entails shedding our sense of personality in every one of its forms and resisting the temptation to refer mind-independent realities.

Instead of interpreting Schopenhauer as admitting that the thing-in-itself may have dimensions that are beyond our apprehension of it as "Will" – an interpretation that undermines his practical philosophy of endless desire and suffering – we have noted how, as a human-derived projection of awareness, the eternalistic consciousness of Christian and Yogic mystics subjectively correlates with our projection of Platonic Ideas. The upshot is to characterize the most enlightened mode of ascetic awareness in Buddhistic terms as simply the privation of desire. The sense of peace attained is a kind of release, relief, liberation, relaxation, calming, or reduction of tension, without any special metaphysical significance. We do not step ultimately into a Yogic, all-absorbing bliss, but finally step away Buddhistically from the nightmare to view it with greater psychological detachment.

Upon hearing that Schopenhauer believes that the world is intrinsically meaningless and that people are ordinarily doomed to suffer, it is natural to react to his philosophy in distaste or aversion. In a sense, his philosophy contains no hope, since it promises no rewarding afterlife as it soberly addresses death and the world's injustices. Despite its denial of an individual afterlife, it remains possible to consider the positive, large-scale practical effects of being able to take the world less seriously, of being able to apprehend other people's sufferings as identical to one's own, and of being able to resist the temptation to fight others for a personal increase in territory, money, and power.

Although our intelligible characters, our egos, are illusory according to Schopenhauer, he nonetheless assigns all responsibility to us, stating that the tribunal of the world is the world that we cannot but make for ourselves. His philosophy is grim, but it harbors the remote possibility that since the future remains unseen, greed and selfishness might significantly diminish and inner peace might govern, at least within the human population. Until that redemptive time arrives, the bittersweet motto of Giordano Bruno may be the most appropriate Schopenhauerian attitude towards the ferocious world that, like a mirage, hovers before us decade after decade, and century after century: *In tristitia hilaris, in hilaritate tristis.*[3]

notes

1 *WWR* (I), Book I, §7, P 31, HK 39, ZA 62.
2 *WWR* (I), Book II, §17, P 99, HK 128, ZA 142.
3 "Cheerful in sadness, sad in cheerfulness" was the personal motto of Giordano Bruno (1548–1600), cited by Schopenhauer sympathetically as expressive of an enlightened attitude towards life. (*WWR* [II], Chapter XXXI, "On Genius," P 381, 383, HK 144, 148, ZA 451, 454).

bibliography

works by schopenhauer

Schopenhauer, Arthur, *The World as Will and Idea*, 3 vols., trans. R. B. Haldane and J. Kemp (London: Routledge and Kegan Paul Ltd., 1883).

Schopenhauer, Arthur, *On the Fourfold Root of the Principle of Sufficient Reason and On the Will in Nature: Two Essays by Schopenhauer*, trans. Mme Karl Hillebrand (London: George Bell and Sons, 1891).

Schopenhauer, Arthur, *Essay on the Freedom of the Will*, trans. Konstantin Kolenda (Indianapolis and New York: The Bobbs-Merrill Company, Inc., 1960).

Schopenhauer, Arthur, *On the Basis of Morality*, trans. E. F. J. Payne (Indianapolis and New York: The Bobbs-Merrill Company, Inc., 1965).

Schopenhauer, Arthur, *The World as Will and Representation*, Volumes I and II, trans. E. F. J. Payne (New York: Dover Publications, 1966).

Schopenhauer, Arthur, *The Fourfold Root of the Principle of Sufficient Reason*, trans. E. F. J. Payne (LaSalle, Illinois: Open Court Publishing Company, 1974).

Schopenhauer, Arthur, *Parerga and Paralipomena: Short Philosophical Essays*, Vols I and II, trans. E. F. J. Payne (Oxford: Clarendon Press, 1974).

Schopenhauer, Arthur, *Arthur Schopenhauer, Zürcher Ausgabe, Werke in zehn Bänden* (Zürich: Diogenes Verlag, 1977).

Schopenhauer, Arthur, *Manuscript Remains in Four Volumes*, ed. Arthur Hübscher, trans. E. F. J. Payne (Oxford, New York, Munich: Berg, 1988).

selected books about schopenhauer's philosophy

Atwell, John, *Schopenhauer: The Human Character* (Philadelphia: Temple University Press, 1990).

Atwell, John, *Schopenhauer on the Character of the World – The Metaphysics of the Will* (Berkeley: University of California Press, 1995).

Bridgwater, Patrick, *Arthur Schopenhauer's English Schooling* (London and New York: Routledge, 1988).

Copleston, Frederick, *Arthur Schopenhauer: Philosopher of Pessimism* (London: Burns Oates & Washbourne, 1946).

Dauer, Dorothy, *Schopenhauer as Transmitter of Buddhist Ideas* (Berne: Lang, 1969).

Fox, Michael (ed.), *Schopenhauer: His Philosophical Achievement* (New Jersey: Barnes & Noble Books, 1980).

Gardiner, Patrick, *Schopenhauer* (Harmondsworth, UK: Penguin Books, 1967).

Hamlyn, D. W. *Schopenhauer: The Arguments of the Philosophers* (London: Routledge & Kegan Paul, 1980).

Jacquette, Dale, *The Philosophy of Schopenhauer* (Chesham, UK: Acumen, 2005).

Janaway, Christopher, *Self and World in Schopenhauer's Philosophy.* (Oxford: Clarendon Press, 1989).

Janaway, Christopher (ed.), *The Cambridge Companion to Schopenhauer* (Cambridge: Cambridge University Press, 1999).

Knox, Israel, *The Aesthetic Theories of Kant, Hegel, and Schopenhauer* (New Jersey: Humanities Press, 1936).

Lauxtermann, Paul F. H., *Schopenhauer's Broken World-View: Colours and Ethics Between Kant and Goethe* (Dordrecht: Kluwer Academic Publishers, 2000).

Luft, Eric von der (ed.), *Schopenhauer: New Essays in Honor of his 200th Birthday* (Lewiston, NY: Edwin Mellen Press, 1988).

McGill, V.J., *Schopenhauer: Pessimist and Pagan* (New York: Haskell House Publishers, 1971).

Magee, Bryan, *The Philosophy of Schopenhauer* (Oxford: Clarendon Press, 1983).

Neeley, G. Steven, *Schopenhauer: A Consistent Reading* (Lewiston, NY: Edwin Mellen Press, 2003).

Safranski, Rüdiger, *Schopenhauer and the Wild Years of Philosophy*, trans. Ewald Osers (Cambridge, MA: Harvard University Press, 1990).

Sedlar, Jean W., *India in the Mind of Germany: Schelling, Schopenhauer and Their Times* (Washington, D C: University Press of America, 1982).

Wallace, W., *Life of Schopenhauer* (London: Walter Scott, 24, Warwick Lane, 1890).

White, F. C., *On Schopenhauer's Fourfold Root of the Principle of Sufficient Reason* (Brill: Leiden, 1992).

White, F. C. (ed.), *Schopenhauer's Early Fourfold Root: Translation and Commentary* (Aldershot: Avebury, Ashgate Publishing Ltd., 1997).

Young, Julian, *Willing and Unwilling: A Study in the Philosophy of Arthur Schopenhauer* (Dordrecht: Martinus Nijhoff, 1987).

Young, Julian, *Schopenhauer* (London & New York: Routledge, 2005).

Zimmern, Helen, *Schopenhauer: His Life and Philosophy* [1876] (London: George Allen & Unwin Ltd.,1932).

other related works

Berkeley, George, *A Treatise Concerning the Principles of Human Knowledge* [1710] (Oxford: Oxford University Press, 1998).

Hume, David, *A Treatise of Human Nature* [1739–40] (Oxford: Oxford University Press, 1978).

Kant, Immanuel, *Critique of Pure Reason*, trans. Paul Guyer and Allen W. Wood (Cambridge: Cambridge University Press, 1999).

Lauer, Quentin, *A Reading of Hegel's* Phenomenology of Spirit (New York: Fordham University Press, 1976).

Locke, John, *An Essay Concerning Human Understanding* [1689] (Oxford: Oxford University Press, 1979).

Marx, Karl, "The Economic and Philosophical Manuscripts of 1844" in *The Marx-Engels Reader*, ed. Robert C. Tucker (New York and London: W. W. Norton & Company, 1978).

Pruss, Alexander, *The Principle of Sufficient Reason: A Reassessment* (Cambridge: Cambridge University Press, 2006).

Schulze, G. E., "Anesidemus" (excerpt) in *Between Kant and Hegel: Texts in the Development of Post-Kantian Idealism*, trans. and annotated by George di Giovanni and H. S. Harris (Albany: SUNY Press, 1985).

Soll, Ivan, *An Introduction of Hegel's Metaphysics* (Chicago and London: The University of Chicago Press, 1969).

Solomon, Robert C., *In the Spirit of Hegel* (Oxford: Oxford University Press, 1983).

index